Praise f... ...e
Bu... ...

WEEK LOA...

// Richard Stutely's clear, no-nonsense writing style ... ...mastery of the subject, makes this a very valuable book indeed. The relation of the material to non-profit organisations definitely helped me in my role at the Chamber.'

MARTIN, F. BRECKNOCK, FORMER DIRECTOR, CANADIAN CHAMBER OF COMMERCE OF THE PHILLIPPINES

// Today's constant turbulence within the economic and commercial landscapes of Europe and Asia calls to attention the importance of effective business planning. This 3rd edition of *The Definitive Business Plan* provides an in-depth and clear framework for the understanding, development, and execution of a world-class business plan. I continue to use *The Definitive Business Plan* as one of the main readings for global business seminars I teach at the university. Moreover, as a CEO & President of a boutique consulting firm, this book remains a trusted reference for business projects. With certainty, I can state that this dynamic book on business planning serves as a valuable asset to both business students and professionals at large.'

JOSEPH S. CABUAY, ASSISTANT PROFESSOR FOR INTERNATIONAL BUSINESS & GLOBAL AFFAIRS, DIVISION OF INTERNATIONAL STUDIES, HANYANY UNIVERSITY, SEOUL, KOREA; CEO & PRESIDENT, OMEGA GLOBAL BUSINESS CONSULTING LTD. – INTERNATIONAL TRAINING & BUSINESS DEVELOPMENT SERVICES, SEOUL, KOREA; SENIOR CONSULTANT AND SALES PARTNER, HOLDEN INTERNATIONAL LTD. – COMPETITIVE SALES STRATEGY & POLITICAL & RELATIONSHIPS ALIGNMENT TRAINING, CHICAGO, USA

// I have read tens of books on business plans and this has got to be the most thorou...
PATRICIA O'SULLIVAN, INNOVATION & ENTERPRISE LECTURER, TRINITY COLLEGE, DUBLIN, IRELAND

// Brilliant book. I wouldn't recommend writing a plan without it.'
DR WADE EDWARDS, MANAGING DIRECTOR, ATL-HYDRO SOUTH AFRICA

// *The Definitive Business Plan* is the only text I have found which offers a clear and sensibly structured approach to business planning. I regularly recommend it to clients and colleagues.'

KIMBERLEY WILLIAMS, MANAGING DIRECTOR, WILLIAMS WROE MANAGEMENT CONSULTANCY, UK

// I have found this book incredibly useful. As a result of the business plan I wrote utilising the book, we have gone from start up to a profitable business and still use the book!'

ADRIAN NEAVE, MANAGING DIRECTOR, GILLIAT FINANCIAL SOLUTIONS, UK

// Invaluable book to clarify the business vision.'

ANSAR BLAKCORI, SENIOR BUSINESS CONSULTANT, LOGICA PLC, UK

The Definitive Business Plan

3rd edition

Richard Stutely

The fast track to intelligent planning
for executives and entrepreneurs

PEARSON

Harlow, England • London • New York • Boston • San Francisco • Toronto • Sydney
Auckland • Singapore • Hong Kong • Tokyo • Seoul • Taipei • New Delhi
Cape Town • São Paulo • Mexico City • Madrid • Amsterdam • Munich • Paris • Milan

PEARSON EDUCATION LIMITED

Edinburgh Gate
Harlow CM20 2JE
United Kingdom
Tel: +44(0)1279 623623
Fax: +44(0)1279 431059
Website: www.pearsoned.com/uk

First published in Great Britain in 1999
Second edition 2002
Revised second edition 2007
Third edition 2012

© Richard Stutely 1999, 2002
© Pearson Education Limited 2007, 2012

Pearson Education is not responsible for the content of third party internet sites.

ISBN: 978-0-273-76114-3

British Library Cataloguing-in-Publication Data
A catalogue record for this book is available from the British Library

Library of Congress Cataloging-in-Publication Data
A catalog record for this book is available from the Library of Congress

10 9 8 7 6 5 4 3 2 1
15 14 13 12 11

Typeset in 10pt Myriad by 30
Printed and bound in Great Britain by Ashford Colour Press Ltd, Gosport, Hampshire

About the author

RICHARD STUTELY During his professional career, Richard has gained unique practical insight into strategic, operational and financial planning from all angles – particularly preparing, approving and using business plans.

When he worked at HM Treasury (the British finance ministry), he dealt with business planning on the grandest scale – relating to the national economy and public expenditure controls. During this period he was also involved with world economic developments, parliamentary affairs and corporate taxation, and was a press officer presenting the then-new monetary policy of the Conservative government.

Subsequently, as a member of the London Stock Exchange, an investment banker and later a general manager of an international commercial bank, he viewed business plans in connection with debt, equity and off-balance sheet funding. More recently, as managing director of multinational technology companies, he has handled business planning focused on exploiting rapid change. He also is director or non-executive director of several companies, and a trustee of two charities – giving him strategic insight into planning for trading, service and non-profit organisations.

Richard has been interviewed in newspapers and on radio and television around the world, he lectures MBA and other audiences, and he has written extensively for publications such as *The Economist, Accountancy* and *The Banker*. He has also been a governor and treasurer of a British private school, a member of Mensa and is a member of The Institute of Directors.

Other books by Richard Stutely include: *The Definitive Guide to Business Finance* (also published by FT Prentice Hall); *The Economist Guide to Economic Indicators* (published in America as *The Economist Guide to Global International Indicators*), which aids understanding of the wider environment for business; *The Economist Numbers Guide* (published in America as *The Economist Guide to Business Numeracy*), which covers many major techniques to assist management decision-making; and *Advanced Desktop Publishing*, a practical guide to desktop publishing. He has also contributed to several other business books.

Acknowledgements

An interesting fact came to light during the preparation of this book. I discussed its content with many senior executives. The people most willing to contribute were those working in enterprises with effective planning procedures in place. The least ready to talk about business planning were associated with organisations sharing at least one common characteristic. Their companies were, it transpired, all in financial difficulty. Some of these are big names in the corporate world. Could it be that there is a link between poor planning and poor performance? I think so.

Brief encounters with, and flashes of insight related to, these struggling corporations contributed to this book. An even greater contribution came from the many friends, associates and business contacts who were willing to talk or brainstorm about business strategy and planning. To you all, I offer my most sincere thanks. This book has benefited immeasurably from your insights and experiences. I am also indebted to those close to me who put up with my quirks and idiosyncrasies. I would not be what I am, and the book would not be what it is, however modest, without their love and support.

My wife made a huge contribution. My son never ceases to amaze me. His intellect, wit and cynicism helped me enormously when writing this book.

Thank you all.

Publisher's acknowledgement

Table 12.1 is courtesy of the World Bank © 2011.

Contents

4 Know yourself 55

5 Know the world 81

6 The core of your plan 107

13 Now make it happen 317

Appendix A *Tetrylus Inc* business plan 341

Foreword

By Sir Paul Judge

Planning is at the heart of good management. We all know that change initiatives in our non-business lives, such as redecorating an apartment, can easily 'cost twice as much and take three times as long'. However, in our business functions we normally have to work with a smaller allowable margin of error and proper planning therefore becomes essential.

Planning is mainly common sense but, like riding a bicycle or painting a picture, it is usually worthwhile to take some advice before starting, which is what this book sets out to provide.

In many countries management has not been seen in the same way as the traditional professions. We do not allow a doctor to prescribe medicines or an architect to design a building unless they have been properly qualified. And yet we have been too ready to allow people to manage important organisations without any equivalent training, even though the ramifications of the decisions made by such managers can have even more important effects on the communities in which they operate. Every manager therefore has a responsibility to become as knowledgeable as possible about the art and science of management.

As planning is such an important part of management, a thorough understanding of planning approaches and documentation is vital. In my own career I have used three simple questions to guide the planning process, whether for large or small organisations, public or private:

- Where are we now?

- Where do we want to be?

- How are we going to get there?

Based on a full understanding of the organisation's situation, this is a goal-driven process which aims to get people to commit to goals and objectives which can then determine implementation and communication both internally and externally.

Planning and knowledge

'When you are a Bear of Very Little Brain, and you Think of Things, you find sometimes that a Thing which seemed very Thingish inside you is quite different when it gets out into the open and has other people looking at it.'

A. A. MILNE, *THE HOUSE AT POOH CORNER*

'Problems that remain persistently insoluble should always be suspected as questions asked in the wrong way.'

ALAN WATTS

Leadership cannot operate in a vacuum. If a leader tries to lead without understanding his or her situation, then he or she will usually be described as reckless or hopeless. The 'Where are we now?' question is the foundation for any plan.

In order to know where you want to go, it is vital to understand where you are coming from, why you are where you are, and what assets you have in your armoury. This book describes a wide range of techniques for doing this so that a proper strategy emerges.

The 'Where are we now?' stage of planning is one which often, in my experience, does not get the proper level of support, and is where it is often quite difficult to get people to be really open and honest. Each department or function will normally see itself as currently well organised and as making a productive contribution to the organisation. Those involved often assume that they know their environment and markets and that they understand the key trends, but in practice operating managers often find it difficult to see the wood from the trees without a formal process. It needs careful questioning to establish the truth and to determine the main strengths and weaknesses. However, it is essential to be honest and to help that honesty by comparing your organisation frankly with your competition and contemporaries.

Planning and leadership

'The significant problems we face cannot be solved by the same level of thinking that created them.'

ALBERT EINSTEIN

'The plan was simple. Unfortunately, so was the chief executive.'

Most plans can be summarised by the answer to the second of the above questions – Where do we want to be? – which is why planning is at the heart of leadership.

Most people in an organisation are mainly involved in their own daily tasks and lives but they prefer to follow someone who has a clear vision which has been effectively communicated. They want to believe that 'someone up there' knows what he or she is trying to achieve for the organisation and that he or she is being broadly successful in getting there. In the modern world, the plan is the description of and rationale for the vision, and the basis for the communication.

The most effective objectives invoke competition (to win the sports cup, to win the war, to increase market share of widgets, to be the most effective charity in the sector) as these give a direct way of measuring achievement. After millions of years of evolution we are all essentially tribal animals with deep instincts of rivalry towards other tribes (those whose genes led them to go off as individuals tended to be eaten by the lions and not survive!). Three very different leaders can be quoted as examples of people who successfully galvanised their 'tribe' by setting stretching objectives:

- St Paul – to convert the world to Christianity;

- Lenin – to improve the peasants' lot through communism;

- Kennedy – to put a man on the moon by 1970.

Such leaders who successfully pursue a clear vision, and who show they believe in themselves, can achieve a huge amount. They are able to create a team with a common purpose. This provides a way of rising above current difficulties and parochial concerns. A new approach is taken to old problems and different questions are asked.

Planning and implementation

'Great ideas need landing gear as well as wings.'

C. D. JACKSON

'Never give up on a dream just because of the time it will take to accomplish it. The time will pass anyway.'

'No plan survives contact with the enemy.'

When you have produced the analysis about where you are and where you want to be, you can move on to the detailed task of deciding all of the things that you have to do to achieve your vision. You will find that these are often in layers, with each strand of the implementation having sub-strands of increasing detail.

Ideally, your organisation also follows this same pattern and you can organise the implementation in line with the strategy. At the least the vision will provide the reason for your organisation structure. You should not just organise the organisation in convenient structures: you should organise it 'to do something', most preferably what you have set out in the plan. If marketing is key then the marketing department must be prominent whereas if technical development is the main competitive advantage then this must be properly staffed. Always remember that if the plan calls for something to be done then it should also identify someone in the organisation who is charged with doing it.

Submitting the plan

'It is not from the benevolence of the butcher, the brewer, or the baker, that we expect our dinner, but from their regard to their own self-interest. We address ourselves, not to their humanity but to their self-love, and never talk to them of our own necessities but of their advantages.'

ADAM SMITH

'Never appeal to man's "better nature". He may not have one.'

A plan does not exist in isolation. It should not be written and then just filed. It will of course be used downwards to communicate the direction of the organisation and the actions required of its members. However, nearly all plans also identify the need for more resources, and these have to be provided from outside the particular organisation preparing the plan. These resources may either come from your parent, if you are part of a larger organisation, or from external sources if you are at the top of your particular tree.

In each case the plan must convince those providers that it is in their self-interest to back it. If you are part of a larger entity then you must show that your strategy will help to meet the objectives of the parent organisation. It must adopt similar ethics and methods and must provide proper returns. It is unlikely that there will be an endorsement of a plan which sets out a development, however worthy, which exposes the parent organisation to new risks or provides a lower return than other potential investments.

When seeking resources externally, it is even more important to understand the parameters of the person to whom the plan is addressed. Some plans will be written in order to identify and correct resource constraints of personnel and will be used to identify people requirements and to enthuse potential recruits. However, most plans going to external audiences are asking for money, whether from a bank or a venture capitalist. These must be carefully prepared with a full understanding of the questions likely to be asked by the recipient. Indeed there may need to be different versions of the same plan as the need of a banker for security is very different from the wish of a venture capitalist for capital growth.

As this book points out, the seeking of venture capital is particularly difficult, with there being many famous successful ideas which have been repeatedly turned down before reaching their potential. As you go outside your own organisation you need strength and stamina to keep to your chosen path and to convince people that you are right. If you have a well-constructed plan which deals with all of the issues then this can give you real support as you deal with the many unbelievers.

People make the difference

'It is not the critic who counts, not the man who points out how the strong man stumbled or where the doer of deeds could have done them better. The credit belongs to the man who is actually in the arena; whose face is marred by dust and sweat and blood; who strives valiantly; who errs and comes short again and again; who knows the great enthusiasms, the great devotions, and spends himself in a worthy cause; who, at the best, knows in the end the triumph of high achievement, and who, at worst, if he fails, at least fails while daring greatly, so that his place shall never be with those cold and timid souls who know neither victory nor defeat.'

THEODORE ROOSEVELT (1858–1919)

'You are the most powerful person in your universe.'

All major human endeavours involve change and this is only achieved by the actions of people. If you want to improve your organisation and lead it to making a greater contribution, then you must be able to produce a plan about why and how it is going to do so.

You are obviously wise because you have bought this book, or at least have got as far as picking it up to browse through it. Please be convinced that good planning is essential to orderly improvement which requires that everyone you need to have on your side can understand exactly what you want to do and why.

May I wish you all the best in your particular project. The techniques in this book will give you all of the technical help you could require. If you can add a dash of your own human inspiration and perspiration then you should be able to produce a comprehensive and visionary plan.

Good luck.

Sir Paul Judge
Former Group Planning Director, Cadbury Schwepps plc
President, Association of MBAs,
President, Chartered Institute of Marketing
Benefactor of the Judge Business School, University of Cambridge

Introduction to the First Edition

'Everyone knew what Walt wanted. Everyone had objectives. Both were communicated all the way down the line. The management layer was flat and responsibilities were clearly defined. We had a good self-image and the company ran well.'

Does this quote from a former Walt Disney executive apply to your business? It could do. It contains two important ideas. The subliminal message is that Walt had to know *what he wanted* before it could be communicated. Knowing *what you want* is what business planning is all about. It is fundamental to business success. The other important suggestion is that when you know what you want you have a useful management tool to help you run a successful business.

Back to Walt. He had two characteristics that are important. First, he knew about planning. The movie business requires meticulous planning to turn a dry script into a lively strip of celluloid. You do not hire a million-dollar actor so that he can sit in his trailer drinking whisky while the set is prepared – you schedule him to appear when you are ready to film. You do not keep changing location to shoot the script sequentially. You take all the shots for one scene at the same time and then juggle them with the other footage to assemble the story in the correct order.

Second, Walt was a visionary. You have to be, in order to take a concept and turn it into a successful movie. This does not necessarily infer that you have to be *a visionary* to run a business, but you do have to develop a vision for the future. An excellent way to do this is by preparing a plan. Let me give you an example.

A few years ago, a famous bank's customers included two with very similar businesses. Both were in their 30s. After serving apprenticeships as printers' devils they were eventually made redundant by changes in technology and working practices. They did not know each other when they used their redundancy pay to start their own small businesses doing what they knew best – printing – in different areas of a busy city. This is where their fortunes began to diverge.

One of them set up in an old garage just off the main shopping area. He started with second-hand equipment. Passing trade kept him busy and he would sometimes work through the night. Within a few years he took on three young assistants. He earned a satisfactory living, had a comfortable house and a new family car, and sent his children to a good private school.

Symbols used

 Fast track boxes provide a rapid path through the topic covered in each chapter.

 Especially important ideas in the main text.

 Other key and useful ideas.

What's it all about?

With careful and detailed planning, one can win;
with careless and less detailed planning, one cannot win.
How much more certain is defeat if one does not plan at all!
From the way planning is done beforehand,
we can predict victory or defeat. SUN TZU, *THE ART OF WAR*, c. 400 BC

You are probably an expert in your field, but I assume that it is not business planning. In other words, you do not really need any prior knowledge to use this book, other than common sense. But bear with me. When I start telling you something that you already know, skim through it to the next section. What you know now is easy to read about. The rest is just as simple – it is just unfamiliar the first time around.

 ## We accept any currency, but no checks

Currencies are a nightmare. Never mind exchange rates, what should I call them in this book? I do not know your favourite currency. I struggled with dollar/franc/sterling (alphabetical – no favouritism implied, sorry if I omitted your currency), but that was too much of a mouthful. I experimented with the euro. I even tried to make up a name for a new currency.

Eventually, as you will see, I drifted to the dollar. It is the unit of account in some African countries, Australia, Canada, Fiji, Hong Kong, New Zealand, Singapore, Taiwan, even the US. This seems to make it a fairly international choice. I hope that it does not distract you.

I do not stick to any particular flavour of English. I use what seems to be most unambiguous and concise. For example, I think that the American word *inventory* is better than *stock* and the British *cheque* is less ambiguous than *check*.

The terms *company* and *corporation* are used interchangeably. In general, I refer to *business areas* – a formal or loose grouping of closely related activities. You will probably want to write a business plan for each business area plus one for the overall collection of businesses. The top-level plan might cover an *enterprise* where the *various* activities are interrelated, or a *holding company* for seemingly unrelated businesses. This is introduced in Chapter 3 and discussed in more detail in Chapter 6.

References to the chief executive should be interpreted as 'the most senior executive'. In the US, this probably means Chairman, President and CEO. In the UK, this person is called simply the MD (Managing Director) – see Chapter 4.

A quick fix or a longer-term tool?

This book is primarily about writing a business plan. Many busy executives confronted with a demand for a plan want only to get one on paper as rapidly as possible. This book provides a fast track to doing just this. At the same time, its pragmatic approach should be of value to those with time for a more considered approach and also to the seasoned veteran of writing business plans.

The fast track through this book

This chapter	Shows you	Gives you
1 What's it all about?	Why plan? Why, what, how, who	Focus for your plan
2 A winning presentation	How to create a standard document to ease the pain of writing your plan	The basis for your current and all your future plans
3 Getting down to it	How to kick off the planning process and get the first words on paper	The first and last sections of your plan – plus some of what goes in between
4 Know yourself	How to come to terms with who you are, what you do, and how you do it	A solid description of the business and its people
5 Getting down to it	How to understand your competitors, customers and operating environment	Critical competitor analysis and market positioning
6 The core of your plan	How to develop a winning strategy and turn it into a plan and objectives	Objectives, a strategy and your operating plan
7 About these numbers	How to think about the numbers that you need	Background to the key financial projections
8 Getting to gross profit	How to project sales and gross profit	Sales, costs of sales, gross profit
9 Getting to net profit	How to estimate operating costs and forecast net profit	Operating costs, capital spending, net profit
10 Funding the business	How to work out your funding requirements and value your business	Balance sheet, P&L/ income, cash flow, funding, valuation
11 Managing risks	How to use uncertainty to your advantage	Evidence that you know what you are doing
12 Getting it approved	How to gain approvals and win the required funding	Approval and funding
13 Now make it happen	How to put the plan to good use	A successful business

You must sit back from the day-to-day pressures of steering the ship around the rocks and take a long, hard look at what lies further ahead. The most successful businesses are those that have proper planning processes in place. This book will show you how it is done.

 Recession-proof your business

Business planning is about a journey. The plan is your starting point. It charts a route to your destination. It identifies the major hazards that you should watch for along the way. It gives you strategies for coping with squalls and obstacles. It gives you landmarks to confirm your progress. It helps you expect the unexpected. With a good business plan, you know where you started, where you are going, and how to get there.

If you are currently in a hole, use this book to help you draw up a plan for climbing out. Take the plan along to your bank manager to demonstrate that you are worthy of that extra loan. If everything is fine, use the plan to make sure that you avoid traps and pitfalls. The business cycle is alive and kicking – do not let a cyclical downturn catch you unawares and kick you into a hole.

Key objectives for your plan

Business plans are used for many different purposes. Essentially, it may be considered that they are:

- a formal expression of the planning process;

- a request for funding;

- a framework for approval;

- a tool for operational business management.

Where does your plan fit? Ideally it will meet all four of these objectives. It is useful to look at each one in a little more detail.

FORMAL DOCUMENTATION

There can be a huge difference between an undocumented and a documented plan. The formal exercise of distilling plans on to paper helps highlight opportunities and risks and helps uncover inconsistencies. Moreover, once formalised, the business plan provides a guide for operating and for reacting to real world events. Writing a plan should never be a bureaucratic exercise – this helps no one. But if as many people as reasonably possible can be involved in developing and reviewing the plan, the management team is more likely to end up with a greater understanding of where it is going, with a better shared vision and common sense of purpose.

FUNDING

There is always a funding motive lurking somewhere behind a plan. The plan might be used to help raise venture capital for a new business, additional equity funding for an existing business, loan capital for an ongoing enterprise, or even trade credit. It might be intended to encourage joint venture participation with a business partner such as a supplier. It might be drawn up to support merger and acquisition activity.

Alternatively, a plan might be used to justify allocating internal resources (probably retained earnings) to a particular business activity – perhaps your pet project. If funds are so allocated, there is an opportunity cost of not investing them elsewhere. It might, for example, be financially prudent to cease operations and place the capital in a bank deposit. The plan helps identify if this is the case – and if so usually demonstrates why there is a good reason for ignoring short-term financial loss in favour of long-term gain or some other objective.

There is a well-known Japanese bank which in the late 1990s had assets of over $8 billion. What was its return on investment (ROI) with that much money available? Perhaps 5%?, or even 25%? In fact, the return was just 0.3% a year. It might have made better sense commercially to have closed the bank, liquidated the assets, and put them on deposit with a rival to earn, at that time, around 5% annual interest. Of course, the bank expected better years ahead and political considerations, including the potential effect on employment, precluded it from closing its doors.

Wherever the funding is coming from in the overall scheme of things, a plan might also be used to justify grabbing a chunk of a bigger, organisational budget.

APPROVALS

It hardly needs to be said that a documented plan provides a framework for approval. The owner of a small business who takes the trouble to document a plan is probably the person who approves it. More usually, a board of directors or management committee approves a plan as a collective statement of intent – or perhaps a lone decision-maker somewhere approves someone else's plan.

The approvals and funding processes are somewhat closely aligned. In a corporate sense, approval of a plan is usually the same thing as approval of the funding. However, the converse is not necessarily true. A capital provider who approves a funding request based on a plan is not saying that the plan is correct. The business owners and executives are always responsible for actually running the business.

The amount of detail in each section will vary depending on the business activity and the intended readership. A plan for a manufacturing unit within a larger organisation will have much more emphasis on product than on marketing. (It might be a useful and salutary exercise to develop a marketing plan for cost centres, such as an information technology department that exists only to support the other departments of the same company.) A plan for the bank manager is likely to need more detail on the product and current status than a plan for your chief executive.

Moreover, the order of the sections will vary depending on the audience and intent. For an internal document you might move the section on the current status right up to the front, while for a business plan for a start-up operation you might put the current status very near the end.

 Five things that belong in annexes

Business plans should be concise and easy to read. How do you cope when you have to include some fairly heavy material? Where possible, summarise it in the text and include the full details in annexes. Examples of things that belong in annexes are as follows.

1 Background material that informs your reader about specialist processes or concepts that are critical to the plan and are more than simple definitions of terms.

2 Detailed product specifications.

3 Marketing brochures and leaflets.

4 Detailed financial analysis.

5 Full biographies (CVs or résumés) of senior executives.

HOW MANY PAGES?

A business plan should be as short as possible. Some people say that 20–40 pages is a good average. Undoubtedly, most executives already have too much to read in this age of information overload. If you add to their problems, your plan will not be given the attention that it deserves. This said, I often find it hard to keep a plan down to this optimum length. There is just so much to say when describing a business.

It depends on your circumstances. You have to provide the documentation and information that readers need. You have to give them enough to make the required decisions or take the required actions. Sometimes you need to give them a little bit more than the minimum in order to demonstrate that you have done your planning properly. In other instances, you need to drop in a taster that shows that you know more than you have written.

The solution is to put in all the information, divided into sections so that it does not all have to be read. Identify what the reader needs to know, what is essential for the plan – and then document it as concisely as possible. Use plenty of clear headings followed by a concise summary and then more detail. This allows readers to be selective, and slow down to read in more detail topics that interest them especially.

 I want to tell you a story

Once, I saw a strategy presented as a series of bullet points. An executive commented *'this is just a shopping list'*. He then read exactly the same points tied together with a few extra words and became excited about *'an excellent strategy'*. It seems that oversimplification can be counterproductive. Always try to tell a story.

Don't trust consultants

I would say that the worst possible thing you can do is to call in management consultants to write a business plan for you. This may be a bit harsh, although a true example illustrates the problems.

The chairman of a medium-sized organisation realised that his business was not performing well. He called in one of the top consulting firms, and let them charge him a handsome fee for preparing a weighty and glossy plan. He followed the first few steps of the plan, recruiting managers to fill new positions as recommended. Then it all fell apart. There was no coherent understanding, no buy-in, no commitment to the plan. The new managers were experienced business people and they had their own ideas about how to run the business. The plan fell into disuse and the whole process failed. Each new manager pursued personal objectives and the company was as badly off as before. Within a year most of the managers left, exhausted by working in an organisation where the chairman continued exactly as he had before the expensive consultants had arrived.

'A consultant is someone who saves his client almost enough to pay his fee.'
ARNOLD H. GLASGOW

There might be occasions when management consultants can usefully be asked to take a fresh, professional look at a company and develop a business plan. This usually happens after an enterprise has grown out of control – such as early in the life of a new business when it starts to get bigger than its entrepreneurial founder. The best that consultants can do in this instance is identify what new management skills should be recruited to try to rescue what is obviously a target for a takeover.

- **Use it as a microscope.** You can use it to help you watch over others. Chapters 7–13 are particularly useful in this respect – how mischievous managers hide things in the figures, ideas about risk management, what to look for when approving or investing, checking performance against plan.

- **Use it to review management mechanics.** This is discussed in Chapter 13.

- **Use it as an investment tool.** Whether you are investing your own savings in a business (see Chapter 10), or are an investment manager or a lender, the book will help you assess the viability of an opportunity.

- **Use it to obtain the funding that you so desperately need.** Chapter 12 contains helpful advice.

Frankly, the list goes on and on. Have fun and be successful.

> *'Make sure you have a Vice President in charge of Revolution, to engender ferment among your more conventional colleagues.'*
>
> DAVID OGILVY

 The fast track to your own plan

A sample business plan is included with this book (see the Appendix), although you should not copy it. As you work through the book, you will see that the layout of your own plan depends on the nature of your business, its stage of development and the expected use for plan.

OK, an admission: if you are really in a rush you could use the framework given here. As you fill in the gaps with your own words you will probably find yourself naturally changing the headings and layout – which will take you fairly painlessly to a unique plan of your own. Try to read or maybe skim this book before you start, or if you are really pushed for time at least read the 'fast track' boxes in each chapter. Also, take a look at Figure 12.3 on page 304 now to see where you are heading.

The key pages from the sample business plan are reproduced throughout this book – as noted on the thumbnail sketches. The sample plan and other supporting material may be downloaded from www.DefinitiveBusinessPlan.com. You can also follow and interact with me on the following networks:

Twitter	www.twitter.com/RichardStutely
Google+	www.gplus.to/RichardStutely
Facebook	www.facebook.com/RichardStutely

A business plan to crib

Section of business plan	Figure
Cover	2.3
Small print	2.2
Contact, document control, definitions	2.4
List of contents	3.1
Executive summary	3.2
Basic data, mission, history	4.1
Business organisation and the management team	4.4
Infrastructure, products	4.5
Market and competitive analysis	5.4
Business strategy	6.4
Sales	8.8
Financials	10.5
Risks	11.8
Annex	
Sales forecast	8.9
Capital outlays	9.2
Employee costs	9.3
Operating costs	9.4
Expenditure commentary	9.5
Profit and loss account	9.7
Balance sheet	10.2
Cash flow	10.3

A winning presentation

Je n'ai fait celle-ci plus longue que parce que je n'ai pas eu le loisir de la faire plus courte.
(I have made this letter longer than usual, only because I have not had the time to make it shorter.)

BLAISE PASCAL, *LETTRES PROVINCIALES*, 1657

On the other hand, a computer word processing application such as MS Word or OpenOffice Writer will reduce the amount of work that you have to do and enhance the professionalism of your output. These are usually more than adequate. Either way, you can set up a standard framework or template that can be used for every report you have to write. You can make simple corrections and revisions and reprint a page easily, and you can track the many versions through which most business plans go.

In addition, a spreadsheet application such as MS Excel or OpenOffice Calc is essential. Nowadays, it is hard to imagine preparing a business plan without one. They take all the hard work out of assembling numbers and performing calculations. If you set it up correctly, it will allow you to make small changes and see how they ripple through your projections. And it will serve you for years, as the numbers change but the calculations and relationships stay the same.

A sample business plan, the spreadsheets from this book and other additional material may be found at: www.definitivebusinessplan.com

---

 ## The fast track to establishing a basic document

Document control

- Establish a procedure for numbering documents and their revisions.
- Keep a record of who receives which version.
- Make sure that contributors and recipients have signed confidentiality agreements.

Presentation

- Select paper and binding that are both practical and good quality.
- Consider using tabbed dividers to identify key sections of the plan.

Page set-up

- Consider formatting the page so that you can print on either A4 or US letter paper.
- Make the left margin wide, so the text itself is no more than 5 inches/ 125 mm across.
- Set up headers and footers – perhaps similar to those in Figure 2.3 (later).
- Choose a font for about three levels of headings – (see Fonts).

Create an outline document

- Type the first few pages, based on the sample in Figures 2.2, 2.3 and 2.4.

Make it feel good

Business plans are usually produced for a very limited circulation, and are often revised several times during their short life. This almost certainly precludes the cost of professional design and printing.

It is most likely that you will print your plan using an office printer and either put it in a ring binder or use a simple binding machine to add a comb or spiral binding. It is advisable to use a binding method that allows the user to open it at any place and lay it flat. You will weaken the reader's concentration if he or she is struggling to keep it flat or scrabbling around collecting up pages that have made a break for freedom.

The quality of the binder and the paper is important. The plan is often the reader's first substantive contact with your business. Do not overdo it, but remember that using good quality material creates a better impression of your business. If you are raising venture capital, the extra cost per plan is probably insignificant in the overall scheme of things. If you take a look at reports produced by or for financiers, you will notice a tendency towards stiff dark blue or green covers and cream paper. You might want to borrow this style of presentation if you are trying to sell to a banker.

High-quality computer printers are so affordable now that there is almost no excuse for poor printing. You can produce a report with near-photographic quality colour pictures for a very small outlay. If you are in an impoverished start-up situation, and you don't have a good printer even for your marketing activities, see if you can borrow one or consider taking your report to a business bureau for printing.

Remember also the little details. Include tabbed dividers to help readers find their way around long reports. A self-adhesive, clear plastic business card holder stuck inside the front cover will make sure that your name, company logo and contact details are conspicuous and available. Insert several cards so that if someone takes one before passing on your plan your details are still there. You can also use stick-on computer disk wallets if you want to include information in electronic format.

'I think it is an immutable law in business that words are words, explanations are explanations, promises are promises – but only performance is reality.'

HAROLD GENEEN

First thoughts on layout

THE OVERALL IMPRESSION

Your business plan should be laid out so that it is inviting, pleasing to the eye and easy to read. Time-honoured rules apply. Aim for a clean layout that is not overburdened with text, without too many distracting typefaces, and with illustrations to aid understanding.

You should probably work on the basis that everyone who will see the plan should first sign confidentiality and non-disclosure agreements. Your employees and fellow executives should already have done so when they started working with you. This should be covered in their employment contracts. Terms for contract staff are more important. Notably, unless explicitly agreed to the contrary, contractors usually own the copyright of any material that they produce while working for you. Generally, you should try to ensure that copyright is assigned to you.

In addition, it is a good idea to mark clearly on every page of the business plan 'copyright and confidential' or 'trade secret' – and also to include an indication of your rights near the front. A sample form of words is shown in Figure 2.2, but check the precise requirements with your legal adviser.

> *'There is no royal road to anything. One thing at a time, all things in succession. That which grows fast withers as rapidly; that which grows slowly endures.'*
>
> J. D. HOLLAND

Creating an outline document

When you begin setting up your first business plan, start by defining the broad details for the page layout. You will probably find that the following characteristics are set in one place on your word processing application.

PAGE SET-UP

Paper size

If you operate in an international environment, you could format the page layout so that you can print your document on A4 paper for ISO-influenced readers and US letter size paper for American-influenced recipients. This simply requires leaving enough space at the bottom of the page so that there is not too much text to fit the shorter US letter paper. US letter paper is 11 inches/280 mm long, A4 is 11.7 inches/297 mm. US letter paper is a touch wider (8.5/216 against A4's 8.25/210) – you can more or less ignore this variation in width, probably by ensuring it occurs in the inner margin.

Margins and columns

Prefer relatively narrow columns. The typographer's rule of thumb is that maximum readability is achieved if lines of text are not more than one-and-a-half alphabets (i.e. 38 characters) long. The eye can skim rapidly down the page without too much lateral movement. However, this is really too narrow for a business plan. Readers associate width with quality, up to a realistic limit.

Figure 2.2 Sample small print

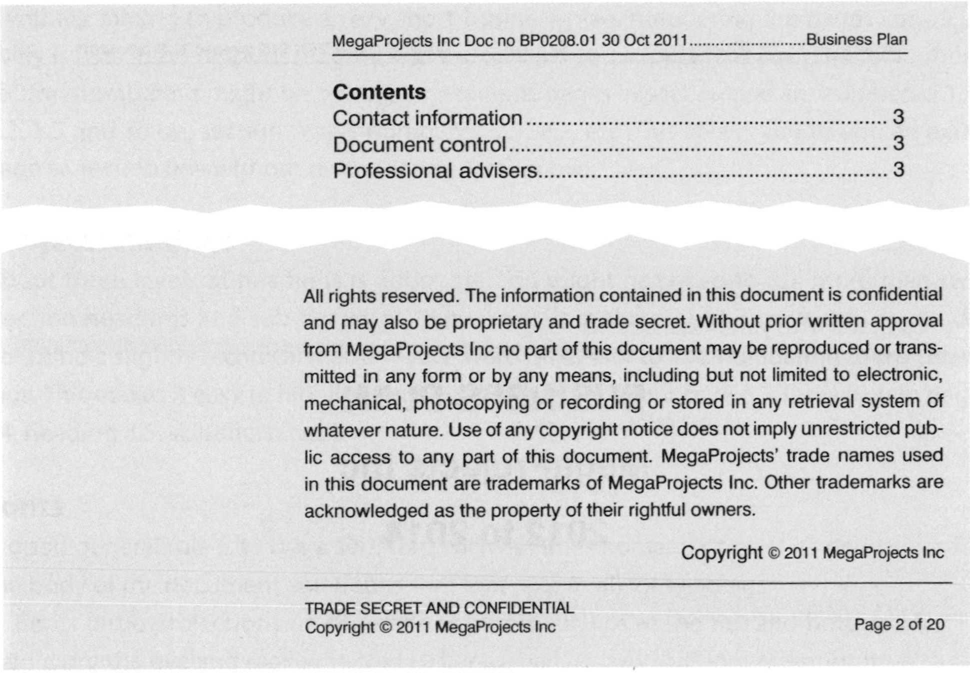

Take a look at well-produced newspapers and magazines. The *Financial Times* is a good example. The number of columns to the page is directly related to the content. Information to be scanned quickly is presented in narrow columns. Weighty editorial to be read and considered is presented in wider columns. The reader slows down and takes in the subject matter.

For a business plan, a single column about 5 inches/125 mm wide works well – setting a good pace for the reader and leaving plenty of white space and a margin for notes.

Headers and footers

Use your word processor's headers and footers option to set up standard information that will appear on each page of your document – similar to the subject header at the top of this page and the page number at the bottom.

You might want to put the document control information that changes in the header, and the static and automated information in the footer. Then you rarely have to change the footer, no matter for what document you use the framework.

For example, the header might read 'Business Plan for MegaProjects Inc. Document no. BP2011.01D released 30 October 2011', while the footer could indicate 'Trade Secret and confidential. Copyright © 2011 MegaProjects Inc Page x of y'. (See Figure 2.3.)

Figure 2.4 Preliminary pages

MegaProjects Inc Doc no BP2011.01 30 Oct 2011....................................Business Plan

Contents

MegaProjects Inc Doc no BP2011.01 30 Oct 2011   Business Plan

Contacts

For further information please contact
Sally McPhearson
Group CEO, MegaProjects Inc
Mega House, 2010 London Road,
Manchester MW12 2DP
Tel: 0161 224 3270
Fax: 0161 224 3275

Document Control

Prepared by: Sally McPhearson
Approved by: Board of Directors

Circulation

Copy 01   Sally McPhearson   1 November 2011

MegaProjects Inc Doc no BP2011.01 30 Oct 2011   Business Plan

Definitions

ABO system   A system of four types (A, AB, B, and O) by which
human blood may be classified, based on the
presence or absence of certain inherited antigens

MegaProjects Inc Doc no BP2011.01 30 Oct 2011   Business Plan

Section 1

Executive Summary

BODY OF THE PLAN

The layout for the body of the report was specified when you set up the master page. The only additional point to consider here is whether you want section dividers – blank pages before each section that say something like 'Section Nine. Analysis of Risks'. If you are aiming for a super-concise report of say 20 pages, omit section dividers and put the section heading information on the first page of text in each section.

If your report creeps much above 20 pages, use section dividers to break it up and make it easier to read. You might want to format them so that you can print them on card or tabbed dividers to help readers jump around the document.

A good way to handle this if you are going to present the business plan in a ring binder is to print the section heading information vertically on the right-hand edge of the page. You can then slide these pages into clear plastic file pockets so that they project from the normal page width and give a clear visual and physical indication of where the sections break.

FINANCIAL TABLES

If you are building a plan with contributions from several departments or business units, you will want to set up some standard spreadsheets at the outset. This will ensure that you receive consistent input that can be consolidated with the minimum effort. The content of these spreadsheets is considered in detail in Chapter 7.

Probably, the financial tables in the main body of the plan will be summaries, with full details going into the annexes.

ANNEXES

Annex dividers can be formatted in the same way as section dividers discussed in the previous paragraphs.

You will need to arrive at a format for the financial data that has to go into your business plan. If you have more than one department head providing you with input, make sure that you establish a standard spreadsheet for them to complete right at the start of the planning process. This will ease the consolidation process later. This is considered in Chapter 7.

CONCLUSION

Having worked through this chapter, you should have a standard framework for documenting your first plan. It might not be perfect yet. You will refine it as you go along. But this preliminary document planning will make subsequent tasks much easier. And, later, you can delete the body text, change the cover, header and document control page, and use the result as a master document for all your reports.

'A man's success in business today turns upon his power of getting people to believe he has something that they want.'

GERALD STANLEY LEE-CROWDS

Getting down to it

Always tell them three times. First tell them what you are going to tell them. Then tell it to them. Then tell them what it was that you have just told them.

times of the year, you can hear a collective sigh of relief at the moment when executives complete the annual planning process and then consider that they can forget about it for another 11 months.

This means that the objectives of the planning process itself are usually different from the priorities in writing the business plan. It would be pleasing to think that they are one and the same; that every planning exercise aims to produce an effective and documented plan that will be used to steer the business. This is the ideal. A written business plan is a formal incarceration of the planning exercise. The very action of writing up the plan usually improves the output of the planning process.

 You will want to order the four broad priorities listed here and then expand on each one. Identify what you are trying to achieve in each instance. Then make a list of each person who will use the business plan and think about what you would say to them if they were sitting in front of you. This should give you a fairly good idea – at the broadest level – of what you have to write about.

The fast track to getting started on your plan

1   Identify your priorities for writing the plan.

2   Identify likely readers and their needs, preferences and prejudices.

3   Draw up a list of contents (see Figure 3.1 later).

4   Write a first draft of the Executive Summary.

5   Think about what the Conclusion will say.

6   Make a start on a list of strengths, weaknesses, opportunities and threats.

When you don't want to be a big fish

Whenever you approach investors, or your boss, it's not really your size or the relevance of your ideas that are important. You have to look at it from the other person's perspective. How big are you and your ideas *relative* to his or her other interests? The less important you are in relative terms, the easier ride you'll have – providing that you know what you are doing and you are not so small that you are overlooked or rejected.

'Intelligence lies in recognising opportunity.'

CHINESE PROVERB

Case study
Three fish on vacation

Three successful entrepreneurs met at an exotic beach hotel. Over sunset daiquiris by the pool they exchanged stories.

- One was a businessman who had needed an extra couple of million dollars to take his ideas to market. He was funded by a company that made a dozen such investments every year, on the basis that nine would fail, two would do reasonably well, and one would be really successful. They didn't have the resources to manage these investments closely. So at the outset they assured themselves that the idea was sound, the market demand was there, and the management team could handle the business. Then they left the business pretty much alone.

- The second tycoon had required $35 million to fund a major expansion. He was financed by one of the big US investment houses. They made only two investments every year, normally for around $50 million each. They had examined his business in minute detail, employed industry experts to analyse it to death, and drawn up their own extensive financial projections. When they did invest, they moved the tycoon aside to be chairman and brought in their own high-profile chief executive with specifically relevant experience.

- The third vacationer was a software developer who had once needed just $50,000 to package his software and deliver it to the public. He was funded by a friend who had just received the golden boot after 30 years in a big manufacturing corporation. The friend had plenty of time on his hands, no other major investments, and thought he knew a thing or two about running a business. He made himself general manager and was a constant irritation to the computer expert.

Note how each one of the entrepreneurs in the example above experienced different levels of interest and interference (and incidentally how none of the financiers could or would have invested in the other businesses). These are the situations that you have to consider when writing and presenting your plan. The smaller you are in the eye of your boss or investor, the more you have to demonstrate that you are capable of surviving alone – and the more you can expect to be left alone once you have proved yourself.

What to do if you have several businesses

This is where a slight complication creeps in. If you are writing a business plan for a small or highly focused business you will work through the steps described here just once. What if you have several business areas or run a group of companies?

- If you are the head of one of those business units or subsidiaries, you need to recognise the areas where you operate independently and those where you take or provide services to the enterprise as a whole.

- If you own the business, or are taking overall responsibility for the plan, you might have to write parts of it several times over – once for each business area and maybe once for activities that are common to all or most businesses. However, in this case, you are likely to be able to delegate most of the work to the heads of the business units.

Essentially, there will be one master plan for the overall business. In addition, there might be a separate plan for each business area (sometimes known as *strategic business areas* or *strategic business units*).

In the top-level plan, the review of the current status, the market and the operating plan will summarise the overall strategy for the sum of the individual plans. The financial section will show the consolidated accounts. The part of the plan that describes the strategy in detail will show how the individual businesses contribute to the enterprise or group of companies as a whole.

In many less developed countries a single entrepreneur (or management team) will often run many, possibly unrelated businesses under a single umbrella. Perhaps I should say under a single sunshade, since I have seen this frequently in the deserts of the Middle East and the tropics of Asia-Pacific. These successful business people have spotted opportunities and gone for them. Unfortunately, the result is often a rather fragmented business overall.

You do not want a fragmented enterprise. You want a cohesive and integrated set of business activities that exploits competencies, synergies and other competitive advantages. One major review and planning exercise will highlight independent activities and dependencies and enable a far more integrated approach in future. This can pay handsome dividends.

This situation is found less often in more mature economies, where the competition and the passage of time have already enabled and encouraged a higher degree of focus.

For the moment, I want to talk about planning as if you had just one tightly focused product line or business area. Examining several products or activities is discussed in Chapter 6 when we look at ways of analysing your overall portfolio of businesses.

'Any corporate policy and plan which is typical of the industry is doomed to mediocrity.'

BRUCE HENDERSON

Your list of contents

When you have defined why you are writing the business plan, sketch out the list of contents. The main objective is to lead your readers logically to the required conclusion. You want them to run through the plan and put it down nodding sagely and thinking that they will back you and your business activities.

As already discussed in Chapter 1, there is no hard and fast order for the contents. Figure 3.1 provides a sample. You do not have to follow this. For example, in a start-up situation you might want to describe the product and market first and save discussion of the business organisation until later. The only essential requirement is that you avoid repetition and that your readers know where to find the information they need.

This book follows broadly the order suggested in the example. Not least, it is convenient because it accords closely with the planning process.

1 You take stock of the factors that are under your control – your current situation – and identify your core competencies.

2 You then consider external factors (the economic environment, your market, your competitors) and identify opportunities and your competitive advantages. Your readers can now picture your business in the context of the market as a whole.

3 In an iterative process, you develop a strategy, set objectives, and create an operating plan. This includes a financial operating plan – usually (misleadingly) known as a budget.

4 You re-examine the risks and confirm or amend your objectives, strategy and plan.

As a slight digression, the word budget originates from the French word *bougette*, itself a diminutive of *bouge*, a leather bag. This indicates the danger inherent in the term. Managers often start the year with the attitude, *I have a bag full of money to spend*. This is incorrect. In the corporate planning context, a budget is a guideline not a commitment.

'The freedom to fail is vital if you're going to succeed. Most successful people fail time and time again, and it is a measure of their strength that failure merely propels them into some new attempt at success.'

MICHAEL KORDA

Figure 3.1 Sample list of contents

MegaProjects Inc Doc no BP2011.01 30 Oct 2011 Business Plan

Contents

Preliminary details	
Contact information	3
Document control	3
Professional advisers	3
Definitions	4
Executive summary	**5**
Current situation	**6**
Basic corporate information	6
Vision, mission, values	7
History	7
Business organisation	8
Products and services	9
Core competencies	10
External environment	**11**
The economy	11
Market analysis	12
Competitor analysis	13
Competitive advantages	14
Strategy and plans	**15**
Objectives	16
Business strategy	17
Operating plan	18
Financial analysis	**20**
Breakeven analysis	20
Sales projections	20
Capital spending	21
Operating costs	22
Profit and loss account	23
Balance sheet	24
Cash flow and funding requirements	25
Risk analysis	**26**
Overview	27
SWOT – strengths, weaknesses, opportunities and threats	29
Limiting factors	29
Critical success factors	29
Alternative scenarios	30
Specific risks and their solutions	31
Conclusion	**32**
Annexes	
A. Current projects	35
B. Detailed financial data	41
C. Biographies for the top management	51

TRADE SECRET AND CONFIDENTIAL
Copyright © 2011 MegaProjects Inc Page 2 of 20

The executive summary

As frustrating as it might seem after you spend weeks crafting the most beautiful plan ever, busy decision-makers may base their assessment of the plan on the executive summary alone. For this reason, you should do everything possible to make this the best part of your business plan.

In fact, the executive summary is the plan in miniature. It is not an introduction. Ideally, it should capture all the pertinent points of the whole plan in just one page. Indeed, if you are looking for funding you might send the executive summary to prospective investors asking them if they would like to see the whole plan (but you probably won't – see Chapter 12).

The summary sets the tone, determines how eagerly the document is read and encourages readers to turn the page (or put the plan down if you pitch it badly). The summary should be a credible marketing statement that sells your visions and objectives. At the same time it must not over-hype the ideas and it should draw attention honestly to any major risks. You will want to consider your readers. How will they interpret understatement or overstatement given their cultural backgrounds, preferences and prejudices?

 Hit with the purpose of the plan in the first sentence. Nascent Industries Inc is seeking funding of $2 million in order to … . Describe who you are, what you want to do, and what you need, including:

- management team, showing how they will make the business succeed;

- products or services, showing why they are special;

- market, indicating your niche and unique factors;

- other assets, strengths, competencies and advantages;

- strategy for success;

- key financial data;

- funding required and how it will be spent, or the approvals required.

Do not worry too much if you cannot express everything at this stage. As you work through this book you will tick off the items on this list and gain greater insight to all of them. You will tighten up your description when you come back to review the executive summary at the end of the planning process.

Figure 3.2 This is what you are going to tell them

AN INTERNAL-USE PLAN

Executive Summary
The Directors of MegaProjects Ltd are invited to review the operating plans for the period 2012–2014. Approval is sought for the business

FOR EXTERNAL USE
This concise introduction describes the purpose of the plan, the offer and the potential rewards.

The Summary then explains:

1 Who

2 What

3 How

and

4 How much

Executive Summary
Tetrylus is offering 40% of its authorised share capital for $1.25m. This is the amount of additional funding that we need to meet orders for our unique industrial computer system and generate net profits of $6m a year by 2013. We are positioning *Tetrylus* for an initial public offering in that year at an expected market capitalisation of $60m. This Business Plan sets out our strategic, operating and financial ...

The Company
Tetrylus was incorporated in February 2010 with issued share capital of $10,000. The founder, Niccolò Machiavelli, is well known for his strategic management. He is supported by René Descartes as Head of Technology. René is famous for his powers of reasoning and he brings important experience from his previous post as Head of ...

The Product
Tetrylus ONE is a package of computer hardware and software that reduces accidents in dangerous working environments and cuts the cost of complying with health and safety regulations. Our first users include major petroleum, mining and construction companies. They recover their full investment in the system within ten months ...

Corporate strategy
Pilot sales confirm that our strategy will be successful. There are five key elements to our strategy ...

Financial projections
Net profit is projected at ... Cash flow will turn positive by month 15 and the potential surplus will reach ... Funding requirements peak at ... On a realistic appraisal ... pushing the potential return on equity to ...

Opinion varies about whether you should write the executive summary first or after completing the remainder of the document. In practice, the answer is a definite yes on both counts. If you have any uncertainty about what you are trying to achieve and what should go into the plan, writing a one-page summary at the outset will help you crystallise your ideas. There will be gaps and you might rewrite most of it later, but you should not regard this as wasted effort. If preparing the plan is a team effort, the summary will help everyone to work to the same goal.

If you are writing a plan for your own use, do not fall into the trap of thinking that the executive summary says it all so there is no need to go any further with the plan. You will learn a great deal about yourself and your business by completing the plan, using it as an operating tool, and carrying out a review a year later to see what went right and wrong.

It is critically important to return to the executive summary when you have completed the remainder of the plan and rewrite the summary with the benefit of hindsight.

 If you are looking for funding, you will not get off the starting block unless your executive summary is solidly convincing and interesting.

I know of a seemingly credible business plan prepared by one of the major US international banks. They presented it to the chief finance officer of a major American investment house. He rejected it without reading more than half of the executive summary when he spotted an error of fact that was perhaps trivial. It was unrelated to the potential success of the business, but it immediately cast doubt on the reliability of all the analysis. Make sure that you avoid such fundamental errors.

Use journalistic tricks if necessary. If there is a useful fact that might or might not be 100% correct, use wording that is less specific. Instead of *demand is $10 billion a year* you might say:

- *Commentators estimate that …*

- *Industry sources indicate that …*

You can also blame somebody else, preferably somebody else with credibility. You can also pump up your opinions:

- Academic sources indicate …, although our market research suggests that commonly accepted estimates are too high/low.

'*Wherever you go, speak the language of that place.*'

CHINESE PROVERB

The conclusion

At this point, you should look ahead to the very end of the business plan. Think for a few moments about what the conclusion will say. What is it that you are building up to? What message do you want to remain in the readers' minds when they put down the plan?

You might attempt to write the conclusion at this point. Going through the thought process now will help you focus on what the plan has to say. You will then find that as you prepare the report you are naturally setting thoughts aside for the conclusion.

Of course, you must return to the summary when you have finished the plan. You will probably rework whatever you might write now – even if you do manage to write what seems to be an entirely satisfactory summary before you really get started (if so, you will be the only person ever to do this). Writing the conclusion twice – at this point and again when you have finished the plan – is not wasted effort. It really does help.

Responsibilities – and the timetable

As indicated in Chapter 1 you need to plan your planning exercise. The final stages of *planning how to plan* are to decide who will contribute to the plan and to set a timetable for its production. You want all your department heads or partners to feel involved and to buy into the strategy. Planning meetings help achieve this (see below). You could set up a schedule such as that in Figure 3.3.

Allow for additional meetings to review sticky issues. Remember also to build in an allowance for the almost inevitable slippage. You or your staff will certainly get dragged into the day-to-day operational and administrative issues described in Chapter 1 and will only return to the 'incidental' planning duties at the last minute.

When the plan is approved, you will want a formal review of progress against objectives every three or six months – or even more frequently if you are in a state of change. This is discussed in Chapter 13.

Planning meetings for planning purposes

1   Conduct a preliminary kick-off meeting, bringing together all the people who will be involved in developing the plan.

2   Schedule the first progress meeting after you have assessed the current status of your business and your external market (Chapters 4 and 5). Contributors can present their findings.

---

3 Allow a period for the information to sink in and then have another meeting – probably a series of meetings – to assess your situation and devise a strategy (Chapter 6).

4 Then allow contributors to go off and develop the operating plan, make the projections and assess the risks (Chapters 7–11).

5 Hold further meetings to review the strategy – followed perhaps by further rounds of amendments and review.

Figure 3.3 Planning to plan

MEMORANDUM

From: Head of Planning

To: CEO, Department Heads

Date: 1st August, this year

Subject: Annual Planning Exercise

Responsibilities

Co-ordination of input	Head of Planning
Historical financial analysis	Head of Finance
Current organisation	Head of Human Resources
Market analysis	Head of Marketing

Preparation of next year's plan

1. Preliminary meeting	16th August
2. Presentation of current status	30th August
3. Setting objectives	2nd September
4. Setting strategy	6th September
5. Presentation of plans	27th September
6. Review: risk, objectives and strategy	4th October
7. Final review	25th October
8. Presentation to Main Board	15th November

Progress reviews

Preliminary review of current year and reassessment of the plan for next year	15th December
Review of current year	15th January
Review of first quarter next year	15th April
Review of second quarter	15th July
Review of third quarter	15th October

.
.
.

Be a SWOT

You should not begin your written plan with an analysis of your strengths, weaknesses, opportunities and threats – the infamous SWOT analysis. This belongs later in the document (see Chapters 6 and 11); however, now is a good time in the planning process to give the matter some preliminary consideration.

- Strengths and weaknesses are internal factors over which you have some control or influence.

- Opportunities and threats are external issues that you cannot control.

For example, an outstanding management team is a *strength*, unless it belongs to your competitors in which case it is a *threat*. The boxes below list ten areas where you might find strengths and weaknesses or opportunities and threats. The lists are a bit over-simplified and generic, but they might help you think about your situation.

Ten places to look for strengths and weaknesses

Area of your business	Strengths	Weaknesses
Processes	High productivity	Slow time to market
Management	Good at acquisitions	Poor staff management
Marketing and sales	Good at direct sales	Poor market research
Other skills	Excellent R&D	Poor maintenance
Experiences	Success overseas	Fingers burnt somewhere
Intellectual property	Branding, trade secrets	Expiring patent
Premises	Excellent location	Unwanted lease
Plant, machinery	Specialist equipment	Worn-out plant
Information technology	Good management information	Poor automation
Finance	Good cash flow	Burden of debts

Ten areas where opportunities and threats can arise

Area	Opportunity	Threat
Market	Your market is growing rapidly	Your market is reaching maturity
Industry	Competition is fragmented	Competitors have strong R&D
Industry association	Compliance with standards strengthens your product	Meeting new standards increases costs
Labour market	Locally available skills	Disruptive strikes
Financial markets	Low-cost funds	Higher borrowing costs will reduce customer spending power
Exchange rates	Cheaper imported raw materials	Cheaper competing products
Green (environmental) lobby	Opportunity to sell, say, water-saving devices	Cost of anti-pollution legislation
Economic trends	Economic expansion will boost demand	Growing unemployment will reduce demand
Government policies	Tax holiday	Incentives for rival company
Natural disasters	Sell specialised equipment or relief supplies	Loss of production or data

For your business, try to list about ten items under each of the four categories. This will give you a good handle on the realities of your business. Keep this list in view as you work through the planning process, and amend it as you go. You will probably add to it considerably as you work through Chapters 4 and 5.

1   Your review of the internal working of your business in Chapter 4 will help you primarily with the list of strengths and weaknesses. But remember that these can also be related to situations in the big wide world (Chapter 5).

2   Your review of the world in Chapter 5 will lead to additions to your list of opportunities and threats. But remember that opportunities and threats do not all come from outside – some arise from within.

When you come to Chapter 6, the SWOT will help you set a strategy. In Chapter 11 it will help you analyse your risks. And of course the SWOT will add great value to your written plan.

 Generally, you want to build on strengths, exploit opportunities, fix weaknesses (before you get trampled by your competitors), and develop a strategy for dealing with threats.

Where now?

So now you have made a real start on your plan. In Chapter 4, we will engage in a period of introspection. I am going to ask you to look closely at the current state of your business. From the perspective of getting your plan on paper, the task is mainly descriptive. However, while doing this you will be reviewing your strengths and weaknesses – and identifying your core competencies.

In Chapter 5, you look outwards to the world at large. Again, the main objective is to document your market and competition. While you are doing this you will be building up your list of opportunities and threats and you will be identifying your competitive advantages.

All this lays the groundwork for what you really want to do – develop your strategy and operating plan, as discussed in Chapter 6.

Know yourself

To know one's self is to know others. CHINESE PROVERB

- Taking stock

- Start with the basics

- The central objective

- Are you visionary?

- How did you arrive here?

- Some numbers to please the bankers

- Building up value

- The all-important management team

- Business organisation

- Business infrastructure

- Products and services

- Core competencies

- The next step

Now that the plan is really under way, it is time to take a close look at your business. This chapter takes you through the process of documenting the current 'internal' status. This is an easy and fairly mechanical exercise. However, it is not unimportant. It helps both you and your readers understand your activities – and, critically, your competencies. It also helps lay the groundwork for the part of the plan that looks to the future. In Chapter 5, we will look out of the window at the world at large.

Taking stock

One of the first activities in any planning exercise is to take stock of where you are today. If you are feeling grandiose you will call this an internal audit. Conveniently you can use the exercise to write a big chunk of the plan.

 Pause for thought – core competencies

Your special mission as you work through this chapter is to identify the core competencies of your business – those things that you are really good at, where you have special skills, knowledge, experience, etc. These are real strengths on which you can build. I define these loosely to include assets, such as special equipment, which give rise to competencies. In Chapter 5, you can compare these with your competitors' and see where you have competitive advantage (or disadvantage).

While you are writing and thinking about the current situation, keep careful track of any strengths, weaknesses, opportunities and threats that you uncover.

Start with the basics

You can make a gentle start on this section of your plan by listing some basic information about your business. Think of this as the 'personal details' page of your company passport. It allows you to be formally identified.

If you are preparing a document for external use or if the business is small you can list the full details. If you are preparing a plan for internal management use and you are working for a long-established multinational it will probably be adequate to include a sensible summary only. Either way, keep it clear and concise.

Give the full corporate name, the legal status (corporation, partnership, sole trader, etc.), the address of the registered office, company and tax registration numbers, the name(s) under which the business trades if different from the corporate name, and the head office address. Depending on your location, you may need to include information such as the states in which you are authorised to operate, details of essential business licences, and other similar information. If you are looking for external funding, you should include a note of all classes of authorised, issued and paid-up capital.

On the basis that a picture is worth a thousand words, or at least livens up any report, there are two charts to consider including at this point. The first is a diagram showing the companies in the group and their relationship to each other. Of course, this is relevant only if there is more than one company or business unit. If you are writing a plan for a subsidiary, this is a good way to show where it belongs in the overall hierarchy of the group.

The second option is to include a simple organisation chart, showing the names of the key executives and their areas of responsibility. Do this if you are going to push the main business organisation section towards the back of the report because, for example, you want to describe your strategies first and then show how reorganising or growing the management team will help. Alternatively, it is unnecessary to include the chart if the immediately following page includes a description of the business organisation. Organisation charts are discussed later in this chapter (see page 69).

 The fast track to knowing yourself

1 **List basic information**

- name of business
- status (sole trader, partnership, etc.)
- capital (authorised, issued and paid-up)
- registered office address
- registration number
- other relevant business licences, tax, social security numbers, etc.
- websites, including links to networking sites used for the business (e.g. LinkedIn, Twitter, Google+, Facebook, etc.)
- head office address
- location of major R&D, factory or retail premises
- perhaps an indication of the number of employees in key locations
- professional advisers (accountants, auditors, lawyers, etc.).

2 **Specify vision, mission, philosophy**

3 **Sketch corporate history**

   ● include summary financial data for the latest five years (full details should be provided in an annex).

4 **Describe the current business organisation**

   ● list directors, general management team, describe line and staff employees.

5 **Outline the business infrastructure**

   ● list major premises, production facilities, business assets.

6 **Describe your products and services**

7 **Identify your core competencies**

The central objective

At this point, it is advisable to take a break from writing so that you can question yourself and perhaps those around you. You need to identify the central objective for the business. This is the overriding force that drives you forwards.

Naïve commentators frequently suggest that maximising profit (a monetary surplus) is the firm's central objective. At the very least this should be restated as 'maximising profitability' (the percentage return on capital employed), which is slightly different. City commentators often seem obsessed with earnings per share (EPS, essentially net profit per ordinary share – profit divided by the number of shares), but this can be a bit myopic. Among other things it favours short-term (and sometimes high-risk) projects over longer-term ventures. These ratios are discussed in Chapter 12. Stock prices are a good measure of shareholder value in the longer term.

Frequently, though, profitability or shareholder value is not the central objective. A number of common central objectives are listed in the box below. Note that the central objectives of shareholders and managers frequently diverge.

Indeed, a major difficulty is that companies do not have objectives – people do. And there can be many personal objectives all pulling in different directions. The chief executive, influential directors, individual general managers, a majority shareholder, or a wealthy individual investor might all be pursuing differing aims.

Ten common central objectives

1 Maximising shareholder value.

2 Maximising profitability (watch for managers with profit-related bonuses).

3 Maximising dividend pay-outs (there goes the working capital).

4 Maximising market share (common in Japan).

5 Maximising total assets.

6 Minimising excitement and risks – perhaps so that the chief executive has an easy ride during his or her final few years in charge.

7 Positioning the company as a takeover target – so that the owner(s) can make a quick capital gain.

8 Building an empire measured by the number of employees, the range of international subsidiaries or some other ego-inflating statistic.

9 Prudence – financial companies often pursue stability and growth.

10 Maximising some altruistic vision – such as social welfare.

Anyway, good luck in your search. I hope that you have, or can find, a single, mutually agreed and rational central objective. Once you have identified it, keep it in mind as you work through the following chapters of this book. It will provide focus for your analysis. The subject of objectives is discussed in more detail in Chapter 6.

Maximising share prices is quite a good central objective. For a public company – in theory at least – the share price reflects investors' aggregate perceptions of all of the factors that affect longer-term performance. If you correctly manage the many things that affect longer-term performance, the market will push your share price to a new peak. Share prices are more difficult yardsticks for private companies, because they are not listed on public stock exchanges.

'The only limits are, as always, those of vision.'

JAMES BROUGHTON

Are you visionary?

Now that you have identified yourself and your central objective, you should state the rationale for your business:

- what you are trying to achieve right now (your mission);

- where you are going (your vision);

- how you will behave along the way (your philosophy).

You have no doubt seen whole books dedicated to writing mission statements. You have probably heard that teams of senior corporate executives lock themselves away for days at a time to debate their vision and mission. You might think that this is going to be a painful experience, but actually it is not.

You should be able to state your vision and mission in one or two sentences each – four paragraphs at most. What do they say? Your mission statement describes what your business will be doing over the next few years. Your vision casts the net further and describes where you would like to end up in the longer term (not the long run because, as the British economist Keynes said, in the long run we are all dead). Personally, I prefer to document these starting with the big picture (vision) and working through to the philosophy. This is what I will do here.

VISION – HOW DO YOU WANT TO BE REMEMBERED?

You ought to be able to document your vision almost without further thought. This is what drives you forward. You might want to grow to be *the world's most profitable airline, have the largest clientele of any hairdresser in Beaconsfield*, or *be the number two gizigit manufacturer* – some companies prefer to let a competitor take the risks associated with being number one.

A relevant story about not being number one concerns the British De Havilland Comet, the trailblazer for passenger jet air travel in the 1950s. It suffered a series of disastrous accidents after its introduction. Months of investigation eventually revealed that the cause was the combined adverse effects of metal fatigue and repeated changes in cabin pressure. This discovery was a masterpiece of troubleshooting.

While this was happening, the US giant Boeing Corporation watched from the sidelines, learnt from events, and went on to be the world leader in passenger jets – having allowed the British company to make the mistakes. This is a clear example of where it sometimes pays to be number two at the beginning.

If you don't have a vision, you should not be writing a plan. Your only problem might be reconciling your personal vision with the corporate vision if you are not the boss but a cog in a corporate machine. In this case, check the machine's vision and slot your own into it. If the corporate vision is to supply the world's best luxury motor cars, your division might want to produce the world's most reliable gearboxes.

Be prepared to stand up for your vision if you believe it to be achievable. A bank manager I know once told a customer not to aim too high for fear of being humiliated in the event of failure. The bank manager ended his career as just that – the manager of a small branch of a big bank. The recipient of his advice ignored it, aimed high and achieved great success. Once you have a vision, do not waver from it. People may laugh, but no one can foretell the future (not businessmen, anyway) and you just might get there. If you do fall short you will always know that you gave it your best shot. Remember the problems that Columbus had getting his business plan funded in 1491.

MISSION – WHAT DO YOU WANT TO DO RIGHT NOW?

Chances are that you have a pretty good idea what business you are in. All you have to do is define this carefully and you have your mission. This is really rather important because your mission statement gives a clear indication to your readers, your employees, your business partners and your customers. It tells them what they should be working towards achieving or what they should be expecting from you.

The trick is to define your mission very precisely. It should describe exactly what you will be doing for the next three to five years (why, where, how) and what you want to achieve. It should be a statement of purpose with specific goals. Generally, it works best to focus on the business and on customer *needs and benefits* rather than on your products themselves. Remember the old adage that people do not want shovels, they want holes in the ground.

Frozen Pizza's mission statement

The *Frozen Pizza Shop* is dedicated to producing the lowest-cost square meals in Alaska. Our goals for the next three years are to:

- improve customer satisfaction by doubling the number of fish-toppings that we offer and reducing the maximum home-delivery time to three days;

- improve working conditions by reducing the working week to 50 hours and providing a fur hat and motorised ski bike for each employee;

- double our market share.

The example above shows that the Frozen Pizza Shop has clear market focus and has set targets and time-scales. In reality, *within three years* would be replaced with a specific date such as *by end 2015*.

PHILOSOPHY AND VALUES

It might be relevant at this point to include a few notes about your corporate values or philosophy. It could be obvious to you that you do not intend to exploit child labour, pollute the environment or pay back-handers, but it might be as well to say so. You might not be as explicit as this, or choose such obvious philosophies, but setting out your company values helps those reading and executing the plan. It helps create a sense of direction among employees. It might also provide a useful marketing angle. *The Body Shop* is known as much for its policies on the environment and animal and human rights as for its products themselves.

Of course, it may be that your current methods of production or sales do not accord with the philosophy to which you aspire, but you are moving towards your ideals. Explaining this will help the reader understand your thinking and how the plan was developed.

Things that are well received include references to looking after your shareholders, forging close and mutually beneficial relationships with business partners, providing career development and training for employees, caring about customers and building long-term relationships with them, being socially responsible, and so on. Avoid the temptation to be trite.

> *'I want to work for a company that contributes to and is part of the community. I want something not just to invest in. I want something to believe in.'*
>
> ANITA RODDICK, FOUNDER OF THE BODY SHOP

Have a look at Figure 4.1.

Figure 4.1 Who you are

This is simple information to find and document.

Basic corporate data

Name of Company:	*Tetrylus Inc*
Status:	International business company Incorporated in the British Virgin Islands (BVI) on 29th February 2010.
Capital	Authorised: 10,000 ordinary $1 shares. Issued: One $1 share to Niccolò Machiavelli
Registered Office:	Frond Chambers, Tortola, BVI.
Company no:	IBC—3471231
Head Office:	2010 Boston Road, Guesswhere

Some blue-sky dreaming here. I'd ask 'how' when I met them.

Vision

Tetrylus is dedicated to becoming the world-leader in industrial health and safety equipment…

The mission statement contains some clear corporate objectives.

Mission

Tetrylus's mission is to provide excellent industrial health-and-safety computer systems in Asia-Pacific. We aim to establish a 5% market share within the next three years, taking sales to over $15 million a year, and net profits to more than $6 million. We will list on NASDAQ by year five. During this time period, we will comply with ISO 13000 environmental standards, provide first-class career development for employees, reduce the maximum customer-response time to three hours, and work closely to meet other objectives of our shareholders.

Given Tetrylus's product and marketing strategy, I expected to see business partners mentioned.

Note the catch-all thrown in to appeal to prospective investors.

Company values

We will operate within strict legal and ethical guidelines … We will not test our product on animals … We will nurture our employee-team and will introduce measures to promote job satisfaction …

This is using every opportunity to provide assurance that the new product is viable.

Brief history and current status

Tetrylus is in a start-up situation. We have successfully completed one pilot project that …

Latest financial data

Financial data are included with the forecasts on page 16.

How did you arrive here?

A short history of the business with a note of the current status will help set the scene. This should be very brief, such as in the following example.

Case study

Walter Schmidt established Schmidt Pacific KallBack (SPK) in March this year after spotting that demand for lower-cost telecommunications could be met by routing calls through Micronesia. The company was incorporated in April and a service agreement was immediately signed with MI Telecoms. This market niche is now fully developed, but SPK is poised for expansion to take advantage of six new routing opportunities.

This section will naturally be shorter for plans supporting new businesses or management buyouts. In these instances its job is largely to set the scene. It will be longer if your business is large, complex or long-established. In such instances, you might be able to draw on a considerable body of knowledge or want to conduct significant research. Knowing where you have come from often helps you see where you are going, or where you have made mistakes. This is not to say that the future depends on the past.

A common mistake is to continue to fund an activity because so much money has been sunk into it already. When you come to assess the future, your opportunities must be assessed in terms of their relative merits. Spend another dollar only if the returns (however you measure them) exceed the opportunity costs of not spending it elsewhere.

Some numbers to please the bankers

During your planning process, you have to look over the finances of the business for the past few years (i.e. the historical financial data). Do not worry if you do not love crunching numbers – most sensible people do not. However, if you can understand your own bank statement, you can analyse your company's financial performance. You might want to skip forward to Chapter 7 on financial analysis before continuing here.

You have two objectives at this moment. One is to understand what has been happening to your business. The other is to communicate this to your readers. If you have a brand new business, you are spared this task and you can consider yourself lucky or hindered. Otherwise, include a brief table showing annual figures for each of the previous five years for each of:

- sales revenue;

- gross profit (sales less the cost of sales);

- gross profit as a percentage of sales;

- operating costs by key areas;

- interest paid;

- net income (net profit) before tax.

Detailed figures should go into an annex. As discussed in Chapter 3, your choice of figures will reflect the nature of your business. You might want to include the balance sheet value of certain assets or liabilities or spending related to specific areas.

> Never include financial figures in a plan without a short written analysis. You might think that the numbers are self-evident, but many readers will ignore tables or miss the important points. As mentioned before, it often makes sense to present important information three times – in a chart or picture, in a table, and in a written commentary.

In a start-up situation, you have no historical data and the business will be valued for the expected income stream with due – probably excessive – allowance for the risks. However, where you do have a track record, you will be judged more on past performance than on the potential of your ideas for the future. In other words, the cost of raising additional finance is going to depend on your past errors and successes.

Occasionally, in these circumstances it is worthwhile developing a two-stage process to create a bit of recovery before going for a large chunk of additional funding. I am not suggesting that you should massage the figures or focus unduly on short-term profits. But if you can put your house in better order before selling or renting it out, it makes sense to do so.

Incidentally, management buyouts are an exception to this rule. The current management might not be hindered in raising cash if they can show that past performance was held back by a disinterested parent.

A quick warning

If your plan is being written to raise additional finance, you must take great care when presenting historical financial data. Your readers will probably consider this to be one of the most important sections of the plan. Many investors will look first at the balance sheet. They want to see if you have:

- tangible value (assets with a genuine net worth);
- a solid core business;
- a reasonable financial situation.

This is covered in the chapters of this book that discuss your financials.

'I come from an environment where if you see a snake, you kill it. At General Motors, if you see a snake, the first thing you do is hire a consultant on snakes.'

H. ROSS PEROT

Building up value

At this point, take another break from writing. Sit back for a moment. Think about the flow of activities that converts an idea into a product or service and then deliver it to a customer. This might involve purchasing, delivery of raw materials, manufacturing, marketing, sales, delivery, after-sales support and much more.

Figure 4.2 shows a simple example of the activities and costs associated with producing an electronic assembly, such as a programmable controller for an industrial machine. Think of it as part of a computer. The total cost in this case is 1000 dollars or yen, or whatever you like. The height of each step (repeated on the right) indicates the value that activity contributes to total output.

For want of a better name I call this a value ladder because if you start at the bottom, you can see clearly how you are adding value as you build your product. We will carry the ladder around with us because it has many uses. Right now we are looking at costs. Later we will bring in selling prices and profits.

This example shows the big rungs only. In practice, you can divide each step into much more detail, highlighting your activities and costs even more precisely. Don't forget to include taxes – included here within administrative costs.

It is well worthwhile sketching a value ladder for your business. Identify in as much detail as you can the sequence of activities that you undertake as you add value to what begins as a concept and ends up as money in the bank. Try to cost each activity as accurately as possible.

Figure 4.2 A sample value ladder

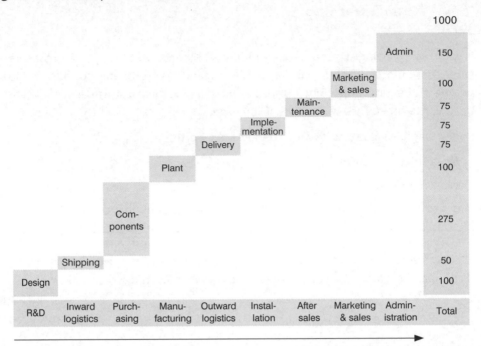

You do not have to include the sketch in your business plan, although it is a useful illustration and it shows that you understand your processes. Right now, you can use it to focus your thinking on the activities that are critical to delivering your goods and services. We will keep coming back to it during the planning process.

> The value ladder helps you identify your key activities, your optimal organisation structure and your core competencies (discussed later in this chapter, see page 78). It also helps you assess which activities can be outsourced, whether you are giving customers what they want, whether you are efficient and competitive – also known as benchmarking – and where you have competitive advantages (see Chapter 5).

BUT IS IT CORRECT?

By the way, having made the effort to draw a value ladder, do not sit back and accept it. Look for alternative steps. An obvious example would be where you buy things to make intermediate components that in turn are part of the final product. Should you instead make the things that you are buying – or go in the other direction and have someone else build the intermediate components for you?

Within each step, consider whether there are other approaches – for example, do you want to buy or lease delivery vehicles, or maybe totally outsource physical distribution? Benchmarking – learning from the best – is touched on in Chapter 5. It is a useful approach to reviewing and building a strong value ladder.

 Vested interests

Always watch out for vested interests and empire building. Your lawyer is not going to propose dispensing with his or her services and outsourcing all legal matters to a big law firm. Your head of manufacturing is unlikely to suggest spending more time with his or her family while you sub-contract production. The same applies all the way through your business. You have to take a hard look at all your activities – including those that you already outsource – and ask whether any (or perhaps which ones) are being championed by vested interests (including your own).

THE VALUE LADDER AND YOUR ORGANISATION

When you are reasonably happy with your value ladder, you can use it to check your organisation chart. Do the *functional* areas correspond to the key steps in your business activities?

Figure 4.3 shows a simple *functional* organisation structure that is found frequently around the world. There are four operating divisions that have line-management responsibilities. The other two divisions shown, quality and administration, are a bit special. They have influence over the whole business but usually no direct power. Quality management is shown out to one side to emphasise this company's commitment to high standards.

Figure 4.3 A simple organisation chart

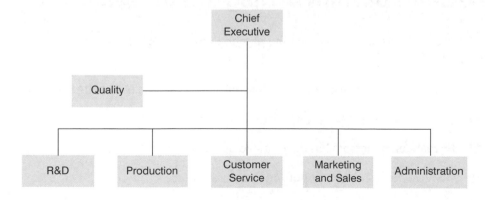

Many businesses start in a similar way to the structure shown. As they grow, each division head gains responsibility for additional products and localities. Large companies sometimes turn this upside down so that the first level below the CEO is allocated by regions or business areas (*divisional* organisation). Within divisions, there is usually a *functional* organisation.

You will have heard no doubt about *matrix* organisations. In essence, people are borrowed (full- or part-time) from their place in the main organisation chart to work on specific projects.

As you review your activities and the world environment, try to form a fresh view about how you should be organised. Do not change for the sake of it, but restructure if required by changing circumstances and if it will enhance performance or morale.

SMALL PARTS ARE MANAGEABLE

For the moment, having examined your organisation structure, think about the most important areas of your business from the viewpoint of people reviewing your business plan. Readers usually want to see costs (and income) broken down by major activities. Choose two or three sensible categories depending on the nature of your business.

A company manufacturing computers might show spending on research and development, production, and sales and marketing. A service-based organisation would include customer support or after-sales service if these were important activities, while a company writing software to order might separate out development, implementation, training and support costs.

It almost always makes sense to identify separately outlays on marketing and sales. Boards and shareholders always want to see that you are spending wisely on these areas. There is no point producing an excellent product if you do not make sales because no one knows about it.

The all-important management team

Your next descriptive job is to explain the organisation of the business. You need to demonstrate that:

- the business is organised in a way that will allow everyone to operate successfully;

- there is good corporate governance (the board is up to its job);

- the management team has the required qualities and skills; and

- you have the necessary supporting structure in place.

There could be two problems at this stage of the planning exercise. One is that you may not have an organisation to document if you are working on a new business start-up. The other is that you might not know yet if the existing organisation is structured effectively. It might appear so, but once you have developed a strategy you may decide that change is needed.

The best approach right now is to document only the current situation – keep this brief. You can return later and either write an additional section showing the changes that you are making or add a paragraph confirming the reasons why the structure is effective.

 When skills and resources are lacking

Your people are key to your success. As already suggested, shortcomings are not killers. You can always recruit. But you must be aware of where you need to use contract staff or find new people – and when. This goes into the operational plan. For the moment, add any shortfalls to the list of weaknesses in your SWOT analysis. Of course, do not forget to include any strengths on the assets side of the SWOT analysis.

Business organisation

This is the best place to include the organisation chart that is discussed earlier in this chapter (see page 69). You need to show the way that the business is structured and identify the general-management team. Name each executive in the chart. Office software usually has built-in facilities for creating charts. You can use your chart to highlight any significant organisational issues, for example:

Case study

The appointment of a Head of Quality reporting directly to the Chief Executive indicates the importance that we attach to achieving compliance with ISO 9000 quality standards. …

DIRECTORS

For a report aimed at raising external funds for a company, list the directors, showing whether they are executive or non-executive. Write a sentence or two about each indicating how their experience and skills will strengthen the governance of the business. Depending on the purpose of the plan, you might add detailed biographies (see *General managers*, below) in an annex. You probably do not need this in a business plan for internal use.

By the way, in a start-up situation directors and managers are often the same people. But they have to wear different hats depending on whether they are in the boardroom or in the production department. Directors govern, managers manage.

 Capital providers are particularly interested in the quality and breadth of the management team, especially when funding start-ups, expansion and – not surprisingly – management buyouts.

By definition, in a new business the managers will not have a track record in that situation. But they have to show that they will not fail in their jobs. You can help perceptions by making sure that the biographies bring out personal successes and achievements – especially those which are relevant to the success of your current venture – as well as important contacts and experience. For example, your head of purchasing might be considered to be able to hit the ground running if in her previous job she had a good business relationship with your intended suppliers.

In other situations, the management team is regarded slightly less critically. Ruthless bosses and investors can be quick to replace or supplement management skills. See Chapter 3 – When you don't want to be a big fish.

GENERAL MANAGERS

Write a paragraph or two about each executive, identifying concisely their duties and responsibilities and spelling out what they bring to the business. This is very important – make sure that you demonstrate the value that the management team brings to the business.

For a plan going outside of the organisation, it is imperative to provide full biographical details in an annex at the back of the plan. Do not include them as part of the main body of the plan, it will be too cumbersome and distracting.

The biographies (résumés or curriculum vitae) should include all the standard mechanical details. Include educational record, professional qualifications, membership of business organisations, a complete employment record showing names of companies, positions held and dates of tenure, and personal details including date of birth, home address and marital status. It may not be politically correct to discuss some of this information in some countries, but it is important to financiers and you gain nothing by withholding it.

> 'The kind of people I look for to fill top management spots are the eager beavers, the mavericks. These are the guys who try to do more than they're expected to do – they always reach.'
>
> LEE IACOCCA

Ownership, governance and management

Shareholders

Shareholders own the company/corporation and appoint directors (or perhaps ratify the CEO's proposal). In Japan the company's president appoints directors, while in Germany employees and unions each elect a proportion of directors.

Board of directors

The board of directors is responsible for setting (or at least approving) strategic direction, monitoring progress, appointing the most senior managers, ensuring that the company complies with legal and ethical requirements, and communicating with shareholders. There is a clear trend towards having a larger proportion of independent directors (i.e. *non-executive* (UK) or *outside* (US) *directors*) – to bring impartiality, independent judgement and additional skills and experience. Surveys suggest that boards with women on them perform better than all-male boards.

Two-tier structures are very uncommon in the US and UK, but elsewhere there are variations ranging from a decision-making (non-executive) board governing an operational (executive) board (Germany and the Netherlands) to a ceremonial board and management committee (big companies in Japan). Very broadly, titles and duties of the top dogs around the world reflect those in the US and UK.

Board committees

For larger companies, operational necessity or legislation might require certain board committees. Most common are an audit committee (safeguarding the financial integrity and risk profile of the business), a nomination committee (making recommendations on the structure of the board), and a remuneration committee (looking after pay and benefits of executives and senior management).

Boardroom top dogs in the US

- *Chief executive officer (CEO)* – often influences board composition to the extent that there are no other executive directors, but he might bring his COO (chief operating officer) on to the board. CEOs are generally all powerful; many are also the *chairman**; usually the figurehead and spokesperson; responsible for executing strategy.

- *President* – older, alternative name for the top man or woman (and frequently the founder), more common in smaller companies or maybe subsidiaries where they report to a group head known as the CEO.

Boardroom top dogs in the UK

- *Chairman* – runs board meetings, is usually the leading representative of the company; might be given executive duties by the board.

- *Managing director* – appointed by the board; is responsible for executing strategy.

* In smaller businesses with tighter budgets the chairman is frequently also the CEO or MD. This is still the case in many larger companies (including perhaps half of major US corporations – down from 75% a decade ago). The trend is towards separation of these responsibilities.

General management

General management is the highest level of management, without constant supervision. In the traditional US model, division or department heads were called (logically) *Vice-Presidents*. Corporate growth and the quest for titles with kudos has spawned amalgams such as Senior Executive Vice-President – probably the CEO's deputy. More recently, a range of CxOs has emerged (COO – chief operating officer, CFO – finance, CIO – information, and so on, sometimes known collectively as the C-suite).

The traditional UK model is much more humble. Most executives are simply referred to as *managers*. Titles such as Marketing Director are creeping into use even where there is no board appointment but are dangerous for all concerned because of the implied authority and responsibility.

OTHER LINE EMPLOYEES

It could be relevant to include selected lower-ranking managers if they complement the more senior managers' skills and experiences.

Figure 4.4 Who you are

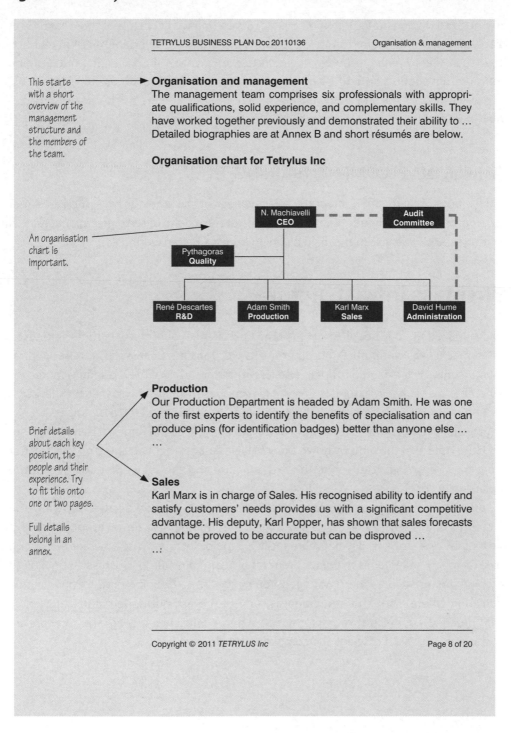

This starts with a short overview of the management structure and the members of the team.

Organisation and management

The management team comprises six professionals with appropriate qualifications, solid experience, and complementary skills. They have worked together previously and demonstrated their ability to … Detailed biographies are at Annex B and short résumés are below.

Organisation chart for Tetrylus Inc

An organisation chart is important.

```
                    N. Machiavelli          Audit
                        CEO                 Committee

         Pythagoras
          Quality

  René Descartes    Adam Smith      Karl Marx      David Hume
      R&D           Production         Sales       Administration
```

Brief details about each key position, the people and their experience. Try to fit this onto one or two pages.

Full details belong in an annex.

Production

Our Production Department is headed by Adam Smith. He was one of the first experts to identify the benefits of specialisation and can produce pins (for identification badges) better than anyone else …
…

Sales

Karl Marx is in charge of Sales. His recognised ability to identify and satisfy customers' needs provides us with a significant competitive advantage. His deputy, Karl Popper, has shown that sales forecasts cannot be proved to be accurate but can be disproved …
…:

ADMINISTRATIVE SUPPORT

You need to demonstrate that you have adequate financial controls and procedures in place, and that other administrative support is available, including information technology, legal affairs, human resources, maintenance, etc. Write a short paragraph describing your internal support structure and those services that you outsource to professional advisers. If you are starting a new business, do not underestimate the burden of processing orders, making payments and collecting amounts due to you.

CAREER DEVELOPMENT, TRAINING, ETC.

Make a note of factors that affect the effectiveness of the whole team – such as career development and training programmes, unions, works councils, restrictive practices, skill shortages. Address these in the main planning exercise before writing your plan.

Business infrastructure

You've looked at your people. Now it's time to describe your infrastructure – premises, plant, machinery, computers and other assets. For Internet businesses, the basic infrastructure may be less tangible, but it is no less important to describe it carefully. Moreover, remember that a major factor in some dotcom crashes in 2000–01 was that they lacked a bricks-and-mortar infrastructure that could be used to deliver product to customers.

You might want to draw up the fixed asset table described in Chapter 9 before continuing here. Note that the written-down book value of assets that you show on the balance sheet may be very different from the market value and this may differ again from the replacement cost.

You should indicate any major plusses or minuses. Include a table showing the addresses of any key premises – a key sales outlet in a high street or shopping mall, a prestigious research and development facility, a major factory. Write a paragraph or two describing any advantages that your premises give and any burden such as an unexpired lease on premises that you do not need. You may want to describe production facilities, indicating where plant and equipment is state-of-the-art, outmoded, underutilised or overburdened. Look also at your information systems. Efficient hardware and software are increasingly critical for efficient and competitive businesses.

Products and services

The description of your products or services might have to be relatively detailed if you have a business start-up with brand new and unknown products, or a more complex mix of products and services. The description can be very short if the products and services are simple or well known by your readers.

Figure 4.5 What you have

For a start-up situation this unexciting infrastructure information is better tucked away near the back of the plan – unless it is more biting ('implementation is currently undertaken using ...')

YAWN. There is a much better product description later in the plan (see Fig. 8.8). Maybe that was written by sales and this was written by R&D.

The writer should be trying to demonstrate what it is that Tetrylus has that is unique. Ownership of intellectual property? A niche product?

TETRYLUS BUSINESS PLAN Doc 20110136   Infrastructure, products

Infrastructure

Tetrylus is currently operating from the founders' residence. We have negotiated a satisfactory lease for office premises in the Millennium Industrial Park. We will relocate in month 1 of our start-up phase. The office is ideally situated close to manufacturing facilities, customers and the airport ...

Products

Our launch product is *Tetrylus ONE* – an automated tracking system for remotely tracking employees in hazardous working environments. The system comprises a computer software application, radio-frequency network cards and identification badges with built-in transmitters ...

The software is licensed from Arthur Andy and Son, a major international consulting house. The software is running ...

The identification badges are modified versions of badges currently produced by ...

At least these paragraphs appear to be working towards demonstrating that production risks have been minimised.

It is best to start with a one-paragraph summary and then repeat this in more detail. You might need to specify raw materials, sizing or packaging in order to build a reasonable understanding, but you probably want to save for later discussion of detailed production methods, pricing and so on. Resist the temptation to be lazy by making weak statements such as 'we manufacture the eight products described in the product fact sheets at Annex A'.

You almost certainly have more than one product or service. Indeed, this is almost essential if you are looking for start-up funding. Venture capital providers are very jumpy about a business with just one line. They have this curious notion that the business will fold and they will wave goodbye to their money if the demand for this single product or service dries up. You know of course that you can expand or modify your lines and that, anyway, you can 'create' many different products by market segmentation (discussed in Chapter 5).

You have to spell this out clearly. Unfortunately the problem is that as soon as you show a range of goods and services, the nice people with money start fretting that you might be losing focus. The middle course is to specify your products judiciously.

Include a table listing your products or services, describing them briefly and indicating the relative importance of each one. Relative importance is best illustrated by contribution to net profit. For example, if you earn the same gross sales revenue from selling computer hardware and software, but you make twice as much profit on the software, then the software contributes twice as much to the bottom line.

Try to make your description less abstract by including a simple picture or diagram. This is less important if the product is well known and probably unnecessary for a plan that is not going outside your well-run organisation. It is critical if you have a new product. You can illustrate services by being creative. A picture of a meeting might serve to illustrate the services of an accountant. This might seem unnecessary, but it is surprising how much a picture helps. Trust me.

Core competencies

You should by now have identified your core competencies – those areas where your business has specific expertise. As already indicated, these competencies reflect the aggregate of the experiences gained and the skills developed when handling specific challenges and opportunities. They may also be derived from investment in particular resources, including facilities, machinery and equipment. I prefer to define them loosely. An alternative approach is to list competencies and assets separately.

This is a good point at which to indicate the unique factors relating to your products and services. Examples include the following.

● If you manufacture, explain your competitive advantage. *We have one of the two looms in the world capable of producing cloth in this width. The capital cost of a new machine at … creates a significant barrier to entry … which tends to prevent competitors from moving into … .*

- If you are in the fortunate position of owning some intellectual property, shout about it. *We own the world wide patent/design rights for …*

- If you buy from a supplier, try to show how you have exclusive rights or some special relationship with the supplier. *Under the terms of our exclusive licence to resell this technology in Italy, the supplier cannot appoint further resellers without …*

- If you own a trademark or servicemark, explain the benefits. *We were first in this market and were able to establish ownership of the trade name which is now recognised as the leading brand … We have further protected our rights by registering this trademark in the following jurisdictions …*

Inspection of your value ladder and the *strengths* section of your SWOT will help you identify your core competencies. Some areas where you might find them are listed in the box below. The list is brief and generic. You should be able to identify much more specific skills and competencies. For example, your company might be good at bringing new products to market rapidly, miniaturising electronic components, managing takeovers and acquisitions, selling to government purchasers or hospitals, and so on.

Identify your competencies honestly, and try to rank them in order of value to you. You will want to bring these out in the written plan. For the moment, keep the details to hand for review in Chapters 5 and 6.

Fifteen areas where you might find competencies

1 R&D capability.

2 Product development.

3 Management of supplies/suppliers.

4 Production.

5 Capacity management.

6 Inventory control.

7 Branding.

8 Management of channels-to-market.

9 Market research/understanding.

10 Sales techniques/account management.

11 Information management.

12 Negotiating.

13 Corporate acquisitions.

14 International operations.

15 Specific areas of management expertise.

The next step

By working through this chapter, you have built up a picture of the business as it exists today – and documented it. You should have a good understanding of what you have that is special. However, before you can draw a line under this, you need to review it in the context of your markets. The external environment is critically important for the pressures that it exerts on you. Chapter 5 explains how to complete the assessment so that you are ready to develop a grand strategy.

Know the world

*Therefore I say: Know the enemy and know yourself, in a hundred
battles, you will never be defeated.
When you are ignorant of the enemy but know yourself,
your chances of winning or losing are equal.
If ignorant of both your enemy and of yourself
you are sure to be defeated in every battle.* SUN TZU, *THE ART OF WAR*, C. 400 BC

- For or against you?
- The next steps
- Collecting information
- Understanding the world at large
- Business partners
- The market – what you are fighting for
- The industry – what you are up against
- Competitive advantages
- Now write about it
- Moving on

Chapter 4 asked you to assess the internal state of your business. In this chapter you will look outwards to try to understand your external environment as well as possible. The aim is twofold. First, when you come to develop your strategic plan you will need a good grasp of what is going on in the big bad world. Second, and more immediate, you want your business plan to include a short description about your existing market and your competition. This will help you understand your competitive advantages.

For or against you?

The world seems to be packed with little spirits and gremlins that influence your business. Most of these are forces over which you appear to have little (or limited) control. Some are helpful. Many are waiting to catch you out. These include your competitors (actual and potential), customers (actual and prospective), business partners and a whole range of other influences.

It is important to understand the working of these external influences. You will find that you can control some of them quite well. You have to learn to work with, and adapt to, those you cannot control. Either way, you can use many of them to your advantage.

You have the greatest ability to influence those things closest to you, *your micro environment* – your company itself, business partners (including suppliers and resellers), competitors, and pressure groups such as labour or trade unions and the media. This contrasts with the world at large over which you have at best very minimal influence – your *macro environment*.

Figure 5.1 Your world environment

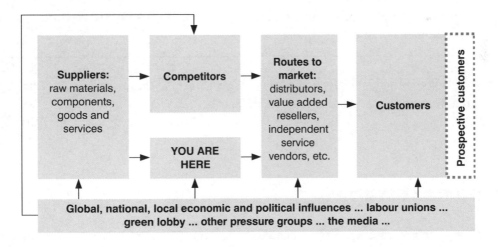

Fast track external analysis

1   Gather information from your customer files, your competitors, public sources, market research, etc.

2   Think about events in the world at large and how they have affected, do affect and could affect your business.

3   Analyse your customer base, understand your market, and think about how it could be expanded.

4   Identify and analyse your existing and potential competitors.

5   Write a short description about your existing market.

6   Write a short description about your competition.

7   Identify your competitive advantages.

 Pause for thought – competitive advantages

In Chapter 4, you identified your core competencies. As you work through this chapter, look for areas where you have competitive advantages over your rivals. Remember that in the short term these can arise from areas where you do not have special competencies – but where your competitors are weak. Alternatively, you might not have advantages even if you are very competent in specific areas if your competitors are as good or better.

Do not forget to continue building your list of strengths, weaknesses, opportunities and threats.

'While you're negotiating for a 35-hour week, remember they have only just got 66 hours in Taiwan, and you're competing with Taiwan.'

VICTOR KIAM

The next steps

For the planning process itself, you need to build a good understanding of your external environment, the extent to which you can control it, how it affects you, and where surprises might come from.

When you write about it in the plan, you need to prove that you understand your industry and market in which you operate, demonstrate where you have competitive advantages and show that you have identified a market niche for your products and services. Your readers may or may not know your market as well as you, but they almost certainly will understand the way that markets work. Moreover, you might think that there is room to replicate one of your competitor's approaches to the market. But you will find that capital providers are resistant to this and will want to see that you have identified a new angle, a fresh approach, a unique niche – competitive advantage alone ('we will do it better') is usually not enough.

Assessing the big bad world requires information, so it makes sense to continue this discussion with a quick digression to review methods of collecting data. Then we will take a look at the big picture, the overall environment in which you operate. I'll do most of the work at this stage – you just have to read and ponder. However, after this we really get down to work. I want to touch on your business partners who help you achieve your objectives, before running through your market and your industry.

You have a great deal of thinking to do, and a little research, analysis and documenting. You probably will read this chapter through completely before you start writing. Your target is to write about two pages for the actual plan. But they are important pages and you will want to get them right. You might also end up with an extensive collection of notes for your SWOT and risk analyses. I find this very interesting; I hope that you have fun also.

Collecting information

I have always been amazed that many people seem unable to collect market information and market intelligence. This must be due to mental blocks rather than any real difficulty. The job is actually surprisingly easy. Be aware though that fears and stumbling blocks can exist and give suitable guidance when you delegate the collection of information.

Market intelligence gathering is wider than market research. Given the difficulties that it can cause and its importance, it is worth running through some sources. The task begins at home.

LOOK IN YOUR OWN FILES

Start by taking a look at your own customer files and you will see that you already have a great deal of information about your customers – and therefore about your existing market. You should be doing everything possible to enhance this database and make information retrieval as easy as possible. This is a valuable marketing tool.

LISTEN

Information gathering from customers does not stop with the files about them. You can gather market intelligence about your competitors just by asking your customers. What do you think about your competitors? What are your competitors good at? Why do they succeed or fail? What are their pricing and discounting policies?

Make sure that your marketing and sales people always follow up properly. Find out why you made the sales that you did and – maybe more important – why you failed to close those sales opportunities that were lost.

Questions to ask your customers

About you and your products

- Why did your customer buy this product or service from you?
- How do they regard your products, service, responsiveness, follow-up, etc.?
- Why did they not buy that product from you? Did they buy elsewhere? Why?
- How much value do they put on specific features, quality, price, installation, after-sales service, warranty, etc.?
- What need do they have for products or product features that are not available (not available at suitable price/quality) now?
- How will their business plans open up new sales opportunities for you in the future?

About your competitors

- Who do your customers regard as your competitors?
- Why is it that your customers buy (do not buy) from your competitors?
- Where do your competitors excel? Why?
- In what areas are your competitors weak? Why?
- What are your competitors' pricing and discounting policies?

About your customers

- How do your customers make their purchasing decisions?
- Do they have strict purchasing policies?
- Do you have to be on an approved list of suppliers?
- Will you be invited automatically to bid in the future?
- Who in the organisation makes the decisions? What are their preferences and prejudices, etc.?

- Who influences decision-making? What are their preferences and prejudices, etc.?
- Who chooses product features? What are their preferences and prejudices, etc.?
- Who approves the spending – and what are their spending limits? What are their preferences and prejudices, etc.?
- What names, contact details, anniversaries and events should you have in your database?

Create a list of basic facts that you want to know (see *Questions to ask your customers*) and make sure that everyone in contact with customers (engineers and support staff – not just account managers) tries to solicit some new information about the customer's profile, decision-making processes, purchasing habits and needs.

Market intelligence also comes from people who are not your customers. You will find that some industries are fairly closed and some of your employees may well have worked for your competitors before falling off the jobs merry-go-round at your door. They will give you insight, but make sure that you do not infringe any confidentiality agreements or laws. Check with your legal adviser if necessary.

Talk to anyone who buys from competitors to find out why, even if you think they will never buy from you. In addition, your competitors' employees will usually help you – at seminars, conferences, trade shows, job interviews. People love to talk and there is no need to do anything underhand, unethical or illegal – just listen. Remember, though, that the same works both ways and this is how your competitors find out about you.

LOOK

Published information is helpful. You can also read your competitors' brochures and reports, which are often very informative. Better still, you can visit competitors' websites and check out networking sites (see overleaf), which often contain amazing details about products, sales successes, major customers, company strategy and financial performance.

You can also check prices at wholesale and retail outlets and trade shows. You can buy your competitors' products and examine them, fly on their airlines, stay in their hotels, use their services and see how their customer-related processes work.

There is a wealth of other public information, including newspaper reports, magazines, trade journals, investment bankers and stockbrokers' research reports, government statistics and other published material. You can also buy information from specialist providers of company information and independent market surveys. Take care, though, not to pay excessive amounts for out-of-date and inadequate data. Again, look out for the websites of these organisations.

Use the web

Think of websites as virtual offices or showcases on the Internet – a global network linking millions of computers. The web is wonderful. It did not exist when I started a business in 1990. When I started another business for another product in 1997, I was able to sit at home and collect volumes of information from websites all over the world.

I gathered names, addresses and contact details, product information, details of sales contracts – a vast wealth of information – for several hundred potential business partners and competitors as well as for specialised press contacts and trade fair organisers. This all stacked up very neatly and gave me an excellent insight to the market.

A decade or two later the amount of useful competition information on the web has increased exponentially.

The key to successful research on the web is understanding how search engines and directories work. It is worth spending 20 minutes looking at the advanced options on your favourite search site – click on advanced search, search tips, etc. to see how quotation marks or a plus sign might enhance your query. Then do a bit of lateral thinking while you are punching in key words, and look particularly for results which take you to specialist sites where an enthusiast has generously listed further links to the topic of interest.

Do not forget to scan blogs and networking sites. These can also give fascinating insight to your markets and competitors. You might find details about, say, product development or working practices in blogs or on Twitter. Take a look at Facebook or Google+ to see what people are saying. You can find out about the people working for your competitors if they have thoughtfully posted their career history on LinkedIn or a job search website. And, of course, watch what your own employees are saying (you may want to establish policies about what your own people can and cannot state online).

'Gentlemen: I have not had your advantages. What poor education I have received has been gained in the University of Life.'

HORATIO BOTTOMLEY, SPEECH AT OXFORD UNION, 1920

OTHER RESEARCH

Everyone must have heard of market research where consumers or other groups of prospective buyers are questioned via the Internet (e.g. take a look at Survey Monkey), telephone, postal or personal surveys. You can also observe activity at the point of sale – go and watch what customers ask for, put back on the shelves or buy. You might also test the market by advertising and selling the product – or a prototype – in a limited market area. You can test the potential with an advertisement inviting readers to ask for more information. You can even invite advance orders, so long as you genuinely intend to meet any commitments that you make.

Understanding the world at large

There is an almost frightening range of external influences that affect you. A few things to mull over are outlined in the following paragraphs – demographics, the economy, political factors, pressure groups, globalisation and technology.

These are in a constant state of change. You will find that you can predict trends in most variables and forecast how they affect your business. Moreover, you can develop a strategy to cope with those that cannot necessarily be foreseen, such as a technological breakthrough or a sudden conflict in one of your overseas markets. Major opportunities and threats should be added to your SWOT analysis. You will minimise surprises by understanding the possibilities – quality newspapers, journals and specific country, industry and technology reports all help you keep abreast of developments.

 Disaster recovery

Every business should identify the disasters that could strike and develop a policy for rapid response. Banks have arrangements so that they can recover customer information and keep trading using remote computers if their own systems suffer catastrophic failure. Oil companies operating in hostile territory have response plans for dealing with kidnappings of senior personnel. Airlines have procedures for informing and counselling relatives and managing press relations in the event of air crashes. You can instantly see the best-prepared airlines by watching the news when tragedies do, sadly, occur.

Make a list of the disasters – threats – that might affect you and make sure that you have well-rehearsed plans in place for dealing with them. Then hope that the plans are never needed – but do not forget to keep them current.

'There is no education like adversity.'

PEOPLE

The structure of the population is constantly undergoing change – locally, nationally and globally. This affects consumer markets and the industries that serve them, which in turn affects a broader range of industrial and commercial suppliers. Consumer demands from the new middle classes in emerging economies, especially China and India, will be significant in the coming decades.

The age structure of the population has obvious implications for your products and services. In the developed countries including North America, Europe and Japan, the average age of the population is increasing, due to the trend towards smaller families, healthier lifestyles and longer life spans. As a result, the physical size of these countries' 'grey' markets is increasing.

Less developed economies tend to have high birth rates and very young populations. Various events cause bulges in particular age groups of populations (youths, young married couples, the middle-aged). An obvious example is the post-war baby boom in many countries in the 1950s. Another example reflects the bulge in the birth rate in the oil-producing Middle East Gulf states in the 1970s when rocketing oil prices caused massive increases in regional wealth.

In addition, the stages of economic development of these countries – with varying focus on agriculture, industrialisation and services – affect occupations and incomes. Spending patterns are also affected by movement: immigration, emigration, rural to urban, city to suburbs and so on. Racial and cultural patterns vary, family sizes generally decrease, average income generally increases – except that the arrival or closure of a major industry affects employment and wealth in specific areas.

THE ECONOMY

Economic development and growth alter the structure of the economy. As intimated above, this leads to shifts from agrarian to low-tech industry. In turn, this develops into high-tech businesses, and as wealth increases, service industries become increasingly important. Again, as mentioned elsewhere, watch what happens as China and India become the new economic superpowers.

National competitive advantage

Everyone recalls from school geography lessons that certain countries have specific advantages. I remember learning about Canadian and Scandinavian lumber, Argentinian beef, and Middle East oil. Often, as in these examples, the advantages are based on the availability of a natural resource. Sometimes they depend on historical events or the stage of economic development – for example, London's financial services or low-cost labour in some areas in the Far East. In other instances, the advantages reflect culture – Italian design comes to mind.

All this has two important effects on your business plan.

1   It might influence your business in the geographical areas where you already operate. For example, you might have a production facility in a low-cost country – how might economic, political and social developments (wages, inflation, exchange rates, coups, revolution) affect your business?

2   It might influence where you conduct business in the future. For example, you might want to source skills or materials from new locations. Or you might consider some sort of business relationship with a foreign company which is particularly strong in an area where you are weak.

Imposed on long-term trends is the inevitable economic cycle – recession, depression, recovery, boom. This ripples through the economy, affecting employment levels, overtime, capacity use, demand for raw materials, industrial output, incomes, demand for services, and so on. The business cycle typically runs for five or seven years. Some commentators claim to see longer-term cycles with durations of 11 or even 50 years. The economic situation at the end of the twentieth century might be blamed on these longer cycles. You need to position yourself against any adverse effects from these *inevitable* cycles and exploit them where possible.

GOVERNMENT AND POLITICS

Government policy has far-reaching effects on industrial activity and consumer spending patterns. The list below shows ten ways that governments can hinder your business. Of course, there is an opposite for each of these. You should look carefully for ways that you can benefit from political activity, economic management and bureaucratic meddling.

Ten ways that governments can hold you back

1 **Taxation**. Higher taxes on income/profits decrease the spending power of consumers and companies.

2 **Public spending**. Less spending on, for example, hospitals means lower demand for medical equipment.

3 **Industrial incentives**. Reduced incentives can cut your profits, industry closures mean less employment and lower consumer spending in a specific area.

4 **Monetary policy**. Higher interest rates or a reduction in credit can kill demand.

5 **Exchange rate management** (or mismanagement). This may push up the price of your imported goods or damage your international competitiveness.

6 **Tariffs and quotas on trade**. These can reduce the availability or increase the cost of imported materials, components and finished goods.

7 **Unfair competition and monopoly/antitrust laws**. Can prevent you growing further or undertaking some activities.

8 **Deregulation and privatisations**. More open capital markets could increase the cost of financing (but are usually beneficial); deregulated telecommunications markets might remove your cosy position as a monopoly supplier.

9 **Other regulatory activities** including those affecting the environment and employment (such as the European Community's imposition of a 48-hour maximum working week) could push up your costs.

10 **Politics, diplomacy and corruption**. Military action, coups, elections, new governments reneging on previously agreed contracts, and various hidden costs can all damage your operating environment. Take care not to fall foul of tough new anti-corruption laws around the globe.

PRESSURE GROUPS

Sitting – or perhaps marching – somewhere between public and private sectors are the many and diverse lobbies that promote change. The green lobby rightly clamouring for a clean environment affects attitudes and legislation relating to energy production and use, manufacturing methods and industrial waste, product design and so on. The anti-smoking lobby affects tobacco companies. Less contentious demands for safety and standards affect food-related businesses; packaging and labelling; products with potential electrical, mechanical and thermal hazards; and so on.

Make sure that you understand which lobbies affect your business, and how you can work with them.

GLOBALISATION

The world continues to shrink due to computer and communication technologies, deregulation of exchange rate controls, softer regulations affecting capital flows, reduced tariffs on trade, deregulation of national financial industries, the quest for international harmony, and the arguable success of regional and international bodies including the EU (European Union), UN (United Nations), World Bank, and even the many standards associations including ISO (International Organization for Standardization). It's odds on that you will wake up tomorrow and find a new competitor from overseas in your physical or virtual backyard. How will you respond?

TECHNOLOGY AND THE INTERNET

Technological developments – including communications, computers and biotechnology – are causing the most rapid and dramatic changes ever in business. This exerts internal and external pressures.

Every company, whether in the new economy or not, has to consider the threat of the Internet. New competitors from any part of the globe can arise at any moment. Many are already there, awaiting their chance. As more businesses and consumers worldwide take to online purchasing, the industrial status quo and market shares could change significantly.

Companies that do not have effective information technology will not be able to process orders or understand their businesses efficiently and effectively enough to compete. Outmoded production techniques prevent the necessary customisation of products or speed to market with new products. Step changes, such as the progressions from vacuum tubes to transistors to integrated circuits, displace leading companies almost overnight. Where do you stand in all this? Are you using information technology to your advantage? Does your employee training keep you abreast (or ahead) of development? Could you introduce *disruptive technology*, which would change the way things work in your industry and put you in front of your competitors?

 I don't know what you're talking about

A few years ago, when Asian long horn beetles were found munching trees in New York, the US authorities banned untreated wood packing crates from China. Just weeks before the deadline, a trade official with a top state-owned export company in Beijing was asked what steps his company was taking to comply with the ban. 'I don't know what you are talking about,' he said. You can see how easily this situation could arise. It is easy to miss developments in this world of information overload. Could something similar happen to you?

Business partners

Do not underestimate the extent to which business partners can help you. Your most important partners are your channels to market (those individuals and companies that help you find customers, make sales and provide ongoing customer support) – and your suppliers.

SUPPLIERS

Suppliers provide you with raw materials, components, part-finished and finished goods, and services. It is in their interest that you do well. Form good relationships with your suppliers and you can both win. Do not try to cheat them, or they will do the same to you. Of course, you need to watch competitive pressures among suppliers to ensure that you are buying from the best sources and that their products are not being outmoded by, for example, technological developments elsewhere. In other words, be careful not to fall for their marketing hype. You can get advance warning of changes in the price and availability of your supplies by watching what is happening to your suppliers' inputs (including raw material prices and labour costs).

CHANNELS TO MARKET

Channels to market include simple re-sellers such as wholesalers and retailers, value added re-sellers (VARs) who enhance your product as it passes through their hands, and independent service vendors (ISVs) who use your product in the support or pursuit of sales of their own services. In the new economy, *affiliates* who act mainly as re-sellers or VARs have grown in significance. These channels are very important. Not only do they have customer relationships that often achieve product acceptance more rapidly than if you go in cold, but they also multiply your sales effort.

 Deal with a single distributor and you might be reaching millions of end-users of your product. Great leverage.

INTERMEDIARIES

Other partners, sometimes called intermediaries, include:

- warehousing, haulage and shipping companies that help you physically move your product to market;

- marketing services – including market research, advertising and marketing/media consultants;

- financial intermediaries including the banks that might be the target readers of your business plan; and

- other professional advisers including accountants, auditors and lawyers.

Look for ways that you can use business partners to share your load. In addition to the sales and marketing benefits described above, you can leverage skills, use someone else's economies of scale, cut capital costs, or benefit in many other ways. For example, rather than hiring an in-house attorney, look to see if a law firm can provide you with access to a vivarium of many specialists for much the same cost. Rather than making a big capital outlay buying your own fleet of trucks, explore whether you could sub-contract to another company that can do it for you more cheaply and more reliably.

Look back at your value ladder (see Chapter 4) and consider which parts could be effectively outsourced. Identify which business partners and intermediaries you do or could work with and how. Then assess the associated opportunities and threats, such as:

- the advantages that you can gain by leveraging their skills, experience, contacts and financial might;

- your vulnerability (for example, if a partner goes out of business or its employees strike).

You can help your cash flow by extending your period of trade credit from suppliers while invoicing and collecting early from distributors. You might not be able to do this for long, but business partners can provide assistance during your start-up phase if you help them perceive that you will be a valuable partner in the future.

'All things being equal people will buy from a friend. All things being not quite so equal, people will still buy from a friend.'

MARK MCCORMACK

The market – what you are fighting for

Your market comprises all your actual and potential buyers. While your business partners are on your side, your market is fairly neutral. Most people, frankly, do not care whether they buy from you or not – unless you create some perceived need for your products. This is an essential point to note. How you create the need for your products is a key component of your marketing plan.

For the moment, consider who you are trying to influence. To understand this you have to create order from chaos. You have to define your target market as concisely as possible. Your definition will include a geographical perspective and market segments. Your target might be very broad – *the global consumer market for all computer-related equipment* – or very narrow – *computer modems for business users in a specific town*.

 Some marketing jargon

- The **industry** in which you operate is made up of all the sellers of products that compete with your product.
- Your **potential market** comprises all actual and potential buyers of your products
  - every person or organisation with a professed *interest* in buying.
- The **available market** is those who have both *interest* and the *ability* to buy:
  - **interest** is influenced by advertising and promotions;
  - **ability** depends on spending power and access to the product.
- Your **target market** is the part of the available market that you decide to pursue – perhaps defined by geographical area or type of customer.

WHO ARE YOUR CUSTOMERS?

Start by examining the profiles of your existing customers. This may be fairly self-evident if you are a defence contractor selling to military buyers, a manufacturer of high-tech medical equipment, a software company specialising in government business, or some other tightly focused business. It might be less obvious if you provide consumer goods to a wide and varied market. The trick is to think in terms of segmentation and positioning. Positioning reflects your price–quality mix and is important. For the moment, concentrate on segmentation.

SEGMENTATION

The days are slipping away for mass-marketing of one-size-fits-all products. In many areas, technology increasingly enables customisation and marketing to a market of one customer. You might already do this if you sell very high-value products such as million-dollar computer applications. However, more common is a market segmentation approach where products are targeted at groups of buyers with similar characteristics or requirements. Companies introducing sensible segmentation usually report increased market share and increased efficiency.

What you are really trying to do is divide all prospective customers into groups that are susceptible to a similar approach. This allows you to focus product design and marketing activities. There are countless ways that markets can be segmented. A very few are illustrated in the following box.

Ten examples of market segmentation

Variable	Consumer	Industrial
Business activity	by occupation	by industry sector
Size	family, house	employees, assets, turnover
Location	city, rural, region	region, country
Resources	income groups	assets, profits
Attitudes	supporter, neutral	risk averse, quality seeker
User benefits	saves money	increases efficiency
Relationship	existing buyer	existing customer
Buying practices	impulse, regular user	centralised, decentralised
Financing	hire purchase	leasing
Loyalty	frequent buyer	repeat orders

Consumer market segmentation is most familiar and varied. You might target a segment of *25–35-year-old, single females with post-graduate qualifications working in offices in west Birmingham with incomes above £50,000 pa*. The same approach works for corporate buyers – *machine tool manufacturers with 50–100 employees located in Western Europe*.

The segments have to be effective, measurable (or estimable), accessible and large enough to be worthwhile targeting. There is little point in targeting males over six feet tall with black hair who own blue cars if you are selling baby food – not only is this group unlikely to have any consistent set of buying habits relevant to your product, but how do you identify and reach them? They are unlikely to read the same magazine, watch the same television programmes, or live in a geographical area that you can target easily. Do not overdo it, or you will end up with a confused and fragmented market (and staff).

Your prime objective at this stage of the planning exercise is to identify existing segmentation – and to think about how it might be improved. If resources are limited, you might *concentrate* your marketing on one segment. Alternatively, you might *differentiate* your product offering and marketing to two or more segments.

ARE YOU SPENDING YOUR MONEY IN THE RIGHT PLACES?

Here is an interesting little exercise that you might like to try. In Figure 5.2, the left-hand bar shows a couple of figures extracted from the value ladder in Chapter 4. You will remember that this showed the cost components of manufacturing, selling, implementing and supporting an electronic assembly. The bar on the right shows the results of asking customers how they value the package of goods and services that they receive when they buy the assemblies. Of course, in practice you also want to know full details about all the 'other' components.

In this example, it is clear that customers think that implementation and after-sales service are worth 30% of the price that they pay, yet these two services represent just 15% of your costs. Put another way, logistics, mechanics, administration costs, etc. amount to 85% of your total costs, but the customer only values these at 70% of the price that they pay. There is a clear imbalance. You would perhaps be serving customers better if you could invest more in implementation and after-sales service and cut other costs.

This is a bit oversimplified, but you can see the thought process that this analysis triggers. Even a simple estimation of customer value helps highlight whether you are spending money in the right places.

'Quality is remembered long after the price is forgotten.'

GUCCI FAMILY SLOGAN

Figure 5.2 Cost and value

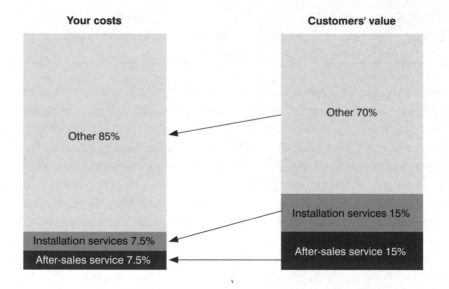

ESTIMATING TOTAL DEMAND – HOW MUCH CAN BE SOLD?

Having segmented your market, you have to estimate the size of the target segments. Well, actually, you want to estimate demand, which is the volume that will be purchased:

- by a specific target segment;
- in a defined time period;
- under defined marketing conditions.

The first two points are obvious. The third reflects the fact that demand is influenced by many factors including advertising, celebrity endorsements and other promotional activities by you or your competitors. In other words, **demand can be managed**.

The classic approach to estimating total demand is to determine the total number of buyers in the market and multiply by the quantity that an average buyer will purchase in a given time period, say one year. For example, if in your geographical market area there are 30,000 target companies and on average, one company consumes one pack of warning labels a week, then the total *volume* of market demand for warning labels is 30,000 × 52 = 1.56 million a year. If the average price is $10 a pack, then the *value* of the market is $15.6 million a year.

There are many variations on this. The most common is to start with a big number and work back using percentages. For example, if consumer spending in a given area is $200 billion a year, and 5% is thought to be on relevant products, then total market demand is 200 × 5% = $10 billion.

You can, of course, increase the complexity of these calculations to any extent, reflecting the degree of intelligent analysis that you can perform on your target segments.

 Benchmark it

Benchmarking is actually quite a useful exercise. Essentially, you compare rungs of your value ladder against the best in the industry to see where and how you can improve your practices and processes.

You do not necessarily benchmark yourself against a direct competitor. For example, you might measure your billing and collection against American Express and your concurrent engineering processes against Boeing. It tends to be the case that industries in the same market have similar value ladders. You want to improve on the industry average. Strive to be the best.

The industry – what you are up against

Having considered your product, customers and target market, the next step is to take a look at the industry in which you operate. This is the sum total of all sellers of the products – in other words, it is your competitors.

 You don't buy a Rolex to tell the time

The chairman of Rolex, when asked about the state of the watch business, replied that he had no idea. He defined correctly that he was not a watchmaker, he was in the luxury business. A classic example of *getting it wrong* is US railroad operators. In the mid-1900s they thought that they were in the railway business. They failed to notice that they were in the transport business, competing against airlines and highways – and have never recovered from that fatal error.

You need to look very carefully at your business from your perspective and from that of your customers. Make sure that you do not omit key competitors from your analysis.

YOUR COMPETITORS

You and readers of your plan must understand what you are up against. You need to identify the major companies operating in your market sector, then assess their products and services, pricing policies, market share, profitability and strategies. Sounds difficult? In fact, you probably have a much better knowledge of this than you think.

In some cases most of this information is readily available. In others you can compile it from sources such as those described above. The easiest competitors to describe are those in existence today. Do not forget to assess the likelihood that other companies might be planning to enter your market sector. There is also a growing possibility that corporations from other regions or countries will enter your territory. You might touch on this here, but you will also want to include it in the risk analysis.

If you find that there are many companies operating in your defined industry, you might want to categorise your competitors. You need to find strategic categories, where all the members will behave similarly or be affected in the same way by certain events.

Size is usually a good characteristic. A given sales situation might be too big for small companies and too tiny for big companies. If you are competing in the middle group, you have narrowed the competition for this particular opportunity. The box below shows some characteristics that differentiate companies.

Ten questions to help you pigeon-hole your competitors

1 On what size sale do they focus?

2 On what market segments do they concentrate?

3 Are they market-led or product-driven?

4 Are they developing their own products or licensing from others?

5 Are they manufacturing or just re-selling?

6 Are they focused on price or product features?

7 Are they diversified or in single industries?

8 Are their products from specific generations of technology?

9 Do they have specific branding or generic products?

10 Do they have full product lines or single products?

For your business plan, you need to summarise your assessment of the industry, and include a table listing your competitors and their market shares (see example in Figure 5.4 on page 106).

Government bodies and industry associations frequently publish estimates of total sales in specific markets. You can work back from these or make estimates using similar techniques to those described above. Figures published by your competitors – look in their annual reports and press commentary – often reveal their own estimates of market shares or give sales figures that enable you to deduce the proportions.

Indicate the reliability of the estimates. If you have to make educated guesses, say so. There is no ignominy. This information can be hard to come by, and if you have been studying it you ought to know about it more than most people.

Trends are important – look for technological developments that will lower costs and increase demand, the availability of substitute products or services, changing patterns of consumption, and so on. Remember to keep a note of opportunities and threats that you uncover when reviewing competitors.

'He gains wisdom in a happy way, who gains it by another's experience.'

PLAUTUS

Eight steps to understanding your competitors

1 Define your business and identify the firms that compete against you.

2 Segment your competitors into strategic groups (see box on page 101).

3 Assess their capabilities – follow the advice in Chapter 4, page 78, on each of them.

4 Assess their market positioning – based on their target customers and pricing policies.

5 Assess their strategies – look at their mission statements, products, pricing, advertising, public statements and so on.

6 Form a view about how they will behave and react in the market place in the future – based on all of the foregoing.

7 Write a couple of paragraphs about each major competitor.

8 Keep this up to date.

 Out of nowhere

Watch out for new competitors. The following are some of the trenches from which they will suddenly emerge.

● **Other geographical areas** – a competitor moving in from another geographical area, often overseas, can take you totally by surprise.

● **Other product markets** – a competitor with a completely different product line might decide to use its technology or marketing skills, brand image or some other competitive advantage to enter your market. Remember also the example about the railroads waking up to find that they were fighting against airlines – competitors might enter your market with a seemingly totally different product.

● **Integration** – customers or their suppliers sometimes decide that they can do what you do, but better.

● **Corporate expansion** – watch out for small companies that suddenly grow very large because they have had an injection of funds (possibly as a result of writing a business plan just like yours) from bankers or corporate mergers and acquisitions.

Competitive advantages

If you understand your business (see Chapter 4) and have analysed your market and competitors thoroughly (following the advice in this chapter), you should have emerged with a clear understanding of where you have advantage over your competitors.

The list on page 104 indicates 12 sources of advantage – but this is not even scratching the surface. If you look hard you might find competitive advantage arising from very obscure areas of your business activities.

Competitive advantage is relative. It arises from the strongest links in your value ladder relative to your competitors. This is not quite the same thing as your core competencies, because your competitors might be more competent in the same areas. Alternatively, they may be bad at something that you do only moderately well. Of course, they or a new competitor might rapidly remedy this. Clearly, the best competitive advantages are those which are sustainable over time.

 The value ladder and competitive advantage

At the risk of being repetitive, look back at the value ladder (see Chapter 4). This is an excellent way to measure yourself against your competitors. The left-hand bar in Figure 5.3 shows selected cost components of a product, with profits added so that the height of the bar shows the total selling price (in, say, dollars). The right-hand bar shows the same analysis for a competitor.

Both of you are selling for the same price (the total height of the bars is the same), but your opponent is sourcing components for less than you. This tends to suggest that your adversary has competitive advantage in the purchasing department. But you are spending less on marketing. So you have competitive advantage in this area. Right? Maybe not. Spending extra on some activities (such as research and development, staff training, marketing and customer service) is an investment that brings long-term returns. It looks as if your slick competitor is buying more cheaply and investing more in future sales.

Of course, it could also be that your underhand competitor is buying cheap unreliable components from overseas (perhaps paying much more in shipping) and pumping money into marketing in order to shift the goods.

We could go on building scenarios around this chart. The immediate message is that you need to know more to reach the correct conclusion. The information required is probably in the public domain – how reliable are your competitors' products, what marketing strategy do you observe, and so on. The broader message is that comparing your costs and profits breakdown with those of your competitors can be extremely instructive. It can highlight your competitive advantages very clearly.

Figure 5.3 Measure against competitors

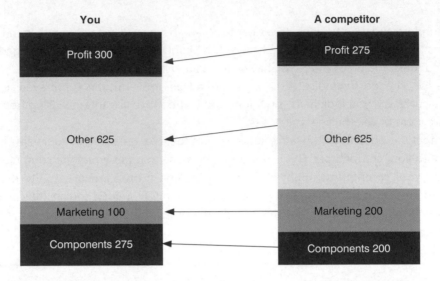

Twelve sources of competitive advantage

1   Strong research and development capabilities.

2   Access to intellectual property – trade names, trade secrets, patents, copyright, etc.

3   Exclusive re-selling or distribution rights.

4   Ownership of capital equipment (specialist machinery, exploration equipment, delivery fleets, surplus capacity).

5   Superior product and/or customer support.

6   Low-cost (and perhaps high-volume) production.

7   Other economies of scale.

8   Superior databases, management information, and data-processing ability.

9   Marketing skills related to specific customer types (e.g. defence), market segments (teenagers), channels (retail, telesales), etc.

10   Access to working capital.

11   Other excellence in management, operations, administration, etc.

12   Barriers to entry.

Moreover, make sure that you think cross-industry. An unusually large warehouse might be converted into a retail outlet for any business, an entertainment complex, a housing development, etc. Equipment that you acquired for making one item might be applied in a totally different industry. And beware that competition against you might emerge from exactly the same lateral thinking.

Once you have identified your competitive advantages, you have just about everything you need to develop a competitive strategy.

Now write about it

By now, you should have a fairly thorough view of the external environment in which you operate. If you have created a suitable framework for analysis, you will have brought order to chaos and you will find it easy to document.

Two pages in your business plan usually cover it sufficiently. At the end of Chapter 4, you wrote about your product. You can follow this logically by describing first your market, then your competition. At this stage, the description will be fairly historical and factual. Later, when you have developed a competitive strategy, you will add to these descriptions – and maybe amend them – to take account of your plans for the future. Figure 5.4 shows a sample extract from a business plan. As you can see, writing this section is straightforward enough once you have completed your analysis.

Moving on

I might have misled you when I said that you had only a little research to do when working through this chapter. I didn't want to scare you. However, if you have made it to here without suffering nervous exhaustion you have done very well. You will probably agree that the research was not really too hard. The results are, or will be, well worthwhile. If you got this bit right, it is a downhill ride to business success. Now you can have the fun of converting the effort to date into a strategy. The rewards are very satisfying.

Figure 5.4 Market and competitive analysis in the business plan

Tetrylus seems to have done its homework. This exposition is tackling a complex market and apparently explaining the analysis simply and factually.

Market and Competitive Analysis

Product classification
The product class is industrial health and safety monitoring and compliance equipment (HSMCE). There are two product categories: non-automated and computerised. *Tetrylus* is in the latter category.

Market segments
The market divides into six segments. There are three industry types (construction, mining and petroleum) each divided into large and small companies (the boundary being 2,000 manual workers and above). *Tetrylus* is targeting primarily large petroleum companies. The other large companies are secondary targets for us, but are not ruled out (see *The economy*). Small companies are currently not viable prospects on cost grounds.

However, it looks worrying that Tetrylus is dependent on three highly cyclical industries – although they do not necessarily move in step.

Territory
Tetrylus is operating in Asia-Pacific. Mining and petroleum companies have fairly homogeneous buying characteristics throughout the region, but the construction industry is more fragmented. Hong Kong and China …

A 'heavy acronym' for an unfamiliar reader.

Competitors
Four major international competitors are operating within our territory. Together they dominated 94% of the market last year, as Table 7 indicates:

A table like this is very useful – but it does highlight that Tetrylus is battling three very large players. I'd want to see which companies were in 'other' or maybe even not active in Asia at this moment (the unseen competitors).

Table 7. Asia-Pacific HSMCE sales by competitor

Company	Sales, $m	Market share, %
Pacific Link	166	46
Atlantic Watch	87	24
Indian Continental	74	20
Arctic Assets	13	4
Other	21	5
SafeTRAK	1	1
Total	**362**	**100**

I hope that Tetrylus is leading to a conclusion that supports its expectation of being able to compete.

However, when taken by market segment the picture is rather different. HSMCE sales by competitor, market segment, and territory are shown in Table 8 …

The core of your plan

If one piece is moved wrongly, the whole game is lost. CHINESE PROVERB

- A strategy and an operating plan

- What is strategy?

- Portfolio strategy – what businesses should you have?

- Business strategies to satisfy your desires

- Strategies for department managers

- Resource requirements

- Strategic objectives

- Documenting the strategy

- Creating an operating plan

- Documenting the operating plan

- Onwards

By now, you have a detailed understanding of your business and its operating environment. You have identified your core competencies, competitive advantages and strengths, weaknesses, opportunities and threats. Now you can have fun devising a strategy, setting objectives, turning them into an operating plan and documenting it. This is the focus of this chapter. In the ones that follow you can cost the plan, make cash flow projections and develop a budget.

A strategy and an operating plan

If you have been writing your business plan while working through this book, you have so far described the current status of the business and its external environment. Along the way you have documented your:

- central objective;

- vision and mission;

- core competencies;

- competitive advantages;

- strengths, weaknesses, opportunities and threats.

You now have everything that you need to develop a strategy, turn it into a plan, execute it, and bask in your success. Start by reviewing the items on the above list. Have a good hard think about how they fit together and make your business unique. Ponder also on how to cover your weaknesses, exploit the opportunities and head off threats. If you look carefully, you might find ways to turn threats into opportunities and advantages. In the middle of every difficulty lies opportunity.

As you work through the next few pages, keep in mind the fact that your ultimate aim at present is to document your strategy. The five steps that you will undertake are shown below.

Five steps to a well-documented strategy

1   Identify the domain sought – market niche, unique products, etc.

2   Explain your competitive advantages in pursuing that domain.

3   Introduce the strategy that you have devised.

4   Specify your objectives.

5   Identify the potential rewards.

What is strategy?

There seems to be confusion about the definition of strategy. Some business books tell you that strategies relate to issues that are important, long-term or high-priority. What do you think? I take the view that strategy is a route map. It shows you where you want to be and how you intend to get there – but it does not tell you how to drive or how to deal with all the little hassles that you meet along the way. This is covered in your tactical (or operating) plan.

Strategy is every bit as important for the short term as for the longer term. It should drive you through short-term buffeting and on towards your objectives as accurately as possible. It should be documented so that it shows users of your plan how to react when the outcome of some future event becomes known.

A STRATEGY IN ACTION

A new software company devised a strategy with the following steps.

1   Customise a computer application for certain companies.

2   Monitor the success of sales in each of various market sectors.

3   Further tailor the application to suit the most successful markets.

4   Build a business unit serving one of those markets, say hospitals.

5   Sell the business unit to a larger company specialising in medical systems.

6   Repeat steps 4 and 5 in other industry areas.

The strategy did not tell the sales and marketing manager what to do or where to sell. But it provided guidelines which, when supported with suitable feedback and monitoring, allowed her to operate successfully in co-operation with the company's software developers.

'Business, more than any other occupation, is a continual calculation, an instinctive exercise in foresight.'

HENRY R. LUCE

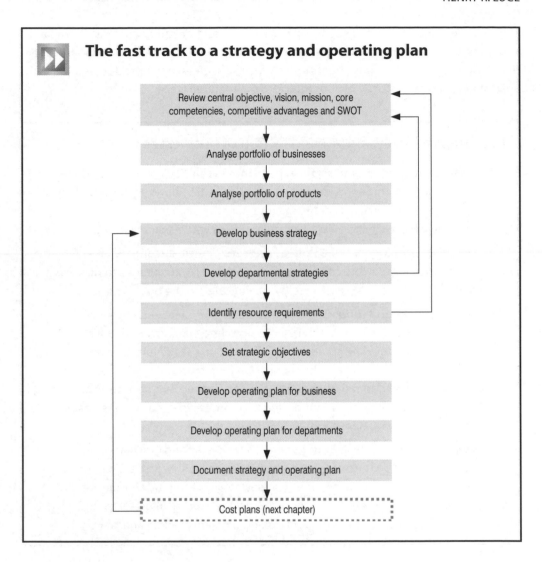

The fast track to a strategy and operating plan

Review central objective, vision, mission, core competencies, competitive advantages and SWOT

Analyse portfolio of businesses

Analyse portfolio of products

Develop business strategy

Develop departmental strategies

Identify resource requirements

Set strategic objectives

Develop operating plan for business

Develop operating plan for departments

Document strategy and operating plan

Cost plans (next chapter)

Portfolio strategy – what businesses should you have?

Up to this point, I have talked mainly as if you had just one product or business area. I touched on the subject of multiple product and businesses in Chapter 3. Now it is time to return to this complication and look at how you might allocate priorities among a *portfolio* of several business interests.

We are discussing *businesses* right now. When you have run an analysis of your collection of businesses, you should repeat the same thinking for the *products* within each business area. In other words, work through this section once, then do it again replacing the word 'business' with 'product'.

There are some wonderfully complex ways to conduct portfolio analysis. Fortunately, you do not have to worry about these. The technique described here is simple and effective. Essentially, you are investigating how your businesses (or products) square up against each other. The following box indicates the required steps.

Four steps to analysing your collection of businesses

1 **Consider the attractiveness of each business area**. You have already done this on your way through Chapters 4 and 5. Figure 6.1 shows a way of pulling all this together. Moreover, by drawing blobs over the diagram (as described in the text), you will see a good visual representation of where you are today.

2 **Review the synergy between the businesses**. You are looking for areas where you can exploit your core competencies and strategic advantages to maximum effect. Some obvious areas of synergy are indicated in the box on page 114.

3 **Weigh up risks and returns**. Consider where risks offset each other and where returns are complementary. For example, a company with a wide and mature product line could support better the risks of introducing a new product than a shiny new undertaking. A manufacturer of equipment that does well during boom times would be well balanced by a service company that maintained the equipment during hard times when customers delay spending money on new equipment.

4 **Look for supporting cash flow**. Apparently successful and growing businesses frequently suffer because of the costs of carrying inventory, processing orders and collecting accounts receivable. New businesses need funds for the initial investment. This is where a cash cow (Figure 6.1) can come in useful by providing the cash flow needed to nurture and expand problem children and stars.

Figure 6.1 combines several famous approaches to assessing the attractiveness of a business. It is highly oversimplified of course, but is still useful. It provides an easy way to visualise the forces at play. For each business area, run through measures of industry attractiveness and your competitive strength (some examples are below) and plot your position on the chart.

For example, if the industry is unattractive but you have a strong competitive position, your business belongs in the lower, right quadrant. In this case, you have a cash cow. You will not want to invest heavily, but instead should milk the existing business for all it is worth.

There is a whole range of possibilities between the four extremes. With a bit of intelligent thought you can open up the middle area and plot various interim conclusions and strategies.

'A race horse that can run a mile a few seconds faster is worth twice as much. That little extra proves to be the greatest value.'

JOHN D. HESS

Figure 6.1 How do you rate your businesses?

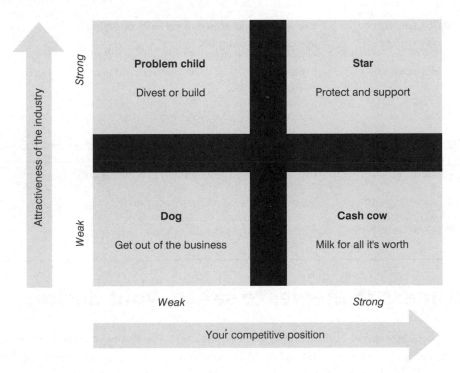

When comparing several businesses, draw blobs on the diagram – large ones for big businesses, small blobs for those that are less important to you. You will see instantly how your business areas compare.

Industry attractiveness:
- the market is large
- the market is growing fast
- competition is weak
- there are barriers to entry, keeping competitors out
- the market is not prone to severe cyclical downturns, etc.

Your competitive position:
- you have good market share
- your product is a success
- you own brands, patents, etc.
- you have low costs/high profits
- you have spare capacity
- you have access to key skills and resources.

It is easy to focus on the businesses that you do have – and overlook the businesses that you could have. You perhaps need to think a bit laterally to make sure that you cover all the options. You will end up with a list of businesses (and products) that you want to: divest; milk; expand; acquire.

Your next action is to develop business strategies to help you pursue each of these desires.

Six examples of synergy

Skill, competence or advantage	Examples of synergy gained from applying it across two businesses
1 Management	Exploitation of skills managing, say, retail outlets, or software development, etc.
2 R&D	Leverage of skills in developing plastics, micro-components, etc.
3 Vertical integration	Benefits from control over supplies and/or channels to market.
4 Branding	Use of an established name to promote a different product.
5 Marketing and sales	Building on resources for direct selling.
6 Administration	Pooling resources to reduce costs.

Business strategies to satisfy your desires

We are back to talking as if you have just one business. You know your desires. Now you need to develop a strategy. To help you organise your thoughts, 12 off-the-shelf business strategies are provided in the boxes on pages 115 to 118. As always with such lists, there has to be an element of generalisation and oversimplification. They are intended primarily to stimulate ideas. There are three each of:

● *integration strategies* (backward, horizontal and forward);

● *market-intensive strategies* (market penetration, and market and product development);

● *diversification strategies* (concentric, horizontal and conglomerate);

● *defensive strategies* (joint ventures, retrenchment and divestment).

Do not get hung up on the names. For example, forming joint ventures with other business partners is listed as a defensive strategy. Yet the purpose is often an offensive attack.

Moreover, do not forget that there is an inverse for each strategy listed here. Consider the very first one – backward integration, where you take control of your supply chain.

This often makes good sense, but at the same time the opposite (outsourcing) is very much in vogue. Similarly, breaking up conglomerates tends to feature more in current management thinking than building them (but a solid strategy is often to create a new business unit with the objective of selling it off in a couple of years' time).

Perhaps it is most important to remember that these are not the only business strategies that you can pursue – and your detailed strategy might involve a mix of many approaches. The following list shows criteria that you might use to assess and measure your strategy.

Seven criteria for evaluating strategy

1   Return on investment (ROI).

2   Risk of losing the investment.

3   Ownership and control (what has to be given up?).

4   Potential for growth.

5   Stability of employment and earnings.

6   Prestige.

7   Social responsibility.

Three cost-reduction/integration strategies

Strategy	Action	Consider pursuing if
Backward integration	Take ownership of suppliers	● you need more control over inputs ● there are few suppliers, many competitors ● the market is growing rapidly (converse is more important – in a shrinking market backward integration restricts your ability to diversify) ● suppliers earn high profit margins
Horizontal integration	Take ownership of competitors	● greater market share increases your power (watch monopoly laws) ● the market is growing rapidly ● economies of scale will be beneficial ● your target has key resources or skills that you lack ● you have resources or skills that will benefit the target
Forward integration	Take ownership of channels to market	● existing channels are expensive, unreliable or otherwise inadequate ● scarce supply of channels gives the owner competitive advantage ● the market is growing rapidly (the converse is more important – in a shrinking market forward integration reduces your ability to diversify)

BE OBJECTIVE

When developing or reviewing a strategy, try to be objective. Suppose that you conclude your review today, and then an outstanding opportunity pops up over the horizon. It wasn't part of your strategy, but it looks so tempting. What should you do? Careful analysis, of course. Be flexible, but ask thoughtful questions before changing course. The mermaid might turn out to be a sea cow (that cannot be milked).

Three market-intensive strategies

Strategy	Action	Consider pursuing if
Market penetration	Increase your share of existing markets	• existing markets are not saturated with your product • you could sell more to existing users • markets are growing and/or competitors' market shares are declining • return on marketing investment is high • increased volumes would return economies of scale
Market development	Move into new markets	• there are attractive channels to market • you are very successful in existing markets • untapped markets are beckoning • you have the required human and financial resources • you have excess production capacity • your industry is becoming more global
Product development	Improve existing products or introduce new products	• you have strong research and development capabilities • you can build on existing brand/image • products in your industry change rapidly • your competitors have better products • your market is growing rapidly

A more obvious example might be where you have a sick dog of a business. You hang on to it because it is part of your heritage, or because just a little more investment might turn it around, or for any number of other reasons. The old advice always holds true. Never look backwards when going forwards. Keep your eye on where you are going and how you get there. The past is the past. Continuing to invest in a dying business, or holding on too long in a declining industry, can both prove disastrous.

MAKE IT WORK: GET BUY-IN

Make sure that you obtain buy-in from your managers. For example, if you have a cash cow that you decide to milk, you might find that the business unit's manager is hostile because you are taking away cash that he or she wants to reinvest in his or her own unit. Similarly, if managers do not understand your strategy you may find that they are being obstructive, perhaps not properly executing instructions that 'don't make sense' to them. This is where involving managers in the planning process aids understanding and commitment.

Three diversification strategies

Strategy	Action	Consider pursuing if
Concentric	Introduce new, related products	● existing market is low-growth or saturated ● existing products are mature ● it would help sales of existing products ● core competencies would make these products very competitive (in this instance focus is on existing business areas) ● the new products would balance seasonality or cyclicality of existing products
Horizontal	Introduce new, unrelated products for existing customers	● this would boost sales of existing products ● the industry is highly competitive or low-growth ● it will exploit existing channels to market ● the new products would balance seasonality or cyclicality of existing products
Conglomerate	Introduce new, unrelated products	● existing market is shrinking or saturated ● some unique opportunity exists ● core competencies would make these products very competitive (in this instance focus is more on profits) ● the new products would balance seasonality or cyclicality of existing products ● extended activities would avoid monopoly laws ● could create a new business unit with the objective of divesting it at a profit

Strategies for non-profit organisations

It might appear that the strategies discussed here do not apply to many non-profit organisations. Generally, government departments cannot diversify or merge, charities cannot undercut competitors, and so on.

However, there are considerable opportunities – a social welfare department might outsource job counselling, schools can focus on specific niches, medical care organisations could sub-contract many activities.

Good strategic planning in non-profit organisations can enhance external confidence (through better understanding, performance measurement and accountability) and support requests for funding and other resources.

GAMES PEOPLE PLAY

When you are developing your strategy, you must take careful account of how your competitors will react. You will be unusually lucky if they sit placidly watching while you gobble up their market share. You should expect them to be monitoring you, learning from your mistakes and successes, examining your products and prices, and adapting their strategy accordingly. After all, it's what you are doing to them. Right?

Three defensive strategies

Strategy	Action	Consider pursuing if
Joint ventures and mergers	Join forces with another company	● it will ease entry to a new market (perhaps overseas) ● skills and competencies are complementary ● additional resources are needed for a compelling project ● additional might will help fight a larger competitor
Retrench	Sell assets and cut costs	● (previous!) managers have failed to implement a successful strategy ● you have failed to keep up with rapid growth ● you have persistent low efficiency, low profitability, low staff morale, etc. ● you are swamped by competitors
Divest	Sell a whole business unit	● the unit needs more resources or capital than you can provide ● the unit is dragging down the whole enterprise ● the unit no longer fits into the required portfolio ● threatened by monopoly laws ● the sale is the only way to protect shareholders' investments ● the only alternative is bankruptcy

Strategies for department managers

For the sake of argument, call the strategies outlined above *business strategies*. Once you have decided on a business strategy, the next logical step is to expand it by developing a series of *departmental strategies* – one for each functional area – research and development, production, marketing, and so on. This gives the next level of detail. For example, if your business strategy is to increase market share, your marketing strategy could include a strategy for attacking your competitors.

> Departmental strategies map directly on to your organisation chart. By delegating execution of these strategies to department managers you are halfway to having a smooth-running organisation working towards clear common objectives.

Marketing people – who generally want to wrest control of the whole shooting match – will protest that most of the strategies already outlined are themselves marketing strategies. This is true, but in an operating context I think that it makes sense to define *departmental* marketing and sales strategies at a sufficient level of detail to guide the department manager.

You should of course revisit your organisation chart in the light of your latest thinking (see the value ladder in Chapter 4). Building a business plan is similar to assembling a jigsaw with identically shaped pieces. You might think that you have one part right, but you will want to keep looking back as the picture builds up to make sure that all the components fit together properly.

PRODUCT STRATEGIES

In the process of evolving departmental strategies, you might like to think about an overall product strategy. Take a look at Figure 6.2. It illustrates a simple two-step technique. Step one invites you to select a competitive approach – with the extremes represented by differentiating your product or being the lowest-cost producer. Step two suggests that you define your areas of focus. You then know exactly where you are going.

A product strategy is an excellent bridge between business and departmental strategies. It helps you develop R&D, production and marketing strategies that are fully integrated.

It might seem obvious to us that everyone should be pulling in the same direction, but inspection of many companies suggests that this is not always clear. All too often, marketing, production and R&D are all doing – and promising – different things. Sad but true.

Figure 6.2 Two steps to a winning product strategy

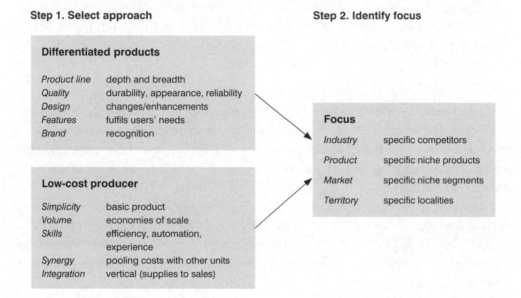

Incidentally, when thinking about your product strategy, take into account where you are in the product life cycle. This is such an obvious point that I almost forgot to mention it here. The cycle is illustrated in Chapter 8 because it is useful to discuss it in detail when forecasting sales. Essentially, sales growth is slow when new products are introduced, it accelerates rapidly as market awareness increases, but eventually levels off and then declines when the market is saturated. The trick is to keep revitalising products to extend their life cycle.

If you've got it, exploit it

It is very fashionable to claim to be market-led, to develop products that your customers want. However, superior profits can result from a well-executed asset-push strategy. In essence, you review your assets (both tangible and intangible) and decide what you can produce that will sell. You should already have a good understanding of your assets, given that you have conducted a full internal audit (see Chapter 4) and identified your competencies, strengths, opportunities and competitive advantages. You will, I hope, understand your market, given the review that is outlined in Chapter 5. This is the classic way that entrepreneurs get started – making profitable use of what they do have, rather than spending on something new. Of course, if asset-push and market-pull coincide, you will be very happy.

Figure 6.3 Marketing strategy

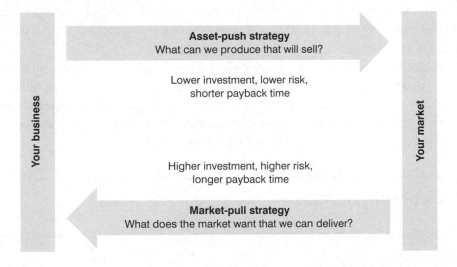

R&D STRATEGIES

As soon as – or even before – you introduce a new product or service, you should be looking for ways to make it obsolete. Your competitors will be. Failure to keep products up to date is usually the major factor that tumbles brand leaders. Another way of looking at the same issue is that new products (introduced within the past five years) often account for up to a quarter of profits.

To some extent, your R&D strategy will fall out of your product strategy. In particular, you will know by now the extent to which you intend to focus on:

● product enhancements; or

● new products.

Your business and product strategies may also have indicated where you need to pay attention to:

● products; or

● processes (the mechanics of production).

The big question, perhaps, is how will you take this forward? Six ways to conduct R&D are shown below. The extent to which you will want to conduct your own research depends partly on your industry.

If technology in your industry is changing slowly *but* the market is expanding and there are barriers to entry, carrying out your own R&D can give you substantial competitive advantages. Your R&D should try to create some trade secret or even a patent that gives you clear competitive advantage (but remember that only about 3% of patents are ever exploited commercially).

At the other extreme, the more rapidly that technology is changing, the greater the risks of spending your own money on R&D. In these circumstances, you might prefer to borrow technology from others – perhaps licensing it from an overseas partner or watching and imitating (legally and ethically) other companies. This approach allows you to reduce the costs and risks associated with developing new products.

Six approaches to R&D

1 Minimal R&D budget	or		big spender?
2 Do your own research	or		copy others?
3 Run your own R&D team	or	outsource to specialist companies?	
4 Employ R&D professionals	or	team up with a local university?	
5 Focus on pure	or		applied research?
6 Have formalised R&D	or	skunk works (unregulated 'creative' research)?	

PRODUCTION STRATEGIES

At first glance, this part of the book might appear to be focused on traditional manufacturing. But the discussion here actually covers any processes that you need to create a product or service. The processes could involve writing software or management reports, conducting biotechnology research for other users, designing educational courses, preparing meals, or providing any other service. Your business and product strategies determine (or result from) a good part of your production strategy. You have already answered questions such as the following.

1 Are you aiming to be a low-cost producer, or are you targeting specific product features, quality, etc.?

2 Will you manufacture or outsource?

3 Are you looking for vertical integration (or disintegration)?

4 Can you exploit strengths related to production capability?

At the next level of detail, some areas of production management activities to consider when developing a production strategy are listed below. Other critical issues worth emphasising include:

● time-to-market when introducing product modifications or new products;

● the ability to run small production volumes to meet specific needs;

● the provision of appropriate customer support.

Five considerations when setting production strategy

Activity	Strategy includes consideration of:
Quality	quality control, sampling, testing, assurance; compliance with ISO quality and environmental standards; compliance with other relevant standards such as US FCC and European CE marking
Process	production methods and technology; location and design of production facilities; requirements for plant, equipment and machinery; automation; process balancing, flow and control; logistics
Capacity	minimum, optimum and maximum capacity levels; actual utilisation; seasonal and cyclical spikes; flexibility and scheduling; effects of future demand
Inventory	optimal levels of raw materials, work in progress and finished goods; purchasing; just-in-time techniques; supplier linkages; materials handling; order processing
Workforce	availability of skills, unskilled workers, and other support staff; job descriptions; performance measurement; training and development; motivation

Do not forget to make sure that your marketing and sales department conducts effective, ongoing market research. Understanding your competitors and customers is critical and, as discussed in Chapter 4, everyone in the organisation has a part to play. Marketing and sales should almost certainly take overall responsibility.

MARKETING AND SALES STRATEGIES

By now, you know in general terms what *marketing and sales* has to achieve. The detailed strategy will support this. Some competitive strategies for marketing and sales are listed below.

On the assumption that you are not retrenching or otherwise reducing activities, your aim is to create demand – a need – for your goods and services. You have already thought about market segmentation. Price, branding, advertising, promotions, channels to market and public relations are other key factors. I have strong feelings about all of these, but the only one to which I want to draw special attention is pricing.

Military-inspired strategies for marketing and sales	
Head-on attack	Sell in same market segments as your competitors
Flank attack	Attack your competitors' weakest products and markets with your strongest
Encirclement	Surround and stifle your competitors by offering a comprehensive range of product options
Guerrilla attack	Mount surprise attacks in favourable markets
Exploit strengths	Focus on one or a small number of products
Stay out of range	Focus on specialised markets where competitors are disinterested
Territorial focus	Dominate a smaller locality
Diplomacy	Form a joint venture or other beneficial relationship

Can you increase prices – or should you reduce them?

It is important to understand the pricing dynamics for your products. What happens to demand when your prices change? This depends on price elasticity (forgive the economics jargon). In summary:

1 **If demand is elastic (very flexible):**
    a. *if you cut prices*, people will buy more and *sales revenue will rise;*
    b. if you increase prices, revenue will decline.

2 **If demand is inelastic (relatively fixed):**
    a. *if you increase prices*, people will still buy the same amount and so *sales revenue will increase;*
    b. if you reduce prices, revenue will fall.

Interesting! Clearly, before pumping up the price you want to know whether your market is price-elastic or not – and the degree of elasticity. Demand will be inelastic if the product is perceived as essential and if there are no substitute products. Remember to think laterally about this. For example, substitutes for the telephone include email, video conferencing, pagers, radios, postal services, courier services, messengers, travel and so on.

'The secret of business is knowing something that nobody else knows.'

ARISTOTLE ONASSIS

 If you increase prices in an elastic (price-sensitive) market, you will have to find additional buyers to make up for the reduction in purchases by existing buyers.

What the market will bear

The other area of pricing worth spending a couple of moments on is the choice between the well-known 'cost-plus' formula (cost plus a percentage profit margin) and value pricing (i.e. what the market will bear). If you really understand your market, value pricing boosts revenues. A little careful experimentation can sometimes pay dividends (literally).

STRATEGIES FOR ADMINISTRATION AND SUPPORT SERVICES

Effective strategic planning touches on all areas of your business. Do not forget to conduct a thorough review of administrative areas. The box below provides a list of things to think about when setting strategy for your underlying support services.

Five areas to consider when setting strategies for administration and support services

Area	Some factors to consider when developing strategy
Information technology	Availability and efficiency of systems; design and integration of systems; ease of communications; availability of management information; management of databases; security; processing ability; operational effectiveness (not necessarily technical excellence); Internet presence; backup
Human resources	Recruitment and development of personnel; terms and conditions of employment; pay and benefits; collective bargaining methods; morale; employee communications
Finance	Managing cash flow and surplus balances; funding; terms of loans; equity, initial public offerings; managing receivables; bad debts; factoring; processing payments; availability of management information; financial control; audits
Legal	Management and protection of intellectual property; efficient contract administration; protection of the interests of stakeholders (shareholders, employees, partners, customers); product liability; mergers and takeovers
Other	Shareholder relations; public relations; disaster management; order processing; premises management and maintenance; security

'Your legacy should be that you made it better than it was when you got it.'

LEE IACOCCA

Some of these are really rather important! Many impose a heavy operational burden, so you might look for strategies to reduce the overheads and increase the benefits. It is always difficult to choose between children, and I probably do not need to tell you this, but it is increasingly critical to make good use of information technology. Make sure that you are continually building your information resources – about your business, competitors, customers, etc. – and streamlining your processes. Your competitors will be.

Resource requirements

Your strategy will require resources, including some or all of the following:

- investment and working capital;
- direction, management, and operating and support personnel;
- premises, plant, machinery, equipment, etc.;
- raw materials, components, finished goods;
- professional services.

Look back at what you have (see Chapter 4) and list the additional resources that you might need. You will need to confirm the feasibility of obtaining any additional resources. If you think you can get them, draw up a timetable for bringing them on board. If the requirements are unreasonable, it is time to revisit your strategy.

Strategic objectives

So, you have decided on a strategy. Now it is time to specify strategic objectives. These identify what your strategy has to lead you towards and what your plans have to achieve.

If you found setting a strategy exhausting, you will be relieved that deriving the objectives is rather easy. Simply identify the key things that you need to achieve to make your strategy a success, and write them down. Remember to make these objectives as specific and measurable as possible – try to include target dates, and quantities or values to be achieved or milestones to reach.

It might assist your thinking if you consider that objectives are tempered by constraints and responsibilities. Constraints might be an upper limit on the amount of working capital available, restrictive practices imposed by a unionised workforce, an inefficient corporate infrastructure that will take time to change, or other internal factors. Responsibilities are external restrictions such as government regulations that affect the way that you can operate. Both might include your corporate values discussed in Chapter 4.

 Do not understate your objectives. Stretch yourself and your organisation. It is remarkable how clearly defined objectives 'happen', however tough they are.

Figure 6.4 Strategy in the plan

Business strategy

Overview

Domain →

The market analysis on page 10 indicates that we can take advantage of an unexploited market niche – automated safety systems for large petroleum companies operating in Asia-Pacific. The main countries …

Sustained competitive advantage →

We were the first to spot the gap in the market and our exclusive licence for the identification badge locks out the main competitors. We estimate that there will be a 15-month time lag before they are in a position to compete … By which time we will have achieved critical mass and the market will be unattractive to them for the reasons explained … We will also use the revenue from the first sales to develop …

Adaptive strategy

Strategy →

In essence, our strategy is to:

1. Work with ISPs to enable fast deployment of our system using their relationships and resources. We have signed exclusive agreements with …
2. Pursue the strategic sales indicated in Table 16, column C that will take us to critical mass most rapidly and lock out the major competitors.
3. Use revenue for the initial sales to erect barriers to entry as shown in …
4. …

Quantified objectives →

Objectives

The strategic objectives that we have set in relation to this strategy are as follows:

1. Annual sales volumes in the range shown in Table 16, column D.
2. Completion of modifications to hardware as described in Table 17 by the dates indicated.
3. Completion of modifications to software as described in Table 17 by the dates indicated.
4. …

Risks, rewards →

Rewards

The range of possible returns from pursuing this strategy is illustrated in Table 18 …

… and reassurance →

Our pilot sales have ensured that we will achieve the first two sales on the list in Table 16, column C. The third sale will give us control of 55% of our target market, given that these users are also service providers to other oil companies and will require them to use our system for compatibility …

Documenting the strategy

You now should be ready to document your strategy. You will recall that the required five steps are as follows:

1   Identify the domain sought – market niche, unique products, etc.

2   Explain your competitive advantages in pursuing that domain.

3   Introduce the strategy that you have devised.

4   Specify your objectives.

5   Outline the potential rewards (we will really bring out the rewards in the financials – especially in Chapter 10).

An example is shown in Figure 6.4. Over to you again.

'If there's a way to do it better … find it.'

THOMAS A. EDISON

Creating an operating plan

By now, you could be thinking that I have dwelt very heavily on developing the strategic part of the plan. Maybe I have, but for two good reasons. First, business managers rarely seem to have enough time to think about strategy and I thought it was useful to spend more time on this topic. Second, when the strategy and related objectives are carefully defined, the operating plan becomes almost self-evident.

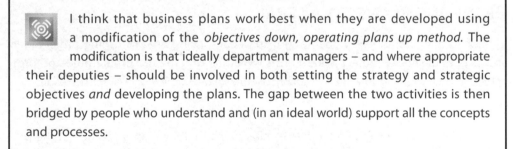

I think that business plans work best when they are developed using a modification of the *objectives down, operating plans up method.* The modification is that ideally department managers – and where appropriate their deputies – should be involved in both setting the strategy and strategic objectives *and* developing the plans. The gap between the two activities is then bridged by people who understand and (in an ideal world) support all the concepts and processes.

You need to develop the following operating plans:

● one at a broad, high level of detail for the business as a whole; and

● one more detailed plan for *each* functional department.

The broad high-level plan will identify major linkages and critical paths. It provides the framework for developing the departmental operating plans. As with every other step in producing a business plan, this is an iterative and interrelated activity. In reality neither the broad, top-level plan nor the departmental plans can be produced in isolation.

The operational plans will each produce a series of operational objectives. Sometimes these are more milestones to be reached rather than targets to be hit, but the more measurable they are the better (this is discussed again in Chapter 13). For example, the plan for the finance department might include a repetitive cycle for paying salaries. The operating objective would be similar to this:

Ensure that all casual labourers are paid their salaries at 3pm each Friday or if it is a public holiday on the preceding working day.

If you then had a standard procedure for paying wages (underpinned by your wages policies), and objectives in the plan were translated into personal objectives for employees, everyone would know exactly what they were expected to do. Carrying this through to the whole business:

- operating employees follow the operating plan, carrying out the standard procedure for each activity;

- department managers ensure that the operating plan is working by ticking off the achievement of the operational objectives;

- the chief executive ticks off the achievement of strategic objectives; and

- the directors play golf.

Everything runs like a well-oiled machine. Well, maybe. But I am getting ahead of myself. Chapter 13 provides guidance on how to execute the plan.

OPERATING PLANS IN GENERAL

It helps to think about every operating plan as comprising one overriding project plan and a series of smaller project plans. Purists will argue that this is a programme-and-projects-plan but we can ignore this complaint for the sake of achieving a practical result.

> The list on page 132 indicates nine steps that you can undertake to help ensure that any plans work. The first step, breaking the required activities into the smallest component activities, is an important initial step. Doing this makes almost anything seem more manageable.

There are many well-known techniques that help you analyse and illustrate the linkages, critical activities and risks. Four of these are outlined below:

PERT (programme evaluation and review)

This was developed by the US Navy in 1958 to help co-ordinate a massive 3000 contractors and agencies working on the Polaris missile and nuclear submarine project. PERT deals well with *unknown* time-scales and incorporates probabilities that activities will be completed on time. It does not include consideration of costs (why should it, the Navy spends public money).

CPA (critical path analysis)

CPA originated on the European side of the Atlantic at about the same time. This has greater emphasis on *known* completion times (expected and fastest or 'crash' times).

Network diagrams

These are spiders' webs, with each thread representing one activity. They are arranged in order and come together at required coincident events. These help plot *critical paths* (see page 132) to completion of the project.

Gantt charts

Developed a century ago by none other than (as you guessed) Henry Gantt, these are bar diagrams that help document a plan.

These techniques can be usefully combined. Figure 6.5 illustrates one way of doing this. The illustration is highly simplified and shows some of the activities that have to be undertaken prior to opening a new retail outlet.

It is very easy to draw up project plans using computer software applications for project planning. These allow you to record information about the project, make changes with relative ease, and view project information in various ways. Options range from the free and relatively simple GanttProject (good, as its name suggests, for making Gantt charts) to the wide-ranging and costly Microsoft Project (which requires some effort to master). You are in a happy situation if you already have project planning software and know how to use it. Do not rush out and get it just because I have mentioned it here, but it can be a pretty useful tool.

The critical path

The linkages (arrows) included in Figure 6.5 show the critical path. Each activity on the critical path has to be completed before the next can begin. This path is actually the longest path through the diagram – and the shortest possible time to completion of the project.

Assuming a 7-day week, this critical path requires 52 days (allowing 1 day for delivery). This is the *expected time* to completion. Unless the time taken for these activities can be shortened, the project cannot happen any faster than this. If the target is to open on 1 June, the slack time in the overall project is 9 days.

Fastest and slowest completion times

If for each activity the minimum and maximum completion times are noted, you can then identify the earliest and latest likely completion dates. Remember to check that these extremes do not change the critical path. For example, if the legal adviser can shorten step one (completing the premises lease) to 5 days, the critical path becomes the 43 days defined by the inventory activities numbered 9 to 12. If you assign probabilities to each time period, you can calculate the probability of opening on time.

Start and end dates for each activity

You can also work through the chart identifying the earliest and latest start dates for each activity. As shown, the inventory planning can begin on any date between 1 and 9 April. Activities such as this with *slack time* may yield resources for other tasks.

Figure 6.5 Charting your way through a project

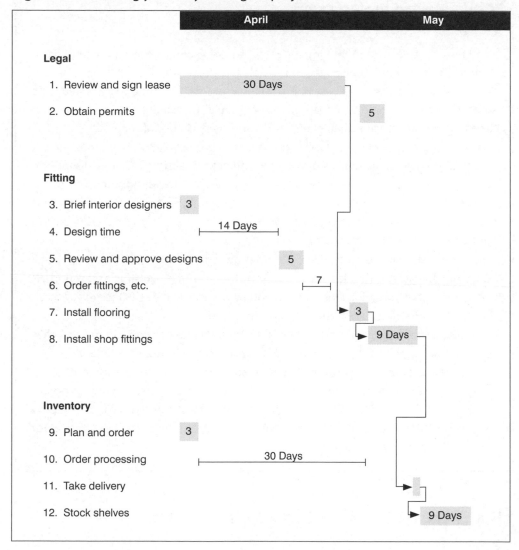

Making it more useful

In practice, all other linkages would also be drawn – such as those linking activities 3 to 7 in sequence. You can also include responsibilities, probabilities, maximum and minimum times, costs and so on. We will look at costs in the following chapters about *financials*. Chapter 11 introduces techniques for assessing probabilities relating to completion time, costs, etc.

Making projects work

You know as well as I do that large projects are rarely completed on time or within budget. The bigger the project, the more likely it is that it will overrun. In fact, therein lies the reason. Projects work best when divided into smaller components or steps. The smaller the better. Moreover, if the steps are very small, measurable and reversible, you have a perfect approach with minimised risks and every chance of success.

For example, if one of your R&D teams is sent off to develop a new super whatsit and told to report back in six months – the project will almost certainly disappoint you and cost you a lot of money. On the other hand, if the assignment is broken into small steps, each with clear targets, and if the highest-risk steps are tackled first, you always know where you stand and as time passes you have increasing confidence that the project will succeed.

My ideal situation is to have targets that are spaced no more than one week apart. Any longer and things start to go wrong. This is not as extreme as it sounds. It is fair to say that you might relax this as you move up the ladder. Once every three months to six months might be acceptable for more senior executives.

I deplore the progress reports that many managers demand for no reason other than the sake of reporting. In practice, the best reporting is quantified confirmation that targets are being met together with instant alerts about possible problems, delays or cost overruns. You will almost certainly need to massage your corporate culture in order to achieve this. It seems to be part of human nature to report missed deadlines no sooner than the date of the deadline, even if the overshoot became apparent weeks earlier.

Documenting the operating plan

When you have devised an operating plan, you will find it relatively straightforward to document. The amount of detail required will depend on your target readers. You need enough to satisfy them that you have an effective operating plan. In some instances, the high-level operating plan for the business as a whole will be enough for the business plan document. In others, you will need to include departmental plans.

 One venture capital provider told me that he likes a plan to tell him what the business managers will start doing on the day after the funding is paid into their account.

A simplified Gantt chart helps illustrate the key steps. You can then write a brief line-by-line commentary describing why key activities are required when. These become your operational objectives. If you have drawn up highly detailed Gantt charts by departmental/functional area, they can go in an annex. If you write a one-paragraph commentary about each line in your charts, tying them into the financial operating plans, you will have a clear, logical and very detailed operating plan. Chapter 13 further discusses the use of the objectives when steering the business.

Onwards

You have now completed the very core of your business plan. The hard part is over. The next step is to cost your plans and draw up budgets and cash flow forecasts. This is not to say that these are separate processes. All the steps in preparing a business plan are interactive. You cannot consider any one in isolation. You may have had to prepare financial estimates in order to develop the strategy and operating plan. Or you might decide to revise these parts of the plan after looking at the costs. Let's move on.

> 'If one wants to be successful, one must think; one must think until it hurts.
> One must worry about a problem in one's mind until it seems there cannot be another
> aspect of it that hasn't been considered.'
>
> LORD THOMSON OF FLEET

About these numbers

The bank's accounts show its true position.
The actual position is a little better still.
Chairman, London and County Bank. THE ECONOMIST, FEBRUARY 1901

- 'The time has come,' the walrus said, 'to speak of other things'
- Varying views of the same numbers
- The way that bean counters think
- The planning horizon
- Looking back
- Estimating the present
- Crystal ball gazing
- Software tools
- Putting it to good use

Probably, this is the best part of the book. We are about to arrive at the bottom line. How much money is going to be spent? How much funding is required? For commercial ventures, how much profit will be made? We also see how mischievous planners sometimes massage the figures and hide away the bad news.

I promise a gentle start. We will take a look at the numbers that you need and discuss the way that they build up into the financial statements. Along the way you will have to put up with some of the terminology that accountants use. But then, it is just as well to be able to speak their language. I will also warn you about some of their preconceptions and unique way of thinking – and how these affect your business planning.

We will also take a preliminary look at how you produce your summaries and forecasts. In Chapter 8, the focus shifts mainly to forecasts rather than historical data. This is because summarising the past is very easy once you have worked through a forecasting exercise.

- Chapter 8 looks at forecasting sales and the cost of sales to arrive at gross profit.

- Chapter 9 takes you through forecasting capital and current spending to arrive at net income/net profit.

- Chapter 10 describes a mechanical restatement of the figures from Chapters 8 and 9 – into balance sheet and cash flow forecast. It then discusses how you can fund a deficit and how you should use a surplus.

- Chapter 11 reviews the risks and threats that affect your business activities and (sorry about this) that will probably cause you to revise your forecasts.

- Finally, Chapter 12 looks at the way that others will interpret your financials – which is rather important.

'The time has come,' the walrus said, 'to speak of other things'

The time has arrived to work through the financials in the business plan. This is not difficult. It requires a little careful thought and some sensible estimating. It can be time consuming. But if you approach it in the right frame of mind, it is straightforward and, dare I say, enjoyable. Moreover, with the correct approach on the first pass, you have a framework to simplify all future financial analysis and forecasting. Always aim to automate or mechanise repetitive activities.

The financial analysis is the easiest part if you are numerate. If you shrink from dealing with numbers, do not be alarmed. Just work through these chapters step by step and it will fall into place. You will be surprised how easy it is.

Rightly or wrongly – usually wrongly – the numbers in the financial plan take on a spurious air of accuracy and importance. They usually become key targets for measuring performance. Retain a healthy scepticism. The numbers are only best guesses. We are going to see how the same numbers can be made to tell different stories and how you can help your readers to understand your message.

The fast track to financial basics

1 Start by remembering that business professionals are familiar with three types of financial transactions – those relating to sales, operating costs and capital spending.

2 Review the way that the three types of transactions relate to the three financial statements – the balance sheet, profit and loss account and cash flow statement.

3 Remember that you are dealing with the past, present and future. You usually have incomplete information for the present – such as when you are preparing next year's business plan *during* the current financial year.

4 Before going on to start analysing sales and costs, make sure that you understand some basic accounting principles.

5 Finally, take a look at the way that you can use computer spreadsheets to simplify your work.

Varying views of the same numbers

THREE VIEWS OF FINANCIAL TRANSACTIONS

You were promised a gentle start. So let me begin by stating the obvious. You are interested in the following three types of transactions.

1 Sales
In fact, you should be obsessed with sales volumes, selling prices and the direct cost of buying, developing or producing the items that you sell. This is what business is all about.

2 Capital outlays
These are primarily spending on productive assets with a life of more than one year; the secret to future income. I will talk mainly about fixed assets (such as plant, machinery and equipment), but the same considerations apply to any investment spending (such as when you take over another company).

3 Operating costs

This is all other expenditure – salaries, wages, stationery, telecommunications – the painful daily costs of running the business.

These figures are not too hard to pull together, as discussed in Chapters 8 and 9.

If you are relatively new to all this, you might find it useful to review the components of various financial statements and see how they fit together. You could take a look at the balance sheet in Figure 10.2, profit and loss account in Figure 9.7 and cash flow in Figure 10.3.

THREE FINANCIAL STATEMENTS

By themselves, the three types of transactions just mentioned are interesting. They take on special meaning when reclassified into three key financial statements. This is a simple matter of mechanical arithmetic. The three statements are as follows and their relationships are shown in Figure 7.1.

1 The balance sheet

Think of this as a snapshot of your finances at one moment in time, say, midnight on 31 December. The balance sheet shows, in financial terms and to the best of the accounting world's ability, the sum total of what you have done in the past and where you are today. See Figure 7.2 and *Balance sheet basics* on page 143.

2 The income or profit and loss (P&L) account

This shows the very important bottom line – net income (American usage) or the net profit or net loss (British usage). US readers will know this as an *income statement* even though it includes expenditure. For the sake of avoiding ambiguity I'll generally refer to it as the profit and loss account. It records financial flows relating to a specific period, perhaps a month or a year. The flows are essentially sales income less production costs and operating costs. The difference is net profit (or loss). Transactions are recorded in the period to which they relate. For example, rent for May is entered in the accounts for May even if it was actually paid in advance in April.

3 The cash flow statement

This shows financial flows as and when they actually happen (rent for May paid in advance in April is recorded in April). It is not unusual for the profit and loss account to look very healthy at the precise moment that negative cash flow (a big borrowing requirement) is strangling the business.

> Most people understand profit and loss accounts. The concepts behind the critical cash flow projection are easy enough to grasp. Balance sheets have managed to take on an unnecessary air of mystery. For this reason, I think it is useful to spend a few moments unravelling them. Take a look at Figure 7.2 and the following text that illustrates the basics.

THREE TIME PERIODS

The familiar transactions in the first list above (sales, operating costs) – and therefore the financial statements in the second list (balance sheet, P&L, cash flow) – apply to three time periods:

- *the past* – historical data from your records;

- *the present* (approximately) – where it is usually necessary to make some estimations;

- *the future* – which you are about to try to predict.

This might seem painfully obvious. I mention it to draw your attention to the fact that rarely do you have complete information for the current period. You might begin your planning in August. Obviously, at that time final figures for the current calendar year are not available. The usual practice is to estimate them before starting the forecast for the year ahead.

Figure 7.1 Basic relationships

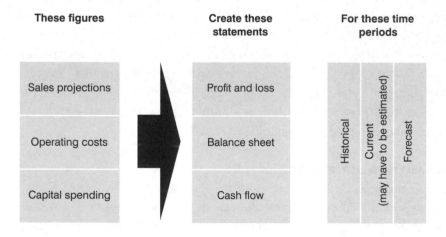

These figures	Create these statements	For these time periods
Sales projections	Profit and loss	Historical
Operating costs	Balance sheet	Current (may have to be estimated)
Capital spending	Cash flow	Forecast

Figure 7.2 The three sections of a balance sheet

Assets	Liabilities
Amounts owned or owed to you	Amounts you owe
Uses of funds	Sources of funds
Debit balances	Credit balances
An increase (a debit) shows use of funds	An increase (a credit) shows source of funds
	Owners' equity
	Capital and retained earnings
	What the stakeholders have put in and left in

 Balance sheet basics

I recall attending a meeting with the general manager of one of the world's top 200 banks. Just before we entered his office, a senior executive of the bank told me 'forget the balance sheet, nobody understands them'. This is largely true. Balance sheets are the least understood of all financial statements.

However, most venture capital providers and most bankers are pretty hot cookies when it comes to reading balance sheets. The discussion in the following pages will help you stay at least one jump ahead. I will show you how the balance sheet reveals if you have enough liquidity – and whether you could sell enough assets to cover your debts if the crunch came.

The company bean counter buries all manner of interesting information in balance sheets. They provide a snapshot of the financial health of a business at a single moment in time. They show what is owned and what is owed. The entries can be classified under the following three headings.

1 **Assets.** There are things you own, such as equipment and cash in the bank, and money that is owed to you by your debtors. You are halfway there if you have spotted the fact that the bank is actually one of your debtors when you have funds on deposit.
2 **Liabilities.** These might seem unwelcome at first glance – amounts that you owe to your creditors, such as bank loans to you and accounts payable by you. In fact, these are the funds that help you build your business.

3 Owners' or shareholders' equity. This is paid-up capital and undistributedprofits (otherwise known as retained earnings). You want to make it grow every year.

It is an immutable rule that **assets = liabilities plus owners' equity** or, put another way, **assets less liabilities = owners' equity**. Bear this in mind for later.

Sources and uses of funds

Balance sheets show *balances*. If you calculate the difference between the figures in a pair of corresponding balances (prepared at, say, the end of June and the end of July) you see the *flows* that have occurred. This is a useful alternative way of looking at the numbers. It reveals sources and uses of funds:

● **An increase in an asset account shows a use of funds.** For example, a $1000 increase in *other assets – deposits paid* indicates that $1000 has been used to make a deposit, perhaps on office rent.

● **An increase in a liability account shows a source of funds**. For example, a $1000 increase in bank loans received means that $1000 has been borrowed (*sourced*) from the bank.

The way that bean counters think

If you are handling a business plan then wherever you are, whatever you do, you need to be familiar with the preconceptions of the accounting profession. Some of their amusing beliefs are listed on page 146. Three other little issues that are worthy of special mention are as follows.

Debits and credits

This might seem to be another obvious thing to say, but make sure that you know the difference between debits and credits (see *Who owes whom?* on page 147). If you are new to company bean counting, you might find that they move in opposite directions to the way that you expect.

Double entry accounting

Double entry accounting is logic that simplifies the preparation of forecasts – it helps make this process as painless as possible. (See page 146.)

Matching

Finally, matching transactions to the correct periods is important from a management perspective (see Figure 7.3). It helps you understand the costs and profits associated with specific activities and revenues.

Figure 7.3 is actually quite useful. If you can follow the logic, you will have no trouble preparing financial statements. Spend a few moments making sure that you follow it. It shows an example of how you deal with *prepayments* (cash paid in advance of the accounting period to which it relates).

Accruals are identical but work in the other direction. They relate to cash payment due but not yet disbursed. For example, suppose that your office rent was due in July but you managed to hide from the rent collector. Your landlord has become one of your creditors. In July you debit *rents* (as usual) and credit *accrued rental payments* (a liability account shown in the liabilities section of the balance sheet). When eventually you are forced to make the payment, you debit *accrued rental payments* to clear the liability and credit *cash at bank*.

> For probably the same reason that Americans call the profit and loss account an income statement (quietly ignoring the fact that it includes expenditure), the practice of matching payments to the relevant periods is known as accruals accounting even though it embraces prepayments and other timing discrepancies.

The techniques for handling prepayments and accruals are applied in other useful ways. Most significant, when you spend money on capital goods (a factory, machine, computer, intellectual property, etc.) the outlay is recorded in an asset account (shown on the balance sheet – debit asset account, credit cash). The recorded value of the asset is reduced over its life and an expense account (in the profit and loss account) is charged with an appropriate amount each month (for example, debit expense account *depreciation of office equipment* and credit asset account *accumulated depreciation*). Do not lose sleep over this, we will cover it in more detail in Chapter 9.

CASH ACCOUNTING

Very small businesses and those which are entirely cash-based might not need to worry too much about accruals accounting. I show the extremes here – allocating every penny to the appropriate period – because it is rigorous and it helps management decision-making. Subject to any requirements of your tax office or accountants, you can exercise a touch of discretion. Passing the book-keeping entries to move $50 by one month probably is not worth the effort. Moving $50,000 definitely would be.

Double entry accounting

Accountants – who sometimes show flashes of brilliance – invented double entry accounting. The concept is simple. For every debit there is a credit (or credits) with an equivalent total amount. For example:

- when you pay cash for a machine, you *debit* machinery and *credit* cash at bank;

- when you pay rent in advance, you *debit* prepaid rents and *credit* cash at bank;

- when you take a bank loan, you *debit* cash at bank and *credit* bank loans.

Do this right and your accounts will always balance. While it might not reflect outstanding brilliance, it is nevertheless a useful technique to bear in mind when preparing forecasts and budgets. It will help you create the financial statements later.

Five of your accountant's top beliefs

1 **Money is everything.** Accountants insist that everything can be measured by money. Accounts do not take account of competitive forces, goodwill, quality, location, etc.

2 **Business is an ongoing concern.** Accountants work on the basis that the business will keep going for ever. The financial statements do not purport to show what you would be left with if you closed the business tomorrow.

3 **The value of something is what you paid for it.** Accountants base all their records on purchase prices. In most cases, it will be an accident if the recorded value of a factory or machine coincides with the current market value or replacement value. Your invaluable boffin in R&D is valued at the cost of his salary package, regardless of what splendid and original ideas are running around in his little grey cells.

4 **Always play it safe.** Accountants steadfastly refuse to anticipate revenue and they include it in the accounts only when a sale is made, but they insist on making provision for every expected expense or loss just as soon as someone thinks about them.

5 **Policies are set in stone.** Honest accountants try to prevent you from changing accounting policies so that your accounts remain consistent from month to month and from year to year.

WHO OWES WHOM?

Here is one little area that sometimes causes confusion. You are no doubt familiar with the terms debit and credit. It helps to remember that the words are derived from *debt* (in this case an amount *owed to you*) and *creditors* (people to whom *you owe* money). Your accountant treats them as follows.

- **Asset accounts have debit balances.** If you extend credit to a customer you *debit accounts receivable* for that customer (indicating that the money is owed to you); similarly – but perhaps stretching the concept – if you buy a clump press you *debit machinery*. The machine owes you money.

- **Liability accounts have credit balances.** If you borrow money you *credit*, say, *short-term loans from the bank* (that is, the bank is your creditor).

- **Expense accounts have debit balances.** This is easy. When you pay out money, you debit the expense account. When you pay office rent, you *debit office rents paid*.

The area of confusion is that when you take money out of your bank deposit account, in your company accounts you show a *credit to the bank* – the bank owes you less. When you show an increase in your bank deposit you show a debit entry – the bank owes you more.

This is the exact opposite of what we normally say. When you go into your bank to put money *into* your account you fill in a *credit* slip not a debit slip. This is because you are then looking at it from the bank's perspective. When you put money on deposit you become one of the bank's creditors. Thus, if you are drawing up a business plan for a bank, customer deposits are liabilities with credit balances and loans to customers are assets with debit balances.

It is straightforward if you look at it from the viewpoint of who owes money to the business.

Figure 7.3 When financial transactions count

Your year planner has the date of your August holiday marked, I would guess, against August. It would not be so helpful for work scheduling purposes if you marked it on the day that you decided on Jamaica, or when you paid the deposit. So it is with financial transactions. For analytical purposes, debits are *matched* against the related credits, and they are each matched to the appropriate period of activity. This is not necessarily the same as the date when money changes hands. One example should suffice. Suppose that:

● you are producing a monthly expenditure plan;

● your office rent is $1000 a month; and

● you pay it once every three months in advance.

For example, on 28 June you pay the $3000 that relates to calendar months July, August and September. The accounting entries are shown on the right.

1 In June, you credit (reduce) your bank balance by $3000 and debit (increase) the asset account *prepaid rents* by the same amount.

2 In each of July, August and September, you debit (increase) *office rental payments* by $1000 and credit (reduce) *prepaid rents* by the same amount.

If the only other transaction is a 10,000 share issue in May, the transactions that show in your financial statements are as follows. Note the way that a change in the balance sheet between two dates (e.g. the change in prepaid rents between the end of June and the end of July) equates to a flow in the intervening period (P&L account – rents paid in July). This is examined in more detail in Chapter 9.

	May	Jun	Jul	Aug	Sep
Balance Sheet *End month*					
Assets					
Cash at bank	10 000	7 000	7 000	7 000	7 000
Prepaid rents	0	3 000	2 000	1 000	0
Total	10 000	10 000	9 000	8 000	7 000
Liabilities and shareholders' equity					
Paid up share capital	10 000	10 000	10 000	10 000	10 000
Profit (loss), current year	0	0	(1 000)	(2 000)	(3 000)
Total	10 000	10 000	9 000	8 000	7 000
Profit & loss account *Whole month*					
Office rental payments	0	0	1 000	1 000	1 000
Net profit (loss)	0	0	(1 000)	(1 000)	(1 000)
Cash flow *Whole month*					
Share issue	1 0000	0	0	0	0
Office rental payments	0	–3 000	0	0	0
Total for month	1 0000	–3 000	0	0	0
Net cash balance	1 0000	7 000	7 000	7 000	7 000

The changes in the balance sheet are flows in the other accounts

The planning horizon

The planning horizon is the most distant point in the future that you will visit in the plan. By the time you start work on the financials, the planning horizon will already have been staked out – probably three or five years hence. If you happen to be working on a plan covering longer than this, you probably will not want to attach much credibility to forecasts more than five years out.

Good business plans usually contain monthly figures for the first year, and quarterly or maybe only annual numbers for the remaining years. Budgets, used for planning and measuring performance, are no more than profit and loss and cash flow forecasts by another name (usually monthly). If you have mixed periods, include a summary for the early part of the plan for ease of comparison. For example, if you have monthly figures for the first year and annual figures for the remaining term, show annual figures for the first year also.

 You can add together financial flows. The sum of the expenditure figures for the 12 months January to December gives you total spending for the calendar year.

Do not add balance sheet figures. They show the end-period balances. The figures for the month ending 31 December are the figures for the end of the fourth quarter and for the end of the whole year.

FORECASTS AND BUDGETS

A budget is a misleading name for a set of financial projections or forecasts that have been formalised as:

- an operating plan; and

- a set of financial targets;

- for a given period of time – usually one year.

The budget is the forecast that you adopt as representing your best guess at the future. Essentially, the budget is saying *if our assumptions about our operating environment are correct this is how much we will spend and receive.* It is preferable to think of a budget as an operational financial plan – not as a budget that must be spent.

Sometimes it does not make sense to operate within a *fixed* budget. For example, when sales are very unpredictable, the production department could operate on a *flexible* budget. The production manager might be authorised to increase spending by $100,000 for every extra 10,000 units of production above a pre-agreed volume.

'If the profits are great, the risks are great.'

CHINESE PROVERB

HOW LONG IS A MONTH?

To save me having to use complicated phrases, please interpret references to *months* as *your shortest accounting period*. Some businesses – such as retailers – use a four-week accounting period to help compare like with like. They always begin on the same shopping day. Also, I tend to use the term *year* to mean the *longer of a year or an operating cycle* – the amount of time that it takes to buy stuff, turn it into a product, and collect cash from the lucky buyer. Most businesses use a 12-month period – fiscal year – that sometimes coincides with the calendar year. It might run for some other period that is convenient for you, perhaps coinciding with the tax year.

If you are starting a new business and you want to spoil your accountant's new year's eve celebrations, choose a fiscal year that matches the calendar year.

 It's the same, even if you are not in it for the money

Much of the discussion here might appear to focus on the financials for business. If you are involved with non-profit organisations, government agencies or similar bodies, your financial statements will look a little different. However, in this case you will almost certainly have or be able to obtain historical examples that you can mimic in your business plan – and the broad principles are exactly the same as those discussed here.

Figure 7.4 Financial relationships exposed

This diagram shows the interrelationships between the three sets of transactions and the three financial statements. Perhaps it looks a little complex, but it is actually quite simple. If you are in doubt, the relationships will become evident as you work through Chapters 7–10 of this book.

Remember that all the accounts show *flows over time*, except the balance sheet, which shows *balances* at a point in time. As discussed in the text, the changes in balance sheet between two dates reveal *flows*.

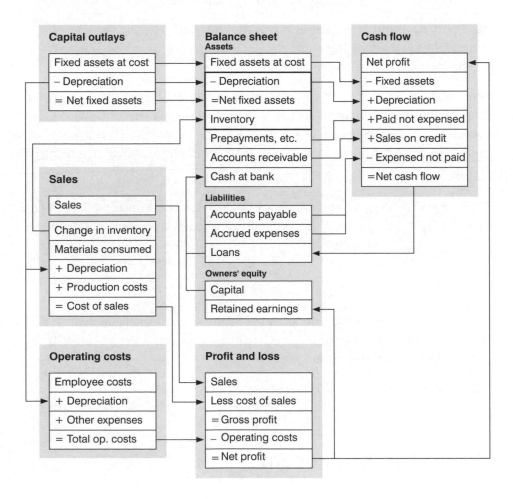

Looking back

There is little need to dwell on how you find the historical figures that you need for your business plan. You just extract them from your records. The only warnings to consider are that sometimes:

- **Summarised figures hide things.** A $10,000 increase in net fixed assets could conceal a $15,000 acquisition and $5000 of depreciation.

- **Policy decisions and changes in practices mislead.** A decision to write off a long-standing bad debt might suggest a reduction in assets when actually nothing fundamental has changed.

In other words, when moving through history to the current figures and on to forecasts, try to make sure that the numbers are presented consistently. Where a change in accounting policies causes lumpiness in the numbers, include an additional line that shows the earlier figures presented on the same basis as the forecast and explain what is going on.

 I am sure that you would never attempt to hide, say, an increase in spending in reclassified or summarised figures. Professional number crunchers are good at spotting this. Don't try it.

The figures that you need were introduced in Chapter 4. I will expand on them in the following pages. When and how you use the data that you extract is also discussed below. It is the same for historical periods and forecasts.

'Consider the past and you will know the future.'

CHINESE PROVERB

Estimating the present

I have mentioned already that you often find yourself preparing forecasts for next year when this year is not yet over.

Filling in gaps in the figures for the current year is more a matter of estimation than forecasting. You will have a reasonable idea of the transactions yet to be recorded in the accounts. You can firm up on these as the planning exercise progresses. To avoid making frequent revisions to the forecast, try not to make it arithmetically dependent on the figures that you are forced to estimate and are likely to change.

Crystal ball gazing

There are six steps to painlessly producing successful forecasts, listed below. The first three steps require varying degrees of thought. The second three are mechanical. It is all much more straightforward than it might appear at first glance.

Cash flow projections reveal your funding requirements – or cash surplus. It may be that when you see the bottom line you will need to work back through the numbers to bring the funding requirement into line with reality – or to put the surplus to good use. This might involve revisiting the marketing strategy or some other part of the plan.

Six steps to painless financial forecasts

1 **Project sales revenue.** This is the most important step. It builds on the market analysis that you have already done. You should forecast sales volumes (quantities). Multiply these by price to convert them into the value of gross sales revenue. Then deduct the cost of those sales (raw materials, payments to suppliers, etc.) to arrive at gross profit.

2 **Identify the capital spending required.** As discussed, you need to treat these slightly differently from other operating costs by spreading the outlays over their assumed operating life. A $30,000 machine with a three-year life 'costs' you $10,000 a year.

3 **Work through the remaining operating costs,** such as sales executives' salaries and telecommunications costs.

4 **Derive a profit and loss (income) statement** – a simple mechanical exercise using basic arithmetic on the results of the first three steps.

5 **Draw up a balance sheet** (another largely mechanical step).

6 **Check your cash flow requirements** (also a mechanical restatement of the foregoing numbers).

'The trouble with facts is that there are so many of them.'

SAMUEL McCHORD CROTHERS

The most dangerous thing you can do if the funding requirement is too large is cheat by adjusting the revenue forecast on the basis that you probably underestimated sales in the first place. You should start out by adopting the policy that you will amend the sales projections only if you first change the sales and marketing strategy and/or plan.

WHAT IF …?

Producing a single financial forecast is not the end of it. Most business people – and all solid business plans – require at least a second pass through the forecasting exercise to produce a worst-case projection. This will show you the amount of funding that you would need if a doomsday scenario plays out. Sometimes even most likely and worst-case forecasts are not enough. It may be that you want to produce a best-case as well to please the boss, or to encourage an investor or banker to pour money into your business. You sometimes hear this referred to as 'scenario planning'.

In fact, the second and subsequent forecasts are the result of common sense *what-if analysis*. What if your competitor introduces a superior product at half the price? What if there is an economic disaster? What if it takes you twice as long to fix the bugs in the new software? If you want to make it sound deep and meaningful, you can refer to *what-if* using the term *sensitivity analysis*. It is a very important part of your business plan, because it shows that you have thought about all eventualities. You might not think that these extremes will happen. Your readers probably do expect them. We will return to this in Chapter 11.

If you make one or two assumptions about your business there is a neat way to show the degree of confidence that you attach to various outcomes. This is also discussed in Chapter 11.

Software tools

The way to tame your numbers and keep them under control is to use a computer spread-sheet, such as MS Excel or OpenOffice Calc. These give you worksheets – tables with blank cells, or boxes, into which you type information – that collect together into workbooks.

You do not need to be a spreadsheet wizard. It is enough to know how to:

● format a cell so that the layout is pleasing;

● enter simple formulas that add, multiply or simply repeat other values.

If you can use the facility to draw charts you are in a strong position. If you are not familiar with spreadsheets, you are certain to have a colleague, friend or relative who loves their computer and will be only too pleased to set this up for you, explain the basic principles and guide you through the groundwork. If not you might consider a short training course.

Which is the first month?

Overheard in a corporate finance department: *Look at the age of this business plan. It shows that the project should have started two months ago. It's still not funded. Maybe 20 other people have seen it and rejected it already?*

Business plans date rapidly – and when they do, they convey a bad impression. This is especially true of plans for new projects or business start-ups. When you start to write the plan in January, you might think that a July launch date is entirely feasible. Corporate bosses and capital providers are rarely so accommodating. In my experience, new ventures nearly always start later than expected. It might take longer to raise capital, maybe other activities cause delays, or perhaps you underestimated the amount of time required for cutting through all the red tape.

To avoid having to revise and reprint business plans, consider replacing dates with numbers. The extracts from sample business plans shown here (for example, see Figure 8.9 later) use *month 1, month 2, month 3*, etc. in the detailed financial projections. These plans will never look out of date

SPREADSHEET TECHNIQUES

You should set up a workbook that essentially contains six tables, one for each of sales, capital outlays, operating costs, profit and loss, the balance sheet and cash flow. These can be six separate worksheets – or you could combine, say, the three financial statements on one page. You might also decide to include worksheets for any additional tables that you produce in pursuit of your analysis and forecasts. Here are four useful tips.

1   **Minimise data entry.** Make sure that you never enter the same information more than once. For example, if you key in the months across the top of one spreadsheet, ensure that all other instances of the dates pick up the values from the first row. Then, if you change the coverage period of the financial statements, you only have to make one amendment and the changes will ripple through all the spreadsheet. The same goes for numerical amounts such as number of employees or spending on salaries.

2   **Automate.** Try to automate data entry further. For example, if you key a month-year (e.g. Jan-2012) into cell one, the next 11 cells could be set as formulas that calculate the value of the previous cell plus one month. Changing the value in the first cell will cause all 12 months to be updated automatically. Again, the same applies to numerical data. If you project that rent will rise in period two, put a formula in the second cell that displays 110% of the first cell.

3 **Carry forward totals.** To ensure a painless interaction between the worksheets, use formulas to carry forward totals. For example, the current-year profit (loss) in the balance sheet should be taken directly from the bottom line on the profit and loss account (which is calculated as the sum of individual entries).

4 **Use colour.** It's a good idea to use one colour to display the characters in the cells into which you key raw data (say, black) and another colour for all automated cells (say, blue). You can then see at a glance which is which. In fact, I take this a stage further and use red print for cells which are mechanical projections so that it is easy to see where the assumptions are that might be modified during a review process. But I usually print the final version in black only – to avoid distracting other users.

When you have a standard workbook, you can give copies to R&D, Marketing, and so on for them to complete during the planning exercise. When you get these workbooks back, you can use an additional identical workbook to automatically aggregate the numbers for the constituent departments. You then have consistent financial plans for the whole business and its constituent parts.

The workbooks can also be used for operational purposes, including tracking actual spending against budget, which is discussed in Chapter 13.

 Squeeze it in

A venture capital provider I knew generally asked for detailed financials for the first six months only, and for broad expectations thereafter. He maintained there are so many variables for a start-up that it is pointless trying to look further ahead. This is a sensible approach. But where you have to show more than 6 months for a financial statement or forecast, you will find that it is usually possible to squeeze in 15 columns (line number, description, 12 months and a total) on one sheet of A4 or letter paper. You can always turn it sideways or spread over two pages.

Putting it to good use

This introduction to accountancy's idiosyncrasies, crystal ball gazing and spreadsheets should have set you in good stead for the rewarding task of working out your financial prospects. I can't wait. Make sure that you have understood the concepts raised in this chapter. When you have, see you in Chapter 8.

Figure 7.5 Spreadsheet magic

What you entered:

Only three new figures

	A	B	C	D	E	F
1						
2	Operating costs					
3	Year	2007	=B3+1	=C3+1	=D3+1	=E3+1
4	Salaries	10 000	=B4	=C4	=D4	=E4
...	...	...	...	...	...	...
14	Telecomms	1 000	=B9*1.02	=C9*1.02	=D9*1.02	=E9*1.02
...	...	...	...	...	...	...
28	Sundry costs	='SUNDRY'!B45	='SUNDRY'!C45	='SUNDRY'!D45	='SUNDRY'!E45	='SUNDRY'!F45
29	Total expenditure	=SUM(B4:B28)	=SUM(C4:C28)	=SUM(D4:D28)	=SUM(E4:E28)	=SUM(F4:F28)
30						
31						
32	=A3	=B3	=C3	=D3	=E3	=F3
33	='GROSS'!A99	='GROSS'!B99	='GROSS'!C99	='GROSS'!D99	='GROSS'!E99	='GROSS'!F99
34	Less expenditure	=B29	=C29	=D29	=E29	=F29
35	Net profit	=B33-B34	=C33-C34	=D33-D34	=E33-E34	=F33-F34
36						

What you see:

	A	B	C	D	E	F
1						
2	Operating costs					
3	Year	2007	2008	2009	2010	2011
4	Salaries	10 000	10 000	10 000	10 000	10 000
...	...	...	...	...	...	...
14	Telecomms	1 000	1 020	1 040	1 061	1 082
...	...	...	...	...	...	...
28	Sundry costs	143	453	122	36	445
29	Total expenditure	23 967	25 333	24 666	24 921	24 921
30						
31	P&L summary					
32	Year	1999	2000	2001	2002	2003
33	Gross profit	45 654	34 566	37 543	35 567	35 468
34	Less expenditure	23 967	25 333	24 666	24 921	24 921
35	Net profit	21 687	9 233	12 877	10 546	10 547
36						

What it means:

	A	B	C	D	E	F
1						
2	Operating costs					
3	Year	2007	Each cell displays the value in the cell to its left incremented by 1			
4	Salaries	10 000	Each cell displays the value from the cell to its left			
...	...	...	...			
14	Telecomms	1 000	Each cell displays the value in the cell to its left increased by 2%			
...	...	...	...			
28	Sundry costs	Each cell displays the corresponding value from the worksheet called 'Sundry'				
29	Total expenditure	Each cell displays the sum of the values above				
30						
31	P&L summary					
32	Year	Each cell displays the corresponding value from row 3				
33	Gross profit	Each cell displays the corresponding value from row 29				
34	Less expenditure	Each cell displays the corresponding value from the worksheet called 'Gross' (profit)				
35	Net profit	Each cell displays the value in row 33 *less* the value in row 34				
36						

Getting to gross profit

The absolute fundamental aim is to make money out of satisfying customers. SIR JOHN EGAN

- Breathe easily

- Forecasting sales volumes

- The big picture – the economy

- Up close and personal – industry and product demand

- Pulling it all together

- Cost of sales

- Gross profit

- Writing it up

The main objective of this chapter is getting to gross profit (sometimes known as the gross margin) – trading income from sales *less* directly attributable costs. These are the *cost of sales* such as the spending directly associated with producing your product – raw materials, components, production costs. If you have a simple product, sales costs might be no more complicated than so-many hours of a consultant's time or the buying price of a gizmo that you re-sell. If you run a manufacturing plant, cost of sales will have a few more elements to take into account – machinery, electricity and so on. Later, you will also deduct indirect costs to arrive at net profit. Indirect costs are expenses (such as those associated with running an office) that cannot be directly attributed to a specific product.

But we are getting ahead of ourselves. Start by looking at how you arrive at a viable sales forecast. Then consider the costs. From these figures, you can calculate gross profit, which is simply *sales* less the *cost of sales*. Always start with quantities (volumes) and then consider the effect of pricing policies to derive sales values.

Breathe easily

Sales revenue is the air supply for your business. Without air, you suffocate. Put another way:

no sales = no revenue = no business.

The exception, of course, is if you are running a cost centre or non-profit organisation that does not make sales in the conventional sense, such as the legal department of a large corporation or a charity providing relief work.

In the case of the charity, there will be some fund-raising or other revenue source which equates to sales revenue. For the legal cost centre, it is sensible to look for some proxy measure of activity (number of contracts reviewed or number of litigations in progress). Better still, cost these activities and charge the department being serviced. In these pages, *sales* and such *proxies* can be taken as synonymous.

For nearly all business plans, forecasts of sales revenue are the key to understanding the future. Existing businesses and products have track records which assist with crystal ball gazing – and sometimes give false credibility to the forecasts. If you are launching a new business or new product you have to start from scratch. In each case, the approach is similar.

For most of this book you and I have pretended that you have just one product. We do the same here. You will need to repeat this forecasting exercise for each of your goods and services. In some cases they will be closely related – for example, maybe you always sell a maintenance contract when someone buys one of your machines.

Volume and values

By and large, you make better sales forecasts when you work in volume terms (the number of items that you sell), and then multiply by the price per item to arrive at sales value. This allows you to separate out the effects of changes in price and the underlying changes in demand.

Forecasting sales volumes

What affects demand for your products? You have already thought about this in great detail while reading earlier chapters. The list on page 164 brings together ten factors, split conveniently into two groups.

- The first four or five influences reflect mainly your operating environment.

- The other items reflect the way that demand is affected by things such as culture, perceptions, needs, styles, fashions and fads.

Demand for a product class belongs in both camps. Perhaps there are plenty of other grey areas. But the point here is that you can make an economic or environmental forecast that relates to areas outside of your control. And then you can paste on top an industry forecast that reflects the way that demand can be managed. The industry forecast will indicate sales of a product class or category *and* – this is where you are heading – sales of your product.

One potential mistake to avoid is forecasting sales on a wish. Venture capital providers in particular shy away from statements such as 'the total market should be worth $10 billion in 2005 and it is not unreasonable to assume that we will win 1% of this …'. You might get away with this proportional forecasting if you have a clear track record, can use historical ratios as evidence, and can demonstrate the likely results of your marketing strategy. Otherwise, resist the temptation.

The fast track to gross profit

1 Forecast economic trends in general (you can *borrow* a free forecast from many sources).

2 Forecast the way that economic trends will affect your product class (such as travel) or category (air travel) – see *Intimate relationships/leading indicators* (page 167).

3 Examine the way that demand for a product class and category is changing.

4 Examine the way that your strategy and plans will affect demand for your product.

5 Put together steps 1 to 4 to forecast your sales volumes and values.

6 Work out your cost of sales.

7 Calculate gross profit (sales less costs).

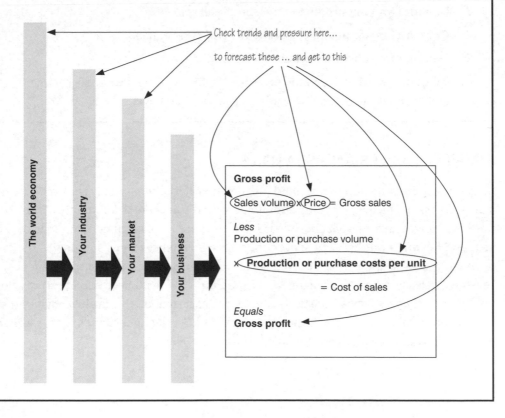

TRENDS, CYCLES AND SEASONS

Recall that around the long-term trend (up, down or flat), there usually is a cycle (recession, depression, recovery, boom). Superimposed on this there is frequently a seasonal pattern. Are you in a seasonal business? Does demand increase at certain times of the year and fall off at others? Almost every business experiences some seasonal variation, even if it is only slight, perhaps caused by vacations or religious festivals. The effects of seasons, cycles and trends is illustrated in Figure 8.1. When you have a long run of sales figures, identifying seasonal variation is one of the easiest and most useful activities that you can undertake. The mechanics are outlined below. A clear understanding of seasonality will help you to manage your operations during the year.

Forecasting with a ruler

If you have a long run of historical sales data you can break it down into a long-term trend, a cyclical component and a seasonal pattern. The time series at the top of Figure 8.1 – which might be sales of your product – is selected deliberately so that you can see the constituent trends in the raw data. Normally, they are not so obvious until you have analysed them.

1   Work with volume (quantities) – the top series in Figure 8.1.

2   Use regression analysis, a moving average or even a ruler to draw a *line of best fit*. This is the long-term trend – the second series in Figure 8.1.

3   Divide each value in the original series by the corresponding value read from the trend line. This gives you an indication of the cyclical component – the third series in Figure 8.1.

4   Identify the seasonal component (simplistically, take the average of all the January figures, all the February figures and so on) – the final series in Figure 8.1.

There will also almost certainly be some unexplained spurious noise that does not fit into any one of these categories. If it is very large, this technique will not work well for the data that you are examining.

From the three components shown, you could produce a reasonable forecast by extrapolation. You might extend the trend with a ruler, continue the cyclical wave freehand, calculate the seasonal variation and then multiply them all back together.

Such forecasting is sometimes adequate, especially if time and money are in short supply. However, a much better approach is to look for intimate relationships between the series and some *leading indicators* – see page 167.

The big picture – the economy

With regard to the big picture, you want to know two things. Where is the economy going and how will it affect you? Generally, a greater level of economic activity boosts sales. A downturn in the economy usually damages sales. You might have recession-proof products. If not, perhaps you should try to add some. When times are hard, people switch to cheaper, basic goods and defer capital spending (focusing instead on maintaining what they already own).

Figure 8.1 All this from one set of figures

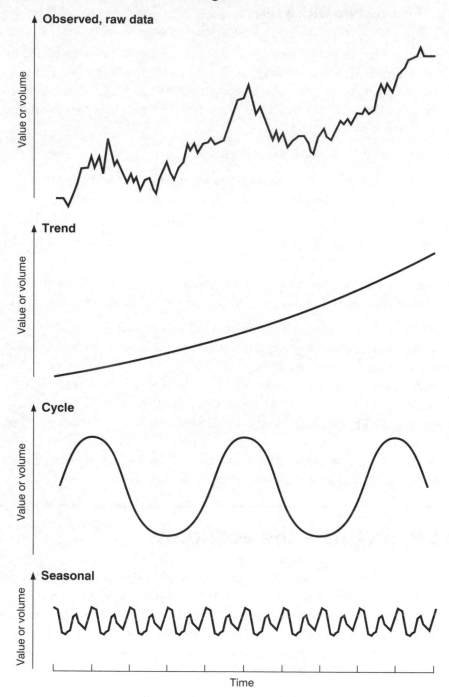

Ignoring the thorny issue of cause and effect, an increase in consumer demand is linked to greater industrial activity overall. Even if your customers are industrial and commercial buyers you will still be affected by demand at the consumer level. For example:

- consumers buy more washing machines, so

- home-appliance manufacturers buy more steel products from your customers, and

- your customers buy more steel from you.

These are examples of companies undertaking successful marketing activities directed at stimulating buying by their customers' customers.

Start by examining your track record if you can. If you do not have a history that you can use to identify the relationships described below, you should be able to develop a reasonable understanding of the forces that will affect sales once you have launched a new product. You can use this to help project sales. Doing so and documenting it carefully will add credibility to your business plan.

INTIMATE RELATIONSHIPS/LEADING INDICATORS

Take another look at your review of the world (Chapter 5). With any luck you will quickly spot several important factors that affect your sales. In particular, you might know about intimate relationships that help you predict the way that demand varies for a particular product or product category.

For example, sales of concrete and carpets are influenced by the level of house-building activity. The time lags are different. Concrete is poured when foundations are started. Carpets are laid several months later. This is a simplistic example, in which house-building activity is used as a *leading indicator* of demand for concrete or carpets.

The relationship is illustrated in Figure 8.2. Carpet sales are shown in the top chart. The lower picture shows housing starts moved forward by a year. Note how the two series move broadly in tandem. You might use the lower chart to predict future sales. It suggests that they are about to rise.

Figure 8.2 Intimate relationships illustrated

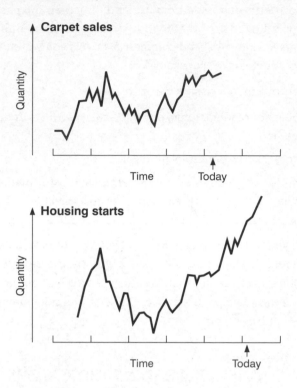

In fact, you usually need to use several leading indicators. For example, demand for carpets will depend on new house sales, office completions, turnover of existing properties, companies' financial surpluses, household disposable income and so on. Each of these indicators will have some influence on demand for carpets, each with a different time lag. Do not forget that the relationships can be turned upside down (for example, if interest rates go up, carpet sales go down).

Governments and some private associations publish enormous amounts of useful economic data for you to explore. Always look for underlying influences – house-building in the example shown here. You might get away with making mistakes such as using sales of concrete to estimate demand for carpets but I am sure that you can see the dangers.

Where you can justify intellectually that relationships might exist, draw graphs to see if they do and how tightly the series are correlated. Use your results for the past few years plotted monthly or quarterly. Sometimes, percentage changes over 12 months (or 4 quarters) magnify trends, making them easier to spot. There are statistical techniques that add rigour to the analysis, such as *correlation and regression analysis*. If you know about this, use it. Computer software, including simple spreadsheets, makes it very easy.

You can usually find leading indicators that help with your forecasting. You might also be able to use them as active management tools. For example, suppose your sales always turn down 18 months after the point at which interest rates reach their trough and start rising again. This makes it fairly easy for you to schedule purchasing, inventory, capacity use and so on.

But watch carefully. Relationships can change. It pays to identify several indicators with different leads and lags – so that you can confirm the signals transmitted by each one. You can track the indicators in a quality newspaper such as the *Financial Times*. If you are really keen, go to the source: check out the websites of your government statistical offices, departments of trade, industry, etc., and the central bank, as well as research bodies and trade associations which produce surveys and figures. International organisations such as the OECD and the World Bank publish very useful data and commentary, especially if you are operating internationally or just want to keep abreast of global developments.

Once you have established a relationship between some external force and your sales, you can use it to predict the future. Leading indicators do not usually show you enough of the future. However, you can follow the linkages all the way to the top. An overall economic forecast will allow you to forecast your key leading indicators which in turn will permit you to forecast your sales.

Watch for surveys of business confidence. Directors and managers just like you are asked leading questions about their current experiences and expectations. The results are summarised and published (I should definitely mention the *Financial Times* again here). Look for indicators such as purchasing plans, investment intentions, distribution activity and so on from bodies such as the Institute of Directors in Britain, confederations of industry in Australia and the UK, the IFO in Germany, government statisticians in the US and Japan, and many other sources.

ECONOMIC FORECASTS

You could produce economic forecasts yourself. However, governments, universities, economic institutes, bankers and consulting houses throw enormous resources into building economic models and forecasts. The results are published, often in great detail and often for free. Why not use them? Beware, though, the only thing that you know with certainty is that the forecasts will be wrong (and I speak as an ex-economist). Examine track records, review the forecasts with healthy scepticism and be prepared to modify them in the light of experience and new information.

If you have found intimate relationships between your sales and indicators that are not included in the forecasts, you need to take one more step. You have to identify a relationship between your leading indicator and an appropriate series that *is* forecast (such as gross national product (GNP) or gross domestic product (GDP), measures of total economic activity – consumer spending, investment, etc.). Sensible judgement is required.

If you want to read more about these subjects, you might like to read two of my other books – *The Economist Guide to Economic Indicators* and *The Definitive Guide to Business Finance*. The title of the first is self-explanatory. The second one considers time series analysis, forecasting and a whole range of interesting analytical methods to assist management decision-making and financial management.

 Estimates, projections and forecasts

In the context of this chapter:

- an **estimate**, as already discussed, happens when you fill in missing knowledge about the present;

- a **projection or extrapolation** is the future predicted using a ruler;

- a **forecast** is a logical view of the future developed using knowledge of relationships between various indicators;

- an **assumption** is a cross between a projection and a forecast. It is a best guess which you use for the sake of the forecast. For example, you might make a series of assumptions about exchange rates that are the basis for various forecasts.

Up close and personal – industry and product demand

As useful as they are, leading indicators have one shortfall. They predict the future using past relationships – and, as Henry VIII with his six wives taught us, relationships can change. As indicated earlier, trends in culture and fashion, fads, advertising, product promotions and so on can cause changes at three levels, in demand for:

- a product class (for example, travel);

- a product category (air travel);

- your product (your specific air travel services).

Test marketing

When starting a new business, planning a new product or entering a new market segment, you should really conduct some test sales. These will help you plan future sales. You might also find it impossible to raise finance without such proof of demand.

An illuminating story comes to mind. The inventor of a well-known household workbench offered it to two major do-it-yourself companies.

- The first company reviewed the product and conducted some market research. The company subsequently wrote to the inventor declining the product on the basis that there was a market for only a few dozen workbenches in the whole of Europe.

- The second company told the inventor to speak to them again when he had proved that there was a market.

The enterprising entrepreneur manufactured the workbenches in his spare bedroom, placed an advertisement in a small newspaper – and immediately sold thousands by mail order. One company lost out, the other could well have done.

This is typical of big corporations – including many venture capital providers. Managers are trained to follow rules and avoid risks. They sometimes appear to lose their feeling for the markets and become a touch myopic. If you are writing a business plan for a new product, you will frequently think that you are the only person who sees the potential. Frankly, this will probably be the case. If you can prove that you are right by making test sales, your plan will almost certainly be approved much more readily.

What do you do? You add a couple of lines to your forecast making additional provision for these changes. You have already examined the external environment (Chapter 5) and developed a marketing strategy (Chapter 6). Now you have to assess how the pattern of product demand might change during the months and years ahead.

Some of this will be judgemental. You might estimate that your competitors' strategies will add 2% to overall demand for the product class, or increase their market share by 5%. However, you may also be able to make some more rigorous forecast based on your analysis. For example, you might know that a given amount of spending on advertising or an additional telemarketing person will boost your sales by a certain amount.

One technique that might help is to examine the life cycle for your product class and category as well as for the product itself.

PRODUCT LIFE CYCLES

In varying degrees, all products, categories and classes go through the following stages of being (illustrated in Figure 8.3). Where does your product fit in?

Development

R&D and marketing people are busy being creative behind the scenes. They are having a good time without having to account for sales – which have not yet begun. Revenue is zero, but cash is being poured eagerly into product development and pre-launch marketing activities.

Introduction

The product is launched, probably with lots of publicity. The marketing people are in their element. R&D is starting a witch-hunt about missed deadlines and overshot budgets and *production* is scratching its collective head over glitches in output. Sales generally increase slowly at first while buyers are learning about the existence of the amazing product. The company starts to recover some of the initial investment.

Growth

Market awareness and acceptance are growing. The production machinery is humming. Sales are expanding strongly and profits are booming – funding R&D's next journey into the unknown. Everyone is having fun.

Maturity

The market is becoming saturated. Laggards are still buying, but the herd is stampeding after new products. Outlays rise as the marketing department struggles to maintain sales. Profits have passed their peak and are beginning to fall off.

Decline

The product has had its day. Ex-prisoners and former commune-dwellers coming back into circulation might buy a few, but sales are dwindling. Profits slump. Production capacity is underused. R&D and marketing people are seen hunched over blueprints for different products. Tempers are frayed.

   Of course, not all products make it out of R&D or through the introductory stage. Many fall by the wayside. You want to get through these first two stages (development and introduction) as rapidly as possible, and extend the growth stage for as long as you can. This is where product and market modifications help – where you can extend the profitable growth period by breathing new life into limp products. Knowing where you are in the product life cycle, and where you are likely to be heading, is a useful aid to planning and forecasting.

Figure 8.3 The five ages of product

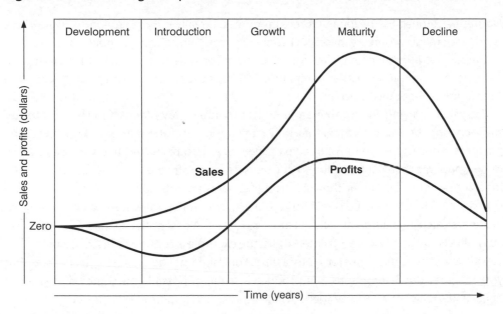

Ask an expert

There are three groups of people that you can turn to for expert opinions:

- Your customers. Surveys of buying intentions can reveal quite succinctly the potential of your market.

- Your sales force. Sales professionals often have a very close handle on their market. Order books might give a very clear indication of projected sales for many months ahead if you are building oil-rigs or aircraft with long order times. Alternatively, your sales people may know about their customers' buying intentions. Otherwise, you might be able to play the numbers game. So-many cold calls will generate so-many leads that will result in so-many sales. You already know your plans, the number of sales staff, the number of calls that they can make – the rest is down to simple arithmetic.

- Other experts. You might want to have a word with trade associations, marketing consultants, distributors, re-sellers, suppliers, other business partners. Nothing is lost by listening and you could gain valuable insight or ideas. You might even find an opportunity for a *co-operative venture*.

IT IS SIMPLE REALLY

Do not be terrified by the idea of forecasting sales. It really is quite straightforward. There is no black magic or sorcery involved. Let me take you through an example.

Recall that *Tetrylus* Inc has developed a computer system that tracks the activities of workers in hazardous industries – mining, oil and gas extraction, construction, accounting (just kidding about this last one).

Tetrylus is playing the numbers game. The planners have identified the number of sales-channel business partners that they can support and the number of sales that the partners are expected to make in a year. They have also projected the average number of components that will be included in each sale (one software package and up to 2500 identity badges). Simple arithmetic produces sales volumes. From volume, costs and prices are built up. These are shown in Figure 8.4. Inventories, sales, cost of sales and gross profit are calculated automatically in Figure 8.6 (later). A descriptive extract from the business plan is shown in Figure 8.8 (later) – and the example is continued in Chapter 9.

This is a simple and consistent forecasting. You might not agree with the numbers, but you can alter the assumptions and produce a range of possible outcomes that you can believe in – which is where our friend *what-if* comes in (Chapter 11).

Pulling it all together

Having arrived here, you have:

- understood your market (Chapter 5);

- developed a strategy and an operating plan (Chapter 6);

- laid down assumptions for the planning period;

- used an economic/environment forecast to predict the path of leading indicators;

- used leading indicators to forecast demand for your product class, category or product itself;

- allowed for changes in the pattern of demand for product class and category; and

- estimated the effects of your strategy and plan on final demand for your product.

Now you need to pull together all of this analysis. Make a table with a row showing forecast sales volumes for each month (or quarter or year). Put your projected sales prices for each period into another row. Multiply one by the other and you have a forecast of gross sales revenue per period. An example is shown in Figures 8.4 and 8.6. Note that all the figures in the second half of the example (Figure 8.6) are calculated automatically. Change a forecast or assumption in the first half, and you see the effect ripple through. This will make your *what-if* modelling in Chapter 11 very easy.

Figure 8.4 Playing the numbers game (1)

Extract from a spreadsheet summarising the first part of a sales forecast.
This company has projected the number of sales partners that it will be working with, the average number of sales that each partner will make, and the average number of hardware components (identity badges in this instance) that will be included in each sale. The company has also calculated cost and sale prices, based on expected volumes. The remainder of the forecast is shown in Figure 8.6 and described in Figure 8.8.

	A	B	C	D	E	F	Notes:
1	TETRYLUS Inc Financial plan						
2							
3	Sales, costs and prices, first five years						
4	Dollars						
5		Year 1	Year 2	Year 3	Year 4	Year 5	
6	Channel arithmetic						
7	No. of channel partners	4	7	11	15	20	
8	No. of sales per partner	1	3	12	12	12	
9	Total no. channel sales	4	21	132	180	240	Line 7 x line 8
10	Direct sales	0	0	0	0	0	
11	Total no. sales	4	21	132	180	240	Line 9 + line 10
12							
13	Average volumes per sale						
14	Hardware	960	2 000	2 500	2 500	2 500	
15	Software	1	1	1	1	1	One package per sale
16							
17	Total sales volumes						
18	Hardware	3 840	42 000	330 000	450 000	600 000	Line 11 x line 14
19	Software	4	21	132	180	240	Line 11 x line 15
20							
21	Cost of production per item						The step reduction in
22	Hardware	25	23	12	11	10	year three reflects new
23	Software	500	500	500	500	500	production techniques
24							made viable by higher
25	Channel price per item						volumes
26	Hardware	80	50	45	41	36	
27	Software	3 500	2 500	3 000	3 000	3 000	Licence fees
28							
29	Markup, %						
30	Hardware	220	122	275	275	275	[(Line 26 + line 22) −1] x 100
31	Software	600	400	500	500	500	[(Line 27 x line 23) −1] x 100
32							
33	Price per package						
34	Hardware	76 800	100 000	112 500	101 250	91 125	Line 14 x line 26
35	Software	3 500	2 500	3 000	3 000	3 000	Line 15 x line 27
36	Total	80 300	102 500	115 500	104 250	94 125	Line 34 + line 35
37							

How does your forecast look? Was it what you expected? Have you made any artificial assumptions? Will the economy perform as expected? Will your competitors play by the rules? Will your customers remain loyal? You will review these issues in Chapter 11 and perhaps modify the forecast – or produce best- and worst-case forecasts, etc. For the moment, assume that you have one perfect forecast. Now look at how you move on to forecast your gross profit.

 Simple services

Perhaps from time to time you will begin to think that this chapter is all about noisy production lines and oily machines. This is because it is useful to consider the more complex situations. If you are re-selling goods that you buy elsewhere or providing services, your forecasting will be much more simple. Cost of sales might be nothing more complex than your buying price including shipping – or so-many hours of your consultants' time at their hourly employment costs.

Some people are notoriously poor at making these calculations. If you add up all the hours invoiced by certain professionals during their lifetimes, you might conclude that they each must live to be several hundred years old.

Cost of sales

Cost of sales is sometimes called *cost of goods sold*, but I am sure that you can cope with this complex variation in nomenclature. Cost of sales is, how can I put this simply, the *direct* cost of what you sell in any one accounting period.

- For a re-seller, the cost of sales is the price paid to acquire the goods that are to be re-sold.

- In manufacturing, the cost of sales is raw materials and other supplies consumed in making the product, plus directly attributed production wages and factory overheads such as heat and light.

- For a software company, the cost of sales might be determined as one-hundredth of the original R&D cost for each unit sold (if lifetime sales are expected to be 100 copies of a program).

It makes sense to run through a more complex example. You can modify this or scale it down for your own business. Figure 8.5 shows an example manufacturing account. To be pedantic, the penultimate line perhaps belongs in a trading account but it is included to show the final cost of sales.

It is not too hard to follow the logic. The manufacturing of a single product takes place at a dedicated facility. It is easy to identify all the costs directly associated with production. These comprise variable costs (such as raw materials) which vary directly with the volume of production, and fixed costs (such as rent paid for the factory).

 Indirect costs cannot be directly attributed to the cost of the product. They include R&D, marketing and sales, and other administrative costs. These are shown separately in trading or operating accounts which we look at in Chapter 9.

COST OF MATERIALS

In just the same way as you explored sales, you can analyse your raw materials, components and other supplies. Again, look for relationships between these and various economic indicators. This time, you are looking both at volumes – for the way that supply and demand affect prices – and at price indicators.

Economic forecasts usually include retail or consumer price and GDP deflators – which are indices of inflation at the consumer and national level – and exchange rates. You will also usually find indicators of labour costs. Obviously, you can use any or all of these to help forecast price movements in your supplies. Trade and commodity producers associations sometimes produce useful data also.

OTHER PRODUCTION COSTS

Some other production costs are shown in Figure 8.5. These are projected in exactly the same way as any other operating costs. To avoid duplication, I will defer discussion of these production and operating costs until Chapter 9. When you read it you will understand my logic. Skip forward now if you want to get straight down to forecasting production costs. The remaining discussion in this chapter assumes that you have already done this.

Figure 8.5 Cost of sales

Sample manufacturing account
Year ended 31 December

		Money (dollars)
Raw materials		
Opening stock		50 000
Purchases		250 000
		300 000
Less closing stock		40 000
Cost of materials consumed		260 000
Production wages		150 000
Prime cost of production		410 000
Factory overheads		
Packers' wages	90 000	
Management salaries	110 000	
Administration salaries	50 000	
Rental and property taxes	100 000	
Electricity and water	12 000	
Maintenance of machinery	8 000	
Depreciation of machinery	10 000	
Depreciation of leasehold improvements	5 000	
Total overheads		385 000
		795 000
Less increase in work-in-progress		5 000
Cost of goods produced		790 000
Less increase in stock of finished goods in factory		10 000
Cost of goods shipped to warehouse		780 000
Less increase in stock of finished goods in warehouse		30 000
Costs of sales		750 000

PRODUCTION (OR PURCHASING) COSTS

You need to understand how much it costs to produce a unit of your product – otherwise you would not know how much to sell it for. The unit might be one widget, one hour of legal advice, one bed occupied (such as in a hospital or hotel), a tonne of coal, 1000 sheep and so on.

Simplistically, divide cost of production by the number of items produced. For example, if the $750,000 worth of activity in Figure 8.5 produced 375,000 widgets, the cost associated with producing one widget is:

$$unit\ cost = total\ cost\ of\ production \div volume\ of\ production$$

$$= 750,000 \div 375,000$$

$$= \$2$$

Figure 8.6 Playing the numbers game (2)

All of the figures here are calculated automatically from the first part of this spreadsheet, which is shown in Figure 8.4. This spreadsheet also shows an example of the effects of using FIFO and LIFO to value inventory when production costs are falling – see *Valuing inventory* on page 181.

	A	B	C	D	E	F	Source:
38	**TETRYLUS Inc Financial plan**						
39							
40	**Sales, costs and prices, first five years**						
41	Dollars						
42		Year 1	Year 2	Year 3	Year 4	Year 5	
43	**Hardware inventory volume**						
44	Opening stock	0	1 160	1 160	1 160	1 160	Line 47, previous period
45	Additions (production)	5 000	42 000	330 000	450 000	600 000	Based on line 18
46	Reductions (sales)	–3 840	–42 000	–330 000	–450 000	–600 000	Line 18
47	**Closing**	**1 160**	**1 160**	**1 160**	**1 160**	**1 160**	Line 44 + line 45 + line 46
48							
49	**Hardware inventory value (FIFO)**						
50	Opening stock	0	29 000	31 900	49 880	87 232	Line 53, previous period
51	Additions (production)	125 000	945 000	3 960 000	4 860 000	5 832 000	Line 22 x line 45
52	Reductions (sales)	–96 000	–942 100	–3 942 020	–4 822 648	–5 756 043	
53	**Closing stock**	**29 000**	**31 900**	**49 880**	**87 232**	**163 189**	Line 50 + line 51 + line 52
54							
55	Hardware inventory value (LIFO)						
56	Opening stock	0	29 000	29 000	29 000	29 000	Line 59, previous period
57	Additions (production)	125 000	945 000	3 960 000	4 860 000	5 832 000	Line 22 x line 45
58	Reductions (sales)	–96 000	–945 000	–3 960 000	–4 860 000	–5 832 000	Line 22 x line 46
59	**Closing stock**	**29 000**	**29 000**	**29 000**	**29 000**	**29 000**	Line 56 + line 57 + line 58
60							
61	**TETRYLUS Inc Financial plan**						((Line 46 – line 47)
62							in previous period)
63	**Gross profit, first five years**						x line 22) + line 53
64	Dollars						in previous period
65		Year 1	Year 2	Year 3	Year 4	Year 5	
66	Gross sales						
67	Hardware	307 200	2 100 000	14 850 000	18 225 000	21 870 000	Line 18 x line 26
68	Software	14 000	52 500	396 000	540 000	720 000	Line 19 x line 27
69	Total	321 200	2 152 500	15 246 000	18 765 000	22 590 000	Line 67 + line 68
70							
71	**Cost of sales**						Line 18 x line 22
72	Hardware	96 000	945 000	3 960 000	4 860 000	5 832 000	Line 19 x line 23
73	Software	2 000	10 500	66 000	90 000	120 000	Line 72 + line 73
74	Total	98 000	955 500	4 026 000	4 950 000	5 952 000	
75							Line 67 – line 72
76	**Gross profit**						Line 68 – line 73
77	Hardware	211 200	1 155 000	10 890 000	13 365 000	16 038 000	Line 77 + line 78
78	Software	12 000	42 000	330 000	450 000	600 000	
79	Total	223 200	1 197 000	11 220 000	13 815 000	16 638 000	Line 77 + line 67 x 100
80							Line 78 + line 68 x 100
81	Gross profit margin %						Line 79 + line 69 x 100
82	Hardware	69	55	73	73	73	
83	Software	86	80	83	83	83	
84	Total	69	56	74	74	74	
85							

Direct costs divide into variable and fixed. Let me state the obvious. *Variable costs* (such as raw materials) *vary* directly with volume. Each cubic metre of *concrete mix A* requires, say, $\frac{1}{2}$ cubic metre of gravel – and for this mix the proportion of gravel is always 50% of the total (except in shoddy construction work when standards slip so that the contractor can save on cement).

On the other hand, fixed costs are *relatively* fixed in relation to production. Factory rent will not vary, whether output is zero or running at maximum capacity. Machine costs might be fixed in relation to smaller quantities of output. If it costs you $15,000 to rent a machine to produce anything between 0 and 100,000 units a month, the fixed costs related to the machines go up in steps of $15,000 every time that production passes a 100,000 barrier.

For general analysis, you will want to *attribute* the portion of indirect costs (such as marketing) that has to be *absorbed* in the production and sale of each of your products. This is discussed in Chapter 11. For the current purposes of assessing production costs we need consider only direct costs.

When you have calculated the cost of producing a unit of your goods or services you can multiply volumes by unit-cost to arrive at total cost of sales. For example, for 375,000 units at $2 a unit:

$$cost\ of\ sales = sales\ volume \times unit\text{-}cost\ of\ production$$

$$= 375,000 \times 2$$

$$= \$750,000$$

The alternative is to do it the long way, to produce a column of figures similar to those in Figure 8.5 for each period in your forecast. You are going to have to do this eventually for the budget exercise – but the unit-value approach is useful for *what-if* analysis (*what if* sales were $500? $10,000? $20,000?) and for 'big-picture forecasting' while you are refining your strategy and plans.

MANUFACTURING, TRADING AND OPERATING ACCOUNTS

Often, the sales and costs of sales figures are included in the overall profit and loss account. We do it this way in Chapter 9. For complex situations, you might separate out chunks of related numbers – otherwise you would need a very long sheet of paper (such as the back of one of those huge computer printouts that for some reason are always stacked up in the accounts department). You might have three accounts.

1 **A manufacturing account** such as in Figure 8.5.

2 **A trading account.** This starts with *costs of goods shipped to warehouse* (brought forward from the manufacturing account) and shows sales and distribution activities resulting in gross sales and gross profit.

3   **An operating account**. Finally, gross profit might be carried forward to a third account, the operating account, and adjusted for the other incomes and costs to arrive at net profit (or loss). These other items are mainly indirect costs such as your accountant's salary that cannot be directly attributed to sales (except sales of someone else's paper).

 Unambiguous inventory

Inventory in the present context is your stockpile of unsold raw materials, work-in-progress, finished goods and services that you intend to sell. I sense that you are wondering whether to quibble about whether you can have a *stock of services*. I think that you could, for example, have an inventory of computer software if this is your business. This is *trading inventory*. It is not what you have in your stationery store cupboard (unless you are in the office supplies business) and it is not your stock of fixed assets (such as machinery and equipment).

Incidentally, this is a situation where I favour the US *inventory*, which is much less ambiguous than the British word *stock*. This could also refer to a unit of stock, which is what Americans call *shares* and I generally prefer to call *equity* – to avoid another ambiguity.

WHEN COSTS VARY

Products purchased or manufactured in, say, July might not be sold until November. The actual purchase or production is recorded in July, the product lives on the balance sheet as 'inventory' until November, when the appropriate amount is charged to cost of sales.

Figure 8.7 shows how your inventory level is derived mechanically from your production/purchases and your sales forecasts. The timing differences between the two might raise a slight problem. How do you value the cost of sales if:

- unit costs are changing over time; and
- you do not or cannot *match specific units* of product to specific sales?

There is no easy, simple answer, as discussed next.

VALUING INVENTORY

Accountants use the following four methods to value the things that you sell.

Figure 8.7 Tracking inventory

	Jan	Feb	Mar	...
Volume, units				
...	...	...	...	...
Production (or purchases)				
Production volume, units	12 000	12 000	6 000	...
...	...	...	...	...
Inventory volume, units				
Opening stock	5 000	7 000	8 000	6 000
Add production	12 000	12 000	6 000	...
Less sales	10 000	11 000	8 000	...
End-month stock	**7 000**	**8 000**	**6 000**	
...	...	...	...	...
Sales				
Sales volume, units	10 000	11 000	8 000	...
...	...	...	...	...

1 Specific unit costs

Specific unit costs (also called specific identification) is where you match exactly the origin of each unit of your product and journey into, through and out of inventory. This is the purest method of valuation, but it cannot be used when units of your product are indistinguishable from each other (grain, paint, talcum powder, jelly beans).

2 Averaging

This is also called *weighted averaging* where each unit of inventory is measured by:

1 *adding up* all the money spent acquiring inventory during the period (the value of the opening stock plus production/purchase costs); and

2 *dividing* the total calculated in step 1 by the number of items available for sale (opening quantity plus quantity purchased/produced).

3 FIFO

First-in first-out (FIFO) is where you track specific unit costs and assume that the earliest items put into stock are the first ones removed. (This is one situation where an accounting concept matches real-life common sense.)

4 LIFO

Last-in, first-out (LIFO) is where you track specific unit costs and assume that the latest items put into stock are the first ones removed. (Unfortunately, this is similar to my document filing system.)

You often find companies using a mix of valuation methods for various categories of inventory. By and large, the first two or three techniques are preferable for analytical purposes. The second two may be more advantageous for tax reasons. Use of LIFO results in the lowest tax bill, although it is not accepted by some tax authorities (for example, in certain European countries).

When stock acquisition costs are rising (perhaps due to inflation), FIFO boosts the value of your closing stock. When prices are falling (such as with many high-tech items and some commodities), LIFO produces a higher valuation for the cost of goods sold and a lower value for closing stock. Figure 8.6 contrasts the effect of using FIFO and LIFO in a computer business where production costs are falling over time.

Clearly, inventory valuation is an example of where the books can be manipulated even when no money is changing hands.

 When is a sale not a sale?

Mischievous managers frequently recognise sales when it suits them. If revenue is running above budget in November or December, a big end-year contract could be booked in January. The year comes in on target and there is a good start to the next one. Alternatively, but more difficult, if income is poor this year it might be boosted by moving back a sale from early next year. I trust you to be honest, but if you are checking someone else's figures this is a trick to watch out for.

There are three other points that will come to mind when you are thinking about inventory. These are discussed under *risks* in Chapter 11.

1   You want to keep inventory as low as possible – it ties up cash that for the moment is not earning for you.

2   Adequate opening and closing stocks do not automatically imply that you can meet demand during the month – if sales run ahead of production there might be an unacceptable delay in meeting orders.

3   You need a buffer stock to meet unexpected changes in demand.

Gross profit

I saved the best for last. The final step is to subtract cost of sales from sales value – to arrive at gross profits. Like this:

	Money
Sale	900,000
Less *cost of sales*	750,000
Gross profit	150,000

You can feel justifiably proud of having arrived at this point. We are almost there. By now, your knowledge and self-confidence should be growing. If you were doubtful of mastering the complexities, you should by now realise that business planning is a matter of simple organisation and logic. It is not an awesome task beyond explanation. You will soon be in a position not only to write a clear plan and explain your financial plans but also to understand and question figures presented to you. Take a break. Then write a summary of all this work for your business plan.

Writing it up

The complexity of acquiring your product dictates the amount of detail required in your business plan. Obviously, there is less descriptive work to do if your sale is a haircut or if you buy widgets and re-sell them. A giant aircraft manufacturing company has a bigger task when calculating *cost of sales*.

The box on page 187 takes you through the ten steps to writing up your sales forecast. The final step, reviewing risks, is covered in Chapter 11. Figures 8.8 and 8.9 show simple examples from a business plan. This is continued in Chapter 9, where we do a little more work to get to net profit.

Figure 8.8 Sales forecasts from the business plan

Some of the background work for this business plan is shown in Figures 8.4, 8.6 and 8.9.

TETRYLUS BUSINESS PLAN Doc 20110136   Sales Projections

SALES

Introduction

Tetrylus ONE reduces the number of accidents at work and cuts the cost of complying with health and safety legislation. Companies will recover in ten months their entire initial investment in buying the hardware, licensing the software and implementing the system. Moreover …

Sales volumes

The limiting factor on sales volumes might be our ability to implement enough systems in a given period of time. We can solve this by selling through ISPs and using *their* technical staff to implement our systems for end-users. This cuts our resource requirements and reduces the sales cycle (since ISPs will leverage existing customer relationships). Moreover, we are increasing the incentive for ISPs to re-sell *Tetrylus ONE* by allowing them to earn a high margin on the product while also earning from sales of their consulting and implementation services.

….

We have already appointed three ISPs, and we expect to recruit one more this year. We will continue to add ISPs – until we have 20 in year 5. We are working with current ISPs to develop specific prospective sales. We have three pilot sales at contract-negotiation stage, and we will make a total of four sales during this year …

Our target is to sell an average of 2500 *Tetrylus ONE* identity badges with each sale by year 3. Initial sales will be smaller because …

Production costs

Identity badges will be produced for us by TechnoWhiz. This will reduce the resources that we require and limit our manufacturing risks – TechnoWhiz have already produced prototypes that meet or exceed our quality specifications. Initial costs of $50 a badge will fall to $23 in year 2. Our projected volumes allow …

Selling price

Longer-term, sales will average a little over $100,000 per package. Pilot sales aimed at establishing references sites will be smaller amounts. The following table shows the composition of a *Tetrylus ONE* package …

Copyright © 2011 *TETRYLUS Inc*   Page 14 of 20

Figure 8.9 Sales forecasts from the back of the business plan

TETRYLUS Inc Financial plan

Production and sales, first six months
Dollars

		Month 1	Month 2	Month 3	Month 4	Month 5	Month 6
G-1	**Costs and prices**						
G-2	Production cost, per unit	0	50	50	50	50	50
G-3	Sales price, per unit	0	78	78	78	78	78
G-4							
G-5	**Inventory volume**						
G-6	Opening stock (prev 9)	0	0	300	800	350	850
G-7	Addition (production volume)	0	500	500	0	500	0
G-8	Reduction (sales volume)	0	–200	0	–450	0	–600
G-9	**Closing stock (6 + 7 + 8)**	**0**	**300**	**800**	**350**	**850**	**250**
G-10							
G-11	**Inventory value**						
G-12	Opening stock (prev 15)	0	0	15 000	40 000	17 500	42 500
G-13	Addition (line 2 x line 7)	0	25 000	25 000	0	25 000	0
G-14	Reduction (line 2 x line 8)	0	–10 000	0	–22 500	0	–30 000
G-15	**Closing stock (12 + 13 + 14)**	**0**	**15 000**	**40 000**	**17 500**	**42 500**	**12 500**
G-16							
G-17	**Gross sales**						
G-18	Hardware (line 3 x line 8)	0	15 600	0	35 100	0	46 800
G-19	Software	0	4 400	0	4 900	0	3 200
G-20	**Total sales (lines 18 + 19)**	**0**	**20 000**	**0**	**40 000**	**0**	**50 000**
G-21							
G-22	**Cost of sales**						
G-23	Hardware (line 2 x line 8)	0	10 000	0	22 500	0	30 000
G-24	Software (from software account)	0	3 591	0	4 683	0	3 979
G-25	**Total cost (lines 23 + 24)**	**0**	**13 591**	**0**	**27 183**	**0**	**33 979**
G-26							
G-27	**Gross profit**						
G-28	Hardware (line 18 – line 23)	0	5 600	0	12 600	0	16 800
G-29	Software (line 19 – line 24)	0	809	0	217	0	–779
G-30	**Total (lines 28 + 29)**	**0**	**6 409**	**0**	**12 817**	**0**	**16 021**
G-31							
G-32	**Gross profit, %**						
G-33	Hardware (line 28 / line 18)	0	36	0	36	0	36
G-34	Software (line 29 / line 19)	0	18	0	4	0	–24
G-35	**Total (line 30 / line 20)**	**0**	**32**	**0**	**32**	**0**	**32**

Ten steps to writing a successful sales forecast

1　Describe the logic underlying your forecast.

2　Show any historical proofs for your methods – such as a chart similar to Figure 8.2 illustrating intimate relationships.

3　Introduce any assumptions that you have made – such as about the level of interest rates.

4　Develop your forecast.

5　Explain how you have modified the forecast to take account of industry trends, your marketing, etc.

6　Show sales forecasts.

7　Show how you arrive at your cost of sales and therefore gross profit.

8　Include a summary table in the text and details in the annexes to your plan.

9　Explain the key risks and indicate alternative sales scenarios if these risks become dominant.

10　Keep it simple, clear and concise.

Getting to net profit

If little money does not go out,
great money will not come in. CHINESE PROVERB

- Where the money goes
- Capital spending
- Capital assets that you already own
- Capital assets that you want
- Accounting for fixed assets
- Operating expenditure
- Net profit
- Other income and expenditure
- Moving on

This chapter looks primarily at the costs associated with operating your business. These can be divided into capital and current spending – also known as investment and consumption. The accounting treatment of each one is slightly different.

Costs are usually split into functional areas (R&D, production, marketing and sales, etc.). In accounting terms, production costs go into a manufacturing or trading account, and all other functional areas are lumped together as operational spending in the rest of the profit and loss account. Methods of analysing and forecasting costs for all functional areas are identical and are considered together here.

Gross profit (Chapter 8) less operating costs (this chapter) leads you to net profit, or net loss if times are tough. Just to complicate matters, there are several definitions of net profit, which are discussed briefly. Then we can move on happily to discuss the critical issues of cash flow and funding.

Where the money goes

Business sometimes seems to be a black hole that sucks in money. Understanding and controlling costs is important. But naïve managers sometimes become obsessed with cutting costs, often to the detriment of the business. As I comment elsewhere, spending can be reduced by 100% maximum. Revenues *could* be increased to almost infinity. Spending wisely to produce the maximum return is what it is all about. This chapter divides logically into three parts.

1 **Capital investment.** First, take a look at capital outlays. This is basically spending on assets with a life of more than a year. It is important, because it represents cash spent today with the expectation of future reward. For this reason, capital spending is singled out for close scrutiny.

2 **Current consumption.** Second, work through current spending. It is straightforward if you break it into functional areas (R&D, marketing and sales) and then into employment and other costs. These two categories divide further (travel, telephones, computers, etc.). You can consider each in turn. The current part of capital outlays – depreciation – is included here. Forecasting tricks are covered below.

3 **Profit and loss.** Third, pull this work together to build up a profit and loss account and reach your bottom line – net profit or loss.

As already emphasised, the method you use to forecast operating costs is identical to the approach for deriving production costs in the *cost of sales figures* – see Chapter 8. It just happens that production costs are directly related to sales and so receive special treatment by the men in grey suits.

My department doesn't make a profit ...

You might not have *sales income* if you are a small cog in a big company, but you will certainly spend money. This chapter is very much for you.

Capital spending

WHAT CAPITAL SPENDING IS AND ISN'T

It is easiest to define capital spending by considering what it is not. We have already looked at the *cost of sales*. These are not capital outlays. *Operating costs* are things that you spend money on and it is gone – advertising, wages and salaries, rents, travel and telecommunications. This is not capital spending either.

Capital spending is spending on *productive items with a life of more than 12 months* such as plant, machinery, vehicles, computers, office equipment, fixtures and fittings and intellectual property. Note that capital assets do not have to be things you can touch and feel. They can also be intangible items.

In accounting terms, your *asset accounts* record other items which for *business planning* purposes it is better to regard as operational (current) spending. For example, you have already noticed that rent paid in advance is recorded as an asset (prepaid rent). This belongs in your cash flow statement, but not in any schedule of capital investment.

WHAT'S IT WORTH?

If you spend a million on machinery that will be used over ten years, how do you show it in your financial accounts? All other things being equal, if you charged the million to today's operational spending your profit and loss account would look rather unhealthy this year, especially if you had not started using the machine. On the other hand, your profit and loss account would be great next year when the machinery was producing output for no apparent outlay (other than perhaps maintenance).

It is usual and rational to divide the purchase cost into several parts and charge them to operating costs over the life of the machine. For example, a $30,000 machine with a three-year life span might be thought of as costing you $10,000 a year for three years. The exact way that you allocate the costs over time is specified by your:

● *depreciation policy* for physical assets;

● *amortisation policy* for intangible assets such as R&D costs; and

● *depletion policy* for natural resources.

Depreciation, amortisation and depletion are different names for exactly the same thing – writing off costs over the working life of the asset. From now on, if I refer to *depreciation* take this to include *amortisation* and *depletion* as appropriate.

You can have a different depreciation policy for each category of assets (plant, machinery, office, etc.) or sometimes even for each asset. You will see how it works in a moment. Essentially, it results in your assets being shown in your accounts at their historic cost, or replacement cost, or some other artificial book value. Watch for somebody revaluing assets when switching between the three values or when bringing recorded values back into line with unexpected inflationary trends. This is a good trick for artificially massaging profits and balance sheet figures. I know that you would not do it.

Capital assets that you already own

As discussed in Chapter 3, your business plan needs to include a summary of your existing fixed assets, together with an indication of their value and an outline of the related depreciation policy. A typical accountant's summary of fixed assets is shown on page 194. You can create this from one (or both) of the following two sources:

1 **Depreciation schedule.** For each asset, your accountant's *depreciation schedule* will show the original acquisition cost, depreciation to date, the current net book value – and probably estimates of current or replacement value for insurance purposes.

2 **Fixed asset register.** Somewhere, often with the people who manage your facilities, you will also find a *fixed asset register*. This might be combined with the depreciation schedule and kept in the bean counter's bottom drawer. Once a year (or more often if things are inclined to walk off the premises on their own) someone in a grey suit will climb over your operations people checking that a physical inventory of assets matches the register.

The box on page 199 shows an example of how you can lay out a combined fixed asset register and depreciation schedule.

Fixed asset summary

This is the information from the box on page 199 presented in a useful summary format. You might want to use this layout in the main body of your business plan with a footnote describing depreciation policy, important assets, etc. The detailed version can go in an annex.

Fixed assets
Book value, dollars

Category of assets	Opening value	Additions in year	Depreciation for year	Closing value
Machinery	0	120,000	4,000	116,000
Office equipment	0	72,000	5,000	67,000
Computers	0	48,000	3,000	45,000
...	...	...	...	...
Total	**0**	**240,000**	**12,000**	**228,000**

Notes: Office equipment is depreciated over three years using the straight-line method ...

DECISION-MAKING VALUES

An excellent way to establish the actual or useful value of your fixed assets is to examine the depreciation schedule and fixed asset register. These show the original cost, current book cost and the age of the assets. The written-down (depreciated) value is often way out of line with current or replacement values. You need to conduct a realistic appraisal to decide what is reasonable.

1 **Market values.** During your management review of the business, you will base decisions on market values. What is the underlying value of plant or machinery? Would it be better to sell it and use the proceeds elsewhere? Do you have competitive advantage because you have already written off the cost?

2 **Insurance value.** For your operational decisions, you will also have to decide whether to insure for current or replacement values.

'Better to wear out than to rust out.'

BISHOP CUMBERLAND

Capital assets that you want

It hardly needs to be said that you need to draw up a list of capital outlays that are required by your strategic and operational plans. For each category of assets (plant, machinery, office, etc.) you should show the expected date of acquisition, total acquisition costs and a depreciation schedule. Some thoughts follow.

WHAT DOES IT COST?

For accounting purposes, the acquisition cost – booked value – of fixed assets is usually taken to include all outlays incurred in bringing them into use. For example, for a computer, booked-value might include the cost of the hardware itself – plus operating software, shipping, installation fees, cabling and so on.

 This is one situation where profits for the current period are inflated – consumables are put on to the balance sheet rather than in the profit and loss account. The downside is that it reduces profits in future periods.

HOW LONG WILL IT LAST?

There are two decisions to be made before you can draw up a depreciation schedule.

1   **Determine the period over which the asset will be written off.** Ideally this will coincide exactly with the operating life of the asset. If you have a machine that will last for exactly three years and then expire, your write-off period will be 36 months. Of course, you rarely know this in advance. Moreover, the depreciation period may be imposed on you by company policy, statutory regulations or the use of generally accepted accounting principles. If you consider such imposition to be unrealistic, you might be bold enough to challenge it or run two sets of accounts – one for economic and management analysis and one for official reporting purposes. Examples of working lives are provided on page 201.

2   **Determine the depreciation method.** The straight-line method is shown in the examples in this chapter (e.g. see Figure 9.1, later). *Units of production* – matching the depreciation of a machine or resource against its output – is a troublesome if attractive alternative. Other methods include the *double declining balance* and *sum of the years' digits*; these are noteworthy techniques for *accelerating depreciation* during the early months of an asset's life when it is falling in value most rapidly.

SHOW OFF YOUR ASSETS

The accounting entries that you pass for one asset in one category are shown in Figure 9.1. By repeating this simple procedure, you can account for any number of assets. A sample extract from a business plan showing capital outlays and depreciation is given in Figure 9.2.

About Tetrylus's capital outlays

The sample extract from a business plan (Figure 9.2) sets out clearly how much this new business will be spending on various categories of fixed assets. *Computers* is the largest single entry – not surprising given that *Tetrylus* deals in computer technology.

The acquisition cost of the computers includes the operating systems and other office software 'bundled' (included in the price) with the computers. The separate $5000 capital outlay on software is for software tools that are used to develop *Tetrylus*'s product. Another entry for software purchases is shown in the operating expenditure accounts (Figure 9.4) – this is for graphics and contact-management packages acquired by marketing, which the company treats as consumption rather than investment. In addition, *Tetrylus* spends on licence fees for software that is sub-licensed to customers – this is recorded as a *cost of sale* in Figure 8.4.

REPLACING FIXED ASSETS

Depreciation is a set of book-keeping entries created at a stroke of the accountant's pen. It does not establish a cash reserve for replacing an asset. If you wanted to do this, you would have to pass a separate set of entries – moving some of your profits from your bank account to a fixed-asset replacement fund each year. Then, of course, the cash in the fund would probably be earning less than your *cost of capital* and so it would be clawing-down your overall *return on capital employed* (see Chapters 11 and 12). Such *replacement* or *sinking funds* tend to be the exception rather than the rule. You should decide if you need one using rational judgement and standard capital investment appraisal techniques (see Chapter 11).

A NEW LEASE OF LIFE

It frequently makes sense to lease rather than to buy. This reduces the up-front demands on your cash flow and is particularly helpful for new businesses. There are two categories of lease:

● **Finance lease** – where the risks and rewards of ownership are passed to the company using the things being leased to them.

● **Operating lease** – all other leases.

As the name implies, a finance lease is a sneaky way of financing an asset. In essence, it produces a *liability* (to pay for the asset) that is hidden off-balance-sheet. Many countries have introduced the generally accepted accounting principle that requires finance leases to be shown on the balance sheet as an asset and as a matching liability. The starting value on both sides of the balance sheet is the *net present value* (see Chapter 11) of the minimum lease payments. Depreciation is over the shorter of the term of the lease or the assets' expected useful life. The excess of annual lease payments over the depreciation charge is charged to the profit and loss account as *interest*.

Operating leases are just charged to the profit and loss account as an expense (such as 'computer leases').

In Chapter 11, I explain some simple arithmetic with an off-putting name. This is the *internal rate of return* (the *discount rate* in *net present value*). It is used in assessing whether or not to acquire an asset. It is also helpful when deciding whether to lease or buy – you use it to compare the relative costs of the two options. Leasing is often especially attractive to new businesses because it averts a big up-front cash outlay.

 Outlays are expenditure

You have probably noticed that I tend to refer to *capital outlays* and *operational expenditure*. This is a rather weak attempt at avoiding another ambiguity. Some bean counters refer to them as *capital* and *expenditure* respectively. I do not know about you, but I class handing over a cheque for an asset as *spending*. Using the word outlay almost exclusively in relation to capital spending, I hope to help you separate it from operational spending.

'Expenditure rises to meet income.'
C. NORTHCOTE PARKINSON. OPENING SENTENCE FROM *THE LAW AND THE PROFITS*

Accounting for fixed assets

This is how you account for fixed assets in your monthly projections. Suppose that:

● in October you will acquire a clumping machine for $120,000 (see Figure 9.1);

● it has an expected life of five years (60 months);

● you are using the straight-line depreciation method.

Fixed assets detailed

Here is an extract summarising expected monthly spending on fixed assets, together with the associated depreciation schedule. It helps to open this list vertically and specify each asset that will be acquired (computer 1, computer 2, etc.) together with some useful descriptive notes. This creates a detailed capital spending plan to include in your business plan. If you are starting a business, you have also created a framework for your fixed asset register and depreciation schedule. The totals for each category can be carried forward into a summary, as shown here.

If you are in an existing business, remember that the schedules for the new assets will have to be merged with the schedules for previously acquired assets.

Spending dollars, whole months		Sep	Oct	Nov	Dec
Capital outlays					
Machinery		0	120,000	0	0
Office equipment		36,000	36,000	0	0
Computers		0	24,000	24,000	0
...		...	...	...	...
Total		**36,000**	**180,000**	**24,000**	**0**
Depreciation schedule	*Term**				
Machinery	60	0	0	2,000	2,000
Office equipment	36	0	1,000	2,000	2,000
Computers	24	0	0	1,000	2,000
...	...	...	...	...	...
Total		**0**	**1 000**	**5 000**	**6 000**

* Term = number of months over which assets are depreciated, in this case using the straight-line method

The accounting entries are as follows.

1 In October you debit *fixed assets – machinery* $120,000 and assuming that you paid cash, credit *cash at bank* by the same amount.

2 Every month commencing in November you debit $2000 (120,000 divided by 60 months) to the operating expenditure account *depreciation of machinery* and credit the asset account *fixed assets – depreciation of machinery* with the same amount.

At the end of the first year:

● the (original) booked value is $120,000;

● the accumulated depreciation is $4000 (two months' depreciation);

● the written-down or net book value is $116,000; and

● your operating costs for the year include $4000 in depreciation.

If the only other transaction in the year was an issue of 200,000 shares, the financial transactions for September to December would be those illustrated in Figure 9.1.

Figure 9.1 Accounting for fixed assets

	Sep	Oct	Nov	Dec
Balance sheet				
End month				
Assets				
Cash at bank	200 000	80 000	80 000	80 000
Fixed assets – machinery	0	120 000	120 000	120 000
Less cumulative depreciation, machinery	0	0	2 000	4 000
Net book value of assets	0	120 000	118 000	116 000
Total	**200 000**	**200 000**	**198 000**	**196 000**
Liabilities and shareholders' equity				
Paid up share capital	200 000	200 000	200 000	200 000
Profit (loss), current year	0	0	(2 000)	(4 000)
Total	**200 000**	**200 000**	**198 000**	**196 000**
Profit and loss account				
Whole month				
Depreciation – machinery	0	0	2 000	2 000
Net profit (loss)	**0**	**0**	**(2 000)**	**(2 000)**
Cash flow				
Whole month				
Share issue	200 000	0	0	0
Assets	0	–120 000	0	0
Total for month	**200 000**	**–120 000**	**0**	**0**
Net cash balance	**200 000**	**80 000**	**0**	**0**

Working life

Machines and things

A quick look through some company accounts shows that typical depreciation periods might be 3 years for computers, 5 years for office equipment, 10 years for some industrial machinery, 20 years for a jumbo jet and 100 years for airport runways (I didn't think that this last example was reasonable either).

Fitting of premises

Spending on fittings that you cannot take with you – fixed partitioning, plumbing, cabling, decorating – is treated as freehold improvements (if you own the premises) or leasehold improvements (if you rent). Such spending is usually amortised over the shorter of the life of the fittings, the lease or the building.

Research and development

Spending on your research and development team and the gizmos that they dissect is best treated as current expenditure. However, where there is clearly identifiable spending on the specific development of a viable product, you may charge the outlays to capital, show the total on the balance sheet as an asset (perhaps as *product X*), and begin writing it off once the product is ready for market. The amortisation might be over the period during which you will be able to sell the product, or over a given number of units sold.

Start-up costs

Identifiable start-up costs for a new business – such as incorporation and professional advisers' fees and management costs – are often *capitalised* and written off over between two and five years.

Goodwill

Goodwill is the difference between the market value of a business and the net value of the assets. It represents the future cash flow that can be generated by, for example, trading on a name or location. You cannot show in your accounts the goodwill value that you attach to your own company. But if you are taken over, the acquiring company can show goodwill and amortise it over up to 20 years (more in some circumstances). It is, however, more common in Europe to charge this directly to shareholder equity.

Other intellectual property

The cost of acquiring patents, copyrights, trademarks and other licences is written off over their expected useful lives – which are often much less than the statutory protection afforded. A copyright, for example, generally lives for 50 years after the originator's death. Will the works have such a long life? You would probably write off the advance for the copyright on a fleetingly famous celebrity's novels over a much shorter period.

Land and building

Generally accepted accounting principles do not allow you to stand depreciation on its head and increase steadily the book value of assets that appreciate. Usually, land and buildings are left in the books at their acquisition costs and revalued from time to time only as an extreme exception (such as when the chief executive wants to make the balance sheet look better).

Natural resources

Natural resources such as oil and gas reserves are *depleted* rather than depreciated using a units-of-production approach.

Operating expenditure

After the complexities of dealing with capital spending, operating expenditure is delightfully simple. There are occasional timing difficulties – but these are easy to deal with as already discussed under accruals and prepayments earlier (see Chapter 7). The following commentary covers both production costs (part of the cost of sales) and operating cost (costs not directly attributable to the cost of sales), because they are both treated identically from an accounting and forecasting point of view.

When looking back at your past performance, all you have to do is copy out the numbers. When looking forward, it is really just a matter of making forecasts for each time period and entering the amounts in your spreadsheet. If you do have a history, the past will help you understand future costs.

If you are starting a new business or new business unit, the forecasting might require a little more thought. If you do not have experience of your likely costs, you need to do some intelligent enquiry. You can check prices with trade associations, utility companies and suppliers. You could also talk to other business owners and advisers to get a feel for what you should expect.

Figure 9.2 Capital outlays at the back of the business plan

TETRYLUS Inc Financial plan

Total capital outlays and depreciation, first six months
Dollars

		Month 1	Month 2	Month 3	Month 4	Month 5	Month 6	H1
	CAPITAL OUTLAYS							
C-11	Office fittings	6 500	0	0	0	0	0	**6 500**
C-12	Office furniture	5 000	0	0	0	0	0	**5 000**
C-13	Office equipment	0	0	750	0	0	0	**750**
C-14	Telecoms equipment	0	0	0	0	0	0	**0**
C-15	Computers, etc.	20 000	1 500	0	1 000	0	0	**22 500**
C-16	Software	5 000	0	0	0	0	0	**5 000**
C-17	Motor vehicles	0	0	0	0	0	0	**0**
C-00	**TOTAL CAPITAL OUTLAYS**	**36,500**	**1 500**	**750**	**1 000**	**0**	**0**	**39 750**
	DEPRECIATION SCHEDULE							
D-11	Office fittings	0	542	542	542	542	542	**2 708**
D-12	Office furniture	0	83	83	83	83	83	**417**
D-13	Office equipment	0	0	0	13	13	13	**38**
D-14	Telecoms equipment	0	0	0	0	0	0	**0**
D-15	Computers, etc.	0	556	597	597	625	625	**3 000**
D-16	Software	0	208	208	208	208	208	**1 042**
D-17	Motor vehicles	0	0	0	0	0	0	**0**
D-00	**TOTAL**	**0**	**1 389**	**1 431**	**1 443**	**1 471**	**1 471**	**7 204**

Notes to the accounts: depreciation policy
Fixed assets are written off over their projected working lives using the straight-line method. Office fittings are depreciated over the 12-month term of the office lease; office furniture and equipment is depreciated over 60 months, computers over 36 months and software over 24 months.

     Page A4 of A10

BREAK IT INTO SMALL PARTS

As always, the key to dealing with any problem (in this case predicting future costs) is to split it into smaller pieces.

- Divide spending into the functional areas identified in your organisational analysis (see Chapter 4) – R&D, marketing and sales, etc.

- For each functional area, separate spending into employee and non-employment costs.

- For each of employee and non-employment, separate spending into related sub-categories – bonuses, premises, office travel and so on.

Then work through each heading at the lowest level of detail, identifying spending requirements month-by-month to meet your operating plan. When you tackle it in this way, what might have seemed to be an obstacle becomes a logical process.

'It is not the employer who pays the wages; he only handles the money. It is the product that pays the wages.'

HENRY FORD

EMPLOYEE COSTS

Employee costs are probably the easiest operating overhead to project. Your operating plan already contains detailed human resource requirements. Just derive the associated expenditure. Some of the employee costs to consider are listed on page 206. You might have others, maybe industry-specific categories such as uniforms. It is a good idea to copy the appropriate headings into a column on a spreadsheet table, and fill in figures for each month working across. Essentially, enter one-twelfth of the annual total under each month, allowing for pay increases, amendments in social security rates and other changes. You might also expand the categories vertically to include details by job title or employee. Figure 9.3 shows an example extracted from a business plan – see also Figure 9.5 later for a commentary.

Figure 9.3 Employee costs at the back of the business plan

Tetrylus Inc Financial plan

Staff costs, first six months

Dollars

		Month 1	Month 2	Month 3	Month 4	Month 5	Month 6	H1
	STAFF NUMBERS							
	Directors/managers	3	3	3	3	3	3	3
	Technical staff	2	4	4	4	4	4	4
	Marketing staff	0	1	1	2	2	2	2
	Administrative staff	2	2	2	2	2	3	3
	Total	7	10	10	11	11	12	12
	STAFF COSTS							
	Staff salaries							
S-1	Technical staff 1	1 200	1 200	1 200	1 200	1 200	1 200	7 200
S-2	Technical staff 2	1 200	1 200	1 200	1 200	1 200	1 200	7 200
S-3	Technical staff 3	.	1 200	1 200	1 200	1 200	1 200	6 000
S-4	Technical staff 4	.	1 200	1 200	1 200	1 200	1 200	6 000
S-5	Sales/distribution manager	.	.	.	1 250	1 259	1 250	3 759
S-6	Marketing assistant	.	750	750	750	750	750	3 750
S-7	Book-keeping, etc.	.	.	.	.	.	750	750
S-8	Receptionist/secretary	600	600	600	600	600	600	3 600
S-9	Messenger/security	300	300	300	300	300	300	1 800
S-00	**TOTAL (sum S1 to S9)**	3 300	6 450	6 450	7 700	7 709	8 450	40 059
S-11	Directors' stipends	10 000	10 000	10 000	10 000	10 000	10 000	60 000
S-13	Contract staff	10 000	10 000	10 000	10 000	10 000	10 000	60 000
S-14	Staff social security	92	162	162	185	185	208	992
S-15	Staff temporary	0	0	0	0	0	0	0
S-10	**TOTAL DIRECT (11 to 19)**	23 392	26 612	26 612	27 885	27 894	28 658	161 051
S-21	Staff pension fund	417	417	417	417	417	417	2 500
S-22	Staff termination fund	0	0	0	0	0	0	0
S-23	Staff rent allowances	0	0	0	0	0	0	0
S-24	Staff transport allowances	0	0	0	0	0	0	0
S-25	Staff other allowances	0	0	0	0	0	0	0
S-26	Staff group insurance	0	0	0	0	0	0	0
S-27	Staff medical insurance	500	0	0	0	0	0	500
S-28	Staff other benefits	0	0	0	0	0	0	0
S-20	**TOT. BENEFITS (21 to 29)**	917	417	417	417	417	417	3 000
S-31	Staff medical expenses	0	0	0	0	0	0	0
S-32	Staff recruitment	0	0	0	0	0	0	0
S-33	Staff relocation	0	0	0	0	0	0	0
S-34	Staff legal expenses	1 500	0	0	0	0	0	1 500
S-36	Staff training	0	0	0	0	0	0	0
S-38	Staff entertainment	70	100	100	110	110	120	610
S-39	Staff sundry	0	0	0	0	0	0	0
S-30	**TOTAL OTHER (31 to 39)**	1 570	100	100	110	110	120	2 110
S-00	**TOTAL STAFF (10+20+30)**	25 879	27 128	27 128	28 411	28 420	29 194	166 161

NON-EMPLOYEE COSTS

Other costs, those not associated with employees, are generally fairly simple to forecast. Again, it is a case of working through categories of spending and making sensible forecasts for each month. Over 50 areas of spending that you might want to consider tracking are listed on page 208. You probably will not use all of these, but there will be other categories specific to your business.

HOW MUCH DETAIL?

You need to decide how much detail to include. In part, this depends on the intended use of the business plan. A forecast that will become an operating budget might have a great many categories of spending for each functional area (marketing, R&D, etc.). A simple projection for review purposes might have all employee costs lumped into one category (although as I have said before it makes good sense to separate out and review separately from other costs those associated with marketing and sales).

Within each category, the detail for monthly figures is based on logic. Take a simple example. Suppose that you estimate that you will spend approximately $500 on stationery each month. Should you just enter $500 for each month? Or should you work out exactly what will be purchased in which months and arrive at a projection such as $534 for January, $405 in February and so on?

The answer is self-evident when you apply cost-benefit logic. How much work is required to arrive at the estimates – compared to the usefulness of the results? How large are the amounts in relation to the overall plan? What is the importance of capturing any erratic patterns?

For example, if you know that total expenditure will be tens of thousands of dollars a month and spending on fuel will vary by around $50 a month you can safely use the same amount for each month (the projected annual cost divided by 12). It would be pointless to spend a day trying to achieve an exact projection. On the other hand, if you expected outlays on fuel to vary by 50% a month you should use a closer projection for each month.

> If you know that seasonal patterns make it a reasonably certain bet that 50% of your sales will occur in January, it would be dishonest to show the monthly average rather than the actual projection (even if this would make your year-to-date figures look very good for the first few months of the year).

DEPRECIATION – AGAIN

By the way, when you built up your capital spending plans you created a depreciation schedule. This gives you several ready-made entries. Just pull the depreciation figures into the production and operating cost tables. For example, leasehold improvements in the operating costs shown in Figure 9.4 (line E-22) are copied directly from the depreciation schedule shown in Figure 9.2 (line D-13). As you can see, the work you do early on feeds into the later tasks. Forecasting becomes easier and easier as you progress.

FORECASTING TRICKS

At this point, you might be saying that it is all very well for me to ask you to forecast operating costs, but more difficult for you to do. Well, in fact, there are some handy rules of thumb that you can apply. The obvious one – I hardly like to mention this – is to assess spending required for the year and divide by 12.

Other operating costs

(Read down under each heading)

Marketing and sales	Occupancy	Office
Delivery, shipping, etc.	Dep'n, lease/f'hold improvements	Depreciation, furniture
Brochures and printing	Premises rental and taxes	Depreciation, equipment
Advertising	Heating and air-conditioning	Leased furniture
Direct mail	Electricity	Small equipment purchases
Exhibitions, seminars, etc.	Water	Stationery and printing
Promotional items and events	Security	Dues and subscriptions
PR, charities, community	Building repairs and maintenance	Books and periodicals
Other marketing and sales	Other occupancy	Other office

Communications	Computers	Travel and subsistence
Depreciation, telecoms	Depreciation, computers	Depreciation, vehicles
Telephone and fax	Leased hardware	Motor vehicle rental
Information services	Software licences	Motor vehicle expenses
Postage and courier	Software maintenance	Travel and subsistence
Messengerial	Computer consumables	Entertainment
Other communications	Other IT	Other TS&E

Professional fees	Other fees and costs	Other adjustments
Accounting fees	Insurance	Amortisation, start-up costs
Audit fees	Bank charges	Profit and loss on disposal of assets
Legal fees	Relocation costs	Bad debts and provisions
Other professional fees	Sundry expenditure	Contingency

Note: PR = public relations, TS&E = travel, subsistence and entertainment

Fixed relationships

Sometimes, one cost has a simple proportional relationship to another. Rental contracts for office premises occasionally cover rent, air-conditioning and water – each charged at a fixed rate per square foot or metre of floor area. Aside from allowing for an annual rent review, each of these rows in the forecast is calculated in the spreadsheet as 'office area in square metres × rate-per-square-metre'. You can often calculate costs in relation to employee head-count. For example, you might find that it is logical to project costs of computer printout paper at some fixed multiple of the number of accountants that you have.

Steady rates of change

When any alternative rationale is absent, it is legitimate to assume a steadily increasing (or more rarely decreasing) pattern, such as a 1% a month increase. Do not forget that this compounds. For example, a 10% increase each month is 127% a year, not 120%.

Seasonal pattern

There might be a seasonal pattern that you can rely on. For example, you might project annual heating and air-conditioning costs, and then allocate them among the months according to some observed pattern (11% of the annual total in January, 9.5% in February, 8.3% in March and so on).

Seasonal with steady change

The effects of a steady rate of change and a seasonal pattern can be combined. A quick fix is to take a fixed change (i.e. +10%) over the same month a year earlier.

 Bad debts

If you give credit, or invoice after delivery, chances are you will have uncollectable debts. Lawyers and other misunderstood professionals realise that their clients do not like to pay. These professionals frequently do not *recognise* their fees in their accounts until payment is safely in the bank. For the rest of us, a percentage of debts, or of debts over a certain age, is usually charged to operating costs as a provision for bad debts. Show this as:

- a charge (debit) entry in the operating expenses account;

- matched by a deduction (credit) to accounts receivable on the assets side of the balance sheet.

Areas where managers massage costs

(Read downwards)

Where no money changes hands	With identifiable costs
Inventory valuation	Capitalising costs (R&D, interest on projects, etc.)
Depreciation	Leasing
Amortisation	Inflating or skimping on maintenance and repairs
Depletion	Discretionary bonuses
Provisions for payments to employees (e.g. termination costs)	Sub-contracting
Provision for bad debts	Service fees
Contingency reserve	Timing errors

CAREFUL!

When you are reviewing financial forecasts produced by others, watch for cheating. The box above shows some tricks used – and watched for – by wily old dogs. Examples include the following.

● **Inventory valuation** – such as using LIFO (*last-in first-out*) valuation where acquisition costs are falling in a high-tech business to boost profits and minimise inventory shown on the balance sheet (see Chapter 8).

● **Depreciation**, amortisation and depletion were discussed earlier in this chapter. *Stretching to ten years the life of the equipment in that new computer centre will make operating costs look much lower this year.* Similar tricks can be played with other accruals accounting techniques, including **capitalising costs**, e.g. *we won't charge R&D outlays to the expenditure account, we will put them on the balance sheet as an asset.*

● **Leasing** was touched on in capital costs above. Other **off-balance sheet liabilities** are considered in Chapter 10. It is not unknown for companies to sell their inventories with an undertaking to buy them back when they are needed – creating cash in the bank quickly and a hidden liability.

- **Provisions** for future payments to employees (such as pensions, redundancy and terminations pay) and bad debts are often covered by statutory regulations. Remember though that no money changes hands when the provisions are created by a stroke of the book-keeping pen – and when they are paid out there is no entry on the profit and loss account.

- **Sub-contracting work or paying service fees** can be ways of shifting money from one business to some other favoured firm. Moreover – since accounts can show only payments actually incurred – outsourcing increases costs. The third party's fee will include a profit that would have been a *saving* if you had done it yourself. You cannot show *savings* in the profit and loss account – only actual spending.

- **Timing errors** can build a useful cash reserve. Getting the seasonal pattern wrong was discussed earlier. **Accruals accounting** is another way that this can be achieved – an entry goes in the cash flow account as a cost early on but the cost can be treated as an accrued cost for a few months.

Net profit

Having worked through your operating costs, you will have built up a table that looks similar to Figure 9.4. You will possibly have one of these for each functional area – production, marketing, etc. The one for production costs goes into cost of sales (see Figure 9.6) as discussed in Chapter 8.

The final monthly versions for the next year are likely to become your budgets, your detailed financial operating plans. They belong in the annexes to your business plan, together with a line-by-line commentary (Figure 9.5 shows an example extract). This is too detailed for the main body of the business plan, where you will want a brief summary, and this is explained in Chapter 10.

The gross profit from Chapter 8 and operating costs considered here take you to net profit. An example of how it all pulls together into a profit and loss account is shown in Figure 9.7. Again, notice that there is no new data to enter, this is just a collection of numbers from your earlier work.

However, although you have arrived at net profit, this chapter is not over quite yet. There are a few additional items to consider. You see, it all depends what you mean by 'net profit'.

'The bigger the headquarters the more decadent the company.'

SIR JAMES GOLDSMITH

Figure 9.4 Operating costs at the back of the business plan

TETRYLUS Inc Financial plan.

Operating costs, first six months

Dollars

		Month 1	Month 2	Month 3	Month 4	Month 5	Month 6	H1
E-11	Premises rental & taxes	1 000	1 000	1 000	1 000	1 000	1 000	6 000
E-12	Amort'n - lease improvem'ts	0	542	542	542	542	542	2 708
E-13	Utilities – electricity, etc.	500	500	500	500	500	500	3 000
E-10	**TOTAL OCCUPANCY**	**1 500**	**2 042**	**2 042**	**2 042**	**2 042**	**2 042**	**11 708**
E-21	Dep'n - office furniture	0	83	83	83	83	83	417
E-22	Dep'n - office equipment	0	0	0	13	13	13	38
E-23	Small equipment	100	100	0	0	0	0	200
E-24	Stationery & printing	100	25	25	25	25	25	225
E-25	Dues & subscriptions	100	100	100	100	100	100	600
E-26	Books & periodicals	50	50	50	50	50	50	300
E-27	Other office	50	50	50	50	50	50	300
E-20	**TOTAL OFFICE**	**400**	**408**	**308**	**321**	**321**	**321**	**2 079**
E-31	Dep'n - coms equipment	0	0	0	0	0	0	0
E-32	Telephone & fax	2 500	2 500	2 500	2 500	2 500	2 500	15 000
E-33	Information services	100	100	100	100	100	100	600
E-34	Postage & courier	250	250	250	250	250	250	1 500
E-30	**TOTAL COMS**	**2 850**	**2 850**	**2 850**	**2 850**	**2 850**	**2 850**	**17 100**
E-41	Depreciation - computers	0	556	597	597	625	625	3 000
E-42	Depreciation - software	0	208	208	208	208	208	1 042
E-43	Other software licences	500	0	0	0	0	0	500
E-45	Computer consumables	50	50	50	50	50	50	300
E-40	**TOTAL COMPUTERS**	**550**	**814**	**856**	**856**	**883**	**883**	**4 842**
E-51	Product distribution	0	0	500	1 000	300	2 500	4 300
E-52	Brochures and printing	0	5 000	2 500	0	0	0	7 500
E-55	Promotional items	0	2 500	0	0	0	0	2 500
E-59	Other marketing	0	5 000	5 000	0	0	0	10 000
E-50	**TOTAL MKTG & SALES**	**0**	**12 500**	**8 000**	**1 000**	**300**	**2 500**	**24 300**
E-61	Depreciation – vehicles	0	0	0	0	0	0	0
E-62	Rental – vehicles	0	0	0	0	0	0	0
E-63	Motor vehicle expenses	0	0	0	0	0	0	0
E-64	Travel & subsistence	5 100	10 100	10 100	10 100	10 100	10 100	55 600
E-65	Entertainment	0	0	0	0	0	0	0
E-60	**TOTAL TS&E**	**5 100**	**10 100**	**10 100**	**10 100**	**10 100**	**10 100**	**55 600**
E-71	Audit fees	0	0	0	0	0	0	0
E-72	Legal fees	1 000	2 500	1,000	0	0	0	4 500
E-75	Other professional fees	0	0	0	0	0	0	0
E-70	**TOTAL PROFESSIONAL**	**1 000**	**2 500**	**1 000**	**0**	**0**	**0**	**4 500**
E-83	Insurance	1 000	2 500	0	0	0	0	3 500
E-85	Sundry expenditure	100	100	100	100	100	100	600
E-80	**TOTAL OTHER**	**1 100**	**2 600**	**100**	**100**	**100**	**100**	**4 100**
E-00	**TOTAL EXPENDITURE**	**12 500**	**33 814**	**25 256**	**17 268**	**16 596**	**18 796**	**124 229**

Figure 9.5 Expenditure commentary at the back of the business plan

This might not be exciting reading, but it is a straightforward commentary that allows readers to understand the basis behind the financial projections.

The directors are trying to make it look as if they are being reasonable. Many venture capital providers will not back a project unless the managers are well paid enough to be able to focus 100% on the business.

Another good sign of sensible planning – minimising commitments during the start-up period.

The detail (see Figure 9.4) has many 'straight-line' entries with the same spending in each month. I might have introduced a seasonal pattern here – not because it makes much difference to the forecast, but because it shows that some thought has been taken.

ANNEX A.1 Commentary on the expenditure details

A.1.1. Staff costs

Line S-00 – Total salaries

Total spending on salaries is based on headcount projections and expected salary levels (as described on page 45).

Line S-11 Director stipends

There is a modest $10,000 a month to cover the directors' basic living costs and commitments. They will be increased towards market levels once the business is generating sustained positive cash flow.

Line S-12 Deliberately omitted

Line S-13 Contract staff

To avoid the commitment associated with increasing the permanent staff complement, and to add to the range of resources available, a number of technical staff will be employed on a contract basis. Their costs are shown on page 45 and the total is included in line S-13.

…

A.1.2. Operational expenditure

Line E-11 Premises rental and taxes

We have a one-year lease on office premises at 115 High Road. This is fixed at $12,000 for the period and it is payable in advance commencing in month 1.

Line E-12 Amortisation – leasehold improvements

This is the initial office fitting costs (described on page 88) written off over the 12-month term of the lease.

Line E-13 Utilities

We estimate that spending on electricity and water will average a little over $500 a month. There will be an annual price increase in month 11 – we have provided for the maximum likely rise of 10%.

….

Figure 9.6 Costs in the profit and loss account

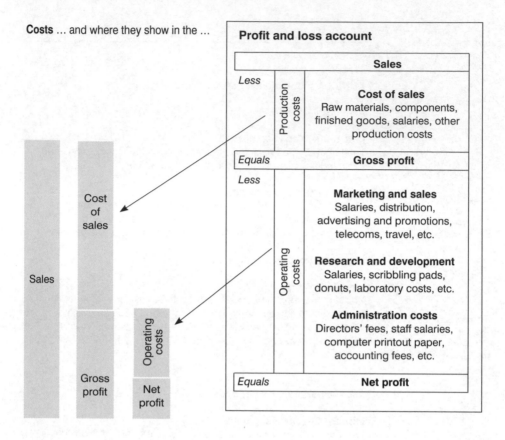

'Trust in Allah but tie up your camels, as the old Arab proverb says.'

 ### 'In that case, I'll have a new carpet please'

One of the nightmares of corporate life (apart from back-stabbing, incompetence, inertia and other routine pleasures) is trusting someone to prepare a budget and operate within it sensibly.

The first problem is that one year's spending is invariably the basis for the following year's. Of course costs are rising (inflation, extra activity and so on). So we add a little – say 10%. And then at the end of the exercise we add a bit more to cover contingencies – say, another 10%. This has added 20% to projected costs in the blink of an eye.

Then, towards the end of the next year, when spending is running well below this generous budget, there is a sudden spending frenzy – *maintenance is down, I'll have a new carpet, with all these unspent professional fees I can commission a salary survey and see how much I could earn if I changed jobs*, and so on. Strangely, entertaining and travel rarely run below budget (if ever). As a result of all this, next year's spending comes in very close to budget, so you add another 10% + 10% and off you go again – setting precedents for ruin.

How do you control this? Some companies resort to zero-based budgeting, where you hide the results of the current spending frenzy and make executives start with a blank sheet of paper. Others indulge in periodic, often damaging cost-cutting exercises. Frankly, though, it's down to having responsible management and keeping a close eye on what they do.

Figure 9.7 Profit and loss at the back of the business plan

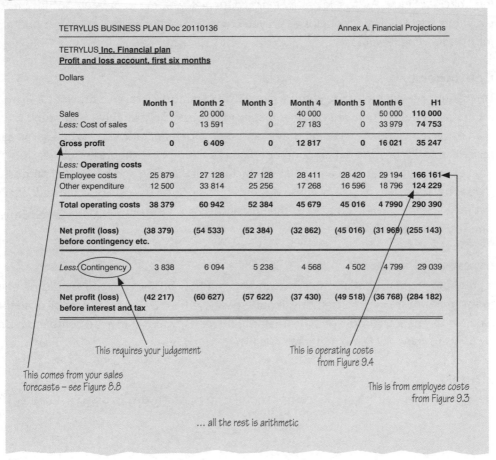

TETRYLUS BUSINESS PLAN Doc 20110136   Annex A. Financial Projections

TETRYLUS **Inc. Financial plan**
Profit and loss account, first six months

Dollars

	Month 1	Month 2	Month 3	Month 4	Month 5	Month 6	H1
Sales	0	20 000	0	40 000	0	50 000	**110 000**
Less: Cost of sales	0	13 591	0	27 183	0	33 979	**74 753**
Gross profit	**0**	**6 409**	**0**	**12 817**	**0**	**16 021**	**35 247**
Less: **Operating costs**							
Employee costs	25 879	27 128	27 128	28 411	28 420	29 194	**166 161**
Other expenditure	12 500	33 814	25 256	17 268	16 596	18 796	**124 229**
Total operating costs	**38 379**	**60 942**	**52 384**	**45 679**	**45 016**	**4 7990**	**290 390**
Net profit (loss) before contingency etc.	**(38 379)**	**(54 533)**	**(52 384)**	**(32 862)**	**(45 016)**	**(31 969)**	**(255 143)**
Less: Contingency	3 838	6 094	5 238	4 568	4 502	4 799	29 039
Net profit (loss) before interest and tax	**(42 217)**	**(60 627)**	**(57 622)**	**(37 430)**	**(49 518)**	**(36 768)**	**(284 182)**

This requires your judgement

This is operating costs from Figure 9.4

This comes from your sales forecasts – see Figure 8.8

This is from employee costs from Figure 9.3

... all the rest is arithmetic

Other income and expenditure

We are not quite finished. There is a small matter of *other* income and expenditure to consider. There are four categories.

1 **Contingency** – an allowance for unexpected costs.

2 **Investment income** – primarily income on shares in other companies.

3 **Interest** – received on bank deposits and paid to bank.

4 **Taxation**.

WHY INCLUDE THEM?

The box opposite shows how they build up in the profit and loss account. You can also look back at Figure 9.7 to see *profit before contingency*. Some people do not bother to show this line. I think that it helps when you come to monitor spending against budgets for the following reasons.

Contingency

You cannot predict the future with certainty. The contingency reserve provides a margin for error. It is here so that you can legitimately inflate cash flow slightly – and spend more than expected without exceeding the budget figure for *profit after contingencies*. You can make the contingency a flat amount, or relate it to some other figures – such as 10% of total operating costs. It is an entry that you include for planning and budgeting purposes. It disappears as time passes, because it is either reallocated to costs or is unused. Watch out for a spending binge on trivia at the end of the year if the unused contingency is not carefully controlled.

Investment income

If you hold share capital or other investments in other businesses, you should be able to estimate future income from these quite easily. You know what interest or dividend payouts to expect. Where you have majority interests, you will instead *consolidate* the accounts to show the combined profit and loss for the group.

Interest

This is easy. It will fall out of your cash flow projections, which are discussed in Chapter 10.

Taxation

This can be more of a minefield, but it is not impassable. It is possibly one of the areas where you get greatest value from paying professional advisers to save you money. Taxes may not relate directly to net profits, because of the effects of timing and differences between management accounting and income tax accounting for items such as depreciation. If you operate in a difficult tax regime or have a complex company situation, take advice. If you have to make your own estimates, play it safe and make an estimate on the high side. Remember that basically you do not pay taxes if you are not making money – and if you are profitable, well, you do not worry so much.

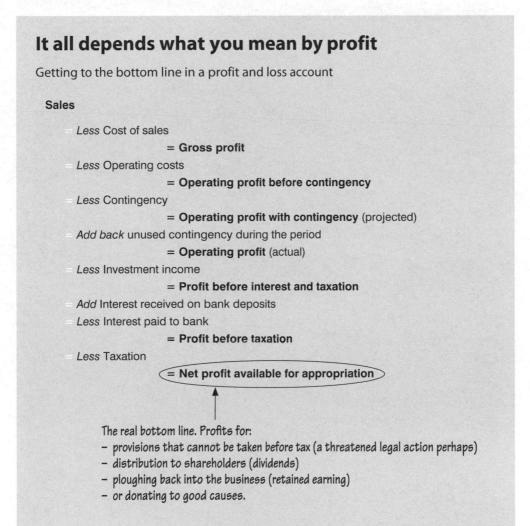

It all depends what you mean by profit

Getting to the bottom line in a profit and loss account

Sales

— *Less* Cost of sales
= **Gross profit**
— *Less* Operating costs
= **Operating profit before contingency**
— *Less* Contingency
= **Operating profit with contingency** (projected)
— *Add back* unused contingency during the period
= **Operating profit** (actual)
— *Less* Investment income
= **Profit before interest and taxation**
— *Add* Interest received on bank deposits
— *Less* Interest paid to bank
= **Profit before taxation**
— *Less* Taxation
= **Net profit available for appropriation**

The real bottom line. Profits for:
– provisions that cannot be taken before tax (a threatened legal action perhaps)
– distribution to shareholders (dividends)
– ploughing back into the business (retained earning)
– or donating to good causes.

Moving on

Once you have made allowances for contingency, tax and interest you really have done almost all of the hard work. You have a detailed profit and loss account. Now it is just a case of reallocating the numbers in order to produce a balance sheet and the all-important cash flow projection. When you have done this once, it will be almost automatic in the future. Moreover, you will be able to change one number in the sales forecast and instantly see the effect on cash flow. Does this sound as if it will be a useful management tool? I think so.

'Those who are prospering do not argue about taxes.'

CHINESE PROVERB

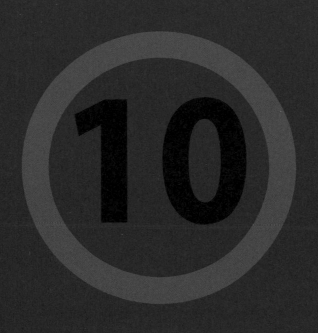

Funding the business

A bank is a place that will lend you money if you can prove that you don't need it. BOB HOPE

- Balancing your cheque book

- Balance sheets and cash flow mechanics

- Balance sheet headings

- Producing the paper

- Watching cash flow

- Using a surplus

- Getting it funded

- Debt or equity?

- What's the deal?

- Putting a price on success

- Does it all hold together?

You have been very patient. You have worked methodically through the forecasting exercise. You have arrived at a forecast of your net profit (or loss). This is an important number, but in many cases cash flow is even more critical. You do not want to go into liquidation for lack of cash in the bank when you are showing a profit on paper. All that remains now is the final mechanical process of creating balance sheet and cash flow forecasts – and at last you will know the size of your cash deficit or surplus.

Essentially, you copy your capital outlay figures into these balance sheet and cash flow formats. Then you work through your profit and loss figures, transferring any non-cash items (prepayments, accruals, etc.) into them.

You end up with a balanced balance sheet, a clear idea of your cash situation, and a basis for valuing your business. Armed with these items, you can determine the mix of funding required or consider how to make best use of any surplus.

Balancing your cheque book

If you have a healthy business that is entirely cash based and you do not spend any money on fixed or long-term assets, your net profit *is* your cash surplus for the period. Your balance sheet will show cash in the bank *balanced* by owner's equity. Ah, but you probably owe taxes that should show as a liability (reducing owner's equity by the same amount).

Unfortunately, life is never this simple. You spend money on things that do not relate to the current period (fixed assets, prepaid rents) and extend credit to your customers. These build up the asset side of the balance sheet. At the same time, you finance this by credit from your suppliers and loans from various sources. Your profits no longer equal cash flow. However, it is a simple process to work through the capital and profit and loss accounts allocating entries to the balance sheet and cash flow forecast. With a small amount of effort and minimal thought, you arrive at the crucial cash flow forecast.

Cash flow is of special interest to you if you have a new business, or if you know that you will need additional funding, or if you are pulling your business out of a crisis of your own making or a cruel twist of fate.

 'But my department doesn't have a balance sheet'

If you are slaving away in a mammoth corporation you might not be required to produce a balance sheet – and your cash flow might be as simple as the sum of your monthly expenditure projections. You will find this chapter easy going. However, you will probably find it instructive to draw up your own balance sheet. It might even support your case for a new photocopier.

The fast track to funding

1   As an aid to your understanding, start by looking at the long way of creating a balance sheet and cash flow projection from your capital and profit and loss accounts. Please do not skip this groundwork unless you are already familiar with the techniques.

2   Now to work. Copy spending on fixed assets and depreciation into the balance sheet and cash flow projections.

3   Work through the profit and loss account, matching any non-cash entries (prepayments, accruals, receivables and payables) into the balance sheet and cash flow projections.

4   Enter a cash surplus as cash at bank, or a deficit as bank borrowing or capital.

5   Value the business on the basis of the future stream of income that you have forecast.

6   Decide how to fund and cash deficit.

7   Decide if the figures are acceptable – otherwise return to revise your strategy and operating plan.

Balance sheets and cash flow mechanics

Creating balance sheets and cash flow is very simple. In practice, you will probably work methodically through the figures that you have produced so far – sales, capital spending, profit and loss – and create the cash flow and balance sheet from them as you go. An alternative is to work in the other direction. To aid your understanding, we will do both.

First, consider how you create balance sheet and cash flow projections from the capital outlays and current expenditure forecasts already in your possession. There is a short cut, but for the moment, imagine that you are going to work through your expenditure forecast line by line. It is useful to see how the balance sheet and cash flow forecasts shape up when you follow this long route.

You will note that spending is always financed in one of three ways.

1   **You pay cash** – the way that you handle this is illustrated opposite.

2   **You accrue** the expenditure (or take credit on an account payable) and pay it later – see page 224.

3   **You prepay** the expenditure and *expense it* (charge it to expenses) later – see page 225.

You can allocate **all** your current spending to the balance sheet and cash flow statements using the three techniques illustrated on pages 223–227. When you buy inventory on credit, the entries work in the same way as an accrual, showing on the liabilities side of the balance sheet in *accounts payable* instead of *accruals*. *Accounts receivable* – money owed to you by customers – work in reverse on the asset side of the balance sheet. Accounting for capital outlays is similar and is described on page 226. In the same way that your balance sheet shows the total of fixed assets at a given date, so it shows the end-period total for inventory lifted straight from your sales spreadsheet (Chapter 8).

Make sure that you understand the logic of the following procedures. But before you rush off and use them to produce balance sheet and cash flow projections, check out the short cuts discussed on page 227.

Balance sheet and cash flow (1) – from cash outlays

Suppose that you projected the following spending on salaries:

Expenditure account, *whole month*	**Jun**	**Jul**	**Aug**	**Sep**
Salaries	12,000	12,000	12,000	12,000

Salaries are normally paid in cash. Assume that this is the case here. There is a direct cash flow implication, but (for our current discussion) no balance sheet effect – see footnote. The matching entry created to balance the expense account charge is as follows:

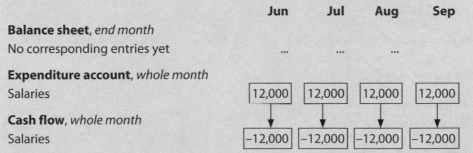

	Jun	**Jul**	**Aug**	**Sep**
Balance sheet, *end month*				
No corresponding entries yet	...	...	...	
Expenditure account, *whole month*				
Salaries	12,000	12,000	12,000	12,000
Cash flow, *whole month*				
Salaries	–12,000	–12,000	–12,000	–12,000

Note: Experienced bean counters will have spotted that the cash flow is actually also the balance sheet effect. In other words, the **total** cash flow will later be reflected in the balance sheet as borrowing or as surplus cash balances.

'Business is many things, the least of which is the balance sheet.'

HAROLD GENEEN

Balance sheet and cash flow (2) – from accruals

Moving on from the previous example, suppose that you had agreed to pay each December an annual staff bonus equivalent to one month's salary. Strictly speaking, you should show one-twelfth of the bonus as an accrued expense each month, as follows (just three months are shown):

Expenditure account, *whole month*	...	**Oct**	**Nov**	**Dec**
Employee bonuses	...	1,000	1,000	1,000

Now put the cash flow effects around this:

1   Starting with the January figures, record a matching $1000 accrual each month (I have only shown three months here because of space constraints).

2   By November, the accruals have reached $11,000.

3   In December, the $11,000 balance on accruals plus the $1000 expenditure charge for the month equals the $12,000 in bonuses that have to be paid from cash (charge $12,000 to cash flow).

This is illustrated below. The plus and minus signs might appear confusing at first glance, until you recall from Chapter 7 that an increase in liabilities is normally a credit entry so the sign moves the opposite way to everything else. That's accountancy for you. The change in the balance sheet (the flow) is added to help clarify what is going on. The first line of figures shows end-month balances (hence *balance sheet*), all the other figures are monthly flows.

Balance sheet, *end month*	**Dec**	**Oct**	**Nov**	**Dec**
Liabilities: accrued bonuses	9,000	10,000	11,000	0
Memo: change in month	...	+1000	+1000	-11,000
Expenditure account, *whole month*				
Employee bonuses	...	1000	1000	1000
Cash flow, *whole month*				
Employee bonuses	0	0	0	-12,000

But that would be misleading ...

Balance sheets show balances on a specific date. Remember that the bank balance, or inventory, or any other figure, might have been very different just a few hours before the balance was struck. Excuse me for being cynical, but I wonder if anyone ever massages balances on purpose?

Balance sheet and cash flow (3) – from prepayments

Now take a look at an expenditure that is prepaid. For simplicity, use the example shown in Chapter 7 (see page 148). This is a situation in which:

● your office rent is $1000 a month;

● in June you pay the $3000 advance for the calendar months of July, August and September.

For this case, when you prepared your spending forecast you would have recorded the following entries under operating expenditure:

Expenditure, *whole month*	**Jul**	**Aug**	**Sep**
Office rental payments	1,000	1,000	1,000

You can put the cash flow effects around this as follows.

1   Starting with cash flow, record the $3000 outflow in June. To be true to double entry accounting procedures, you have to add a corresponding $3000 to the balance-sheet asset-account called prepaid rents.

2   Then you should deduct $1000 from prepaid rents in each of July, August and September to reflect the matching charge to the expenditure account office rents paid.

This is illustrated below, with boxes around the matching entries. The change in the balance sheet (the flow) is added to help clarify what is going on. The first line of figures shows end-month balances (hence balance sheet), all the other figures are monthly flows.

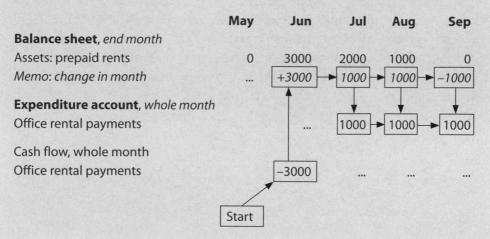

Balance sheet and cash flow (4) – from capital outlays

The example shows how you allocate capital outlays to the balance sheet and cash flow projections. Returning to the example in Chapter 9 (see page 198):

1   In October you acquire a clumping machine for $120,000.

2   It has an expected life of five years (60 months).

3   You are using the straight-line depreciation method.

4   Depreciation is therefore $2000 a month for 60 months.

For these transactions, your capital expenditure projections for this year are as follows:

	Sep	Oct	Nov	Dec
Capital outlays, *whole month*				
Acquisitions – machinery	0	120,000	0	0
Depreciation schedule, *whole month*				
Machinery		0	2000	2000

This is the one instance where I have made you duplicate a little effort. The expenditure forecasts that you created *form part* of the profit and loss account. But the capital outlay account and depreciation schedule can be thought of as *extracts from* the balance sheet – the same information twice. I did it this way because capital outlays are regarded with special interest and you need this extract to wave around in the boardroom or in your bank manager's office.

The easiest approach is to copy the capital outlays and depreciation schedule to the balance sheet (remember that these are *changes or flows* and the balance sheet shows end-month *balances*). You then create the matching entries. Depreciation is matched in the expenditure account (remember that you already put it here when you produced your expenditure forecast). The acquisition is matched in the cash flow account. This is how:

	Sep	Oct	Nov	Dec
Balance sheet, *end month*				
Fixed assets – machinery	0	120,000	120,000	120,000
Memo: change in month	0	+120,000	0	0
Cumulative depreciation, machinery		0	–2000	–4000
Memo: change in month	0	0	–2000	–2000
Expenditure account, *whole month*				
Depreciation – machinery	0	0	2000	2000
Cash flow, *whole month*				
Purchase of machinery	0	–120,000	0	0

Short cut to cash flow

There is a handy short cut for developing cash flow. Most spending is immediate. You pay for most of your operating costs as and when they happen. Prepayments and accruals tend to be in the minority. So, if you take the bottom line on your expenditure account as indicative of the total cash flow and adjust for things that do not involve an on-the-spot cash payment, you arrive painlessly at your actual cash requirement.

For example, if all your spending was cash except for the rent in *Balance sheet and cash flow* (3), you could derive your cash requirement as shown below. Note that the adjustment in the cash flow statement is the *change* in the balance sheet entry for office rent prepayments. A full development of this is shown in Figure 7.4 – which shows the linkages between the various transactions and accounts.

Therein lies an interesting fact. Changes in the balance sheet show *sources and uses of funds* (as introduced in Chapter 7). You are probably thinking right now, if this is the case why all this fuss about cash flow? Why not just derive it directly from the balance sheet? You could do this, but you still have to make adjustments and in my view it is not as convenient or as logically related to the forecasting exercise.

	Jun	Jul	Aug	Sep
Balance sheet, *end month*				
Assets: prepaid rents 0	3000	2000	1000	0
Memo: change in month ...	+3000	−1000	−1000	−10000
Expenditure account, *whole month*				
Salaries	12,000	12,000	12,000	12,000
Office rental payments	...	1000	1000	1000
Other expenses	100,000	100,000	100,000	100,000
Total (including expenses not shown)	**112,000**	**113,000**	**113,000**	**113,000**
Cash flow related to expenditure, *whole month*				
Total expenditure brought forward	−112,000	−113,000	−113,000	−113,000
Adjustment for rental payments	− 3000	+1000	+1000	+1000
Net cash flow requirement	**−115,000**	**−112,000**	**−112,000**	**−112,000**

Balance sheet headings

You have just looked at methods of producing balance sheets and cash flow from your expenditure forecasts. Now is a good time to take a look at the entries that appear in balance sheets. You could, if you wanted, do the opposite and work through the balance sheet pulling in entries from the transaction accounts and churning out the cash flow on the side. Figure 10.1 shows the main headings on a balance sheet. To make sure that you are familiar with them, I will run through each in turn. But first how long is long?

HOW LONG IS LONG?

Unlike other professionals, accountants consider the *long term* to be anything that is not going to happen before their next pay review.

- **Current assets and liabilities** are those which relate to the current year.

- **Long-term assets and liabilities** relate to payments and consumption that will take place after the end of the current year or operating cycle.

Figure 10.1 A snapshot of the balance sheet

The left-hand side always equals the right-hand side: assets = liabilities plus owners' equity

Current assets Cash Inventory/stock Accounts receivable Other (prepaid expenses, deposits paid …)	**Current liabilities** Short-term loans Maturing long-term loans Accounts payable Other (accrued expenses, taxes due …)
	Non-current liabilities Long-term loans and other borrowing Pension fund
Non-current assets Investments Fixed assets (plant, machinery …) Natural resources Intangible assets (patents, goodwill …)	**Owners' equity** Paid-in share capital Retained earnings

CURRENT ASSETS

Current assets are those which will be converted into cash, sold or consumed within one year. There are four categories:

1 cash at bank;

2 accounts receivable;

3 inventory/stock;

4 miscellaneous.

Cash at bank

This includes currency, demand deposits, certificates of deposits and other deposits maturing within 90 days. You probably want to avoid forecasting this total until you have developed your cash flow projections. Generally, you should aim to keep it as small as possible, while providing adequate working balances. Cash in the bank is not generating income in the normal course of your business.

Accounts receivable

This is revenue recognised in your profit and loss accounts, where cash has not yet been received (you will have to deduct an allowance for bad debts). Essentially, the total balance on accounts receivable reflects the length of time that passes between recognising sales and collecting payment.

Inventory/stock

These are your holdings of raw materials, work-in-progress and finished products that will be sold. You produced a forecast of these in Chapter 8.

Miscellaneous

This category is usually small, but it can be significant for a new business. It usually represents cash tied up in payments that you would rather not have made. Try to minimise them. Two such categories, already discussed, are:

- **Prepayments.** These are advance payments for goods and services – rent, insurance, subscriptions. Although classified as current assets, they are often ignored by bankers and others appraising your balance sheet because they are generally unrecoverable.

- **Deposits paid.** These are (supposedly) returnable sums payable when renting premises, machinery, vehicles, etc. Beware that sometimes, especially in less developed countries, it can be remarkably difficult to recover deposits.

LONG-TERM (OR NON-CURRENT) ASSETS

There are four main categories of long-term assets. It is common to hear all of these referred to as 'fixed assets':

1 investments;

2 fixed assets;

3 natural resources;

4 intangible assets.

Investments

This is where you show your long-term *minority* shareholdings in other companies. *Minority* is used loosely in this context. The opposite is where you exert a dominant influence over another company (usually but not always through a majority shareholding) – in which case the investment is not shown here. Instead, you will *consolidate* the accounts and have a consolidated balance sheet showing the total value of combined assets and liabilities.

Fixed assets

These are holdings of property, plant, machinery, equipment, etc. which were more-or-less discussed to death in Chapter 9 (along with natural resources and intangibles). They are shown at cost and also at their net value after deducting accumulated depreciation. You bring in the totals for these amounts from your forecast of capital outlays.

Natural resources

The treatment of these was considered with our discussions of fixed assets (see above).

Intangible assets

These include R&D costs, patents, copyrights, licences and goodwill. Again, the treatment of these was considered with fixed assets (see above).

CURRENT LIABILITIES

Current liabilities represent payments that you will have to make within one year.

1 **Accounts payable** (trade payables/trade credit). This reflects the grace period that you can win between buying and paying for inventory, supplies and other materials. Extend it as much as you can.

2 **Short-term loans** (bank loans, notes payable). These are short-term borrowing – usually secured against inventory or accounts receivable – from banks and trade creditors.

3 **Long-term debt maturing in the current period.** This reflects the obligations of past borrowing coming home to roost.

4 **Miscellaneous.** As with assets, the miscellaneous category is not always as 'unimportant' as it might sound. It mostly covers payments that you know you have to make, but which have not hit your cash flow yet. Three headings are as follows.
   - **Accrued expenses payable.** This is recognition of expenses due but not yet paid – discussed under accruals accounting in Chapter 7. Note that long-term accruals such as those related to pensions belong – obviously – with long-term liabilities.
   - **Provision for taxation.** The tax collector usually grabs your money as fast as possible, but you tend to know ahead of time that you will have to pay up, and you should make provision here.
   - **Deposit received.** If you take returnable cash payments from customers, show them here. Financial institutions take deposits in a different sense and have special categories for deposits.

LONG-TERM (NON-CURRENT) LIABILITIES

1 **Long-term bank loans, bonds, debentures, mortgages.** These sources of credit, together with capital issues, usually provide the major source of loan funding. As with cash at bank, you will return to this heading once we have reviewed your cash flow projection.

2 **Pension obligations.** Another major entry under long-term liabilities is provision for pensions – where they are unfunded (that is, where no specific cash reserve is created). In some countries, legislation requires that pensions are funded – otherwise there might not be cash available to meet obligations when the day comes. Where they are funded, there is often a pool of cash from which erring chief executives have been known to pilfer.

OWNERS' EQUITY

1 **Capital.** The cash injected to a business by a sole trader, partners or shareholders is recorded here. For sole owners and partners, an entry is recorded against each contributor's name. Companies have many shareholders and a summary is needed. You will consider capital under *Getting it funded* below.

2 **Retained profits/earnings.** Profits that have not been withdrawn by sole owners and partners or not distributed as dividends are scored in the accounts as retained earnings. The increase between two balance sheet dates represents the net retained profits for that period. As already discussed, this may bear little relationship to cash in the bank.

Producing the paper

However you choose to approach it you ultimately arrive at a balance sheet and cash flow. You can tie these in with the figures shown for *Tetrylus* in Chapters 8 and 9 to see where the numbers come from. The share capital is shown as a ridiculously low figure to help you identify that loans in the balance sheet equate directly to the net deficit in the cash flow forecast. Let me explain how this was derived.

Off-balance-sheet liabilities

In Chapter 9 you looked at ways that leasing provides finance that may not be recorded on the balance sheet. There are other similar funding tricks, such as selling assets or inventory with an agreement to buy them back at a later date (with interest). This makes the liabilities side of the balance sheet look healthier and reduces the apparent ratio of debt to equity. It is worth considering when you need cash, but you have an obligation to make sure that such liabilities are recorded in notes to the balance sheet.

In a similar way, you should look for any other commitments or *contingent liabilities*. These are actual or probable obligations that may not be recorded on the balance sheet – examples are guarantees or airline 'frequent flyer' loyalty schemes. *Reasonably probable* liabilities should be reported on the balance sheet. *Possible* liabilities should go into footnotes. *Remote* contingencies are often ignored. Why worry about it if it might not happen?

For your business planning purposes, you need to understand fully *all* off-balance-sheet liabilities no matter how remote, how they might affect your cash flow, and what provision you should make for them – in hard cash or in your strategy.

Watching cash flow

Your cash flow projections have a clear bottom line – they show your cash position at the end of each month and, therefore, your cumulative surplus or funding requirement.

If you are in the happy position of having a surplus, you enter it in the cash at bank entry on the balance sheet, and everything should balance nicely. If the surplus is very large, you might want to review your strategy and see how you can make the surplus work for you.

If you have a deficit, make it bigger by deducting a working balance as touched on above. Enter the working balance as the entry for cash at bank, and enter the final deficit as your funding requirement. This can be either additional borrowing as shown, or funding, or a mix of the two. Ways of funding a deficit are considered in a moment. If you have an unrealistically large deficit, you may have to revisit your strategy and hunt for ways to increase revenue – or perhaps look for ways to trim costs. Remember, though, that you can only cut costs so far – when they reach zero the business dies. Boosting revenues is a far more satisfactory approach.

The Yangtse River never turns back but flows forever onwards.

CHINESE SAYING

Figure 10.2 A balance sheet from the back of the business plan

TETRYLUS Inc Financial plan

Balance sheet

Dollars

		Month 1	Month 2	Month 3	Month 4	Month 5	Month 6
	ASSETS						
B-1	Cash at bank	1 000	1 000	1 000	1 000	1 000	1 000
B-2	Accounts receivable	0	20 000	0	40 000	0	50 000
B-3	Deposits paid	2 000	2 000	2 000	2 000	2 000	2 000
B-4	Prepayments (rents)	11 000	10 000	9 000	8 000	7 000	6 000
B-5	Inventory	0	15 000	40 000	17 500	42 500	12 500
B-6	Fixed assets at cost	36 500	38 000	38 750	39 750	39 750	39 750
B-7	Less accumulated depreciation	0	−1 389	−2 819	−4 263	−5 733	−7 204
B-8	**Memo: net fixed assets**	**36 500**	**36 611**	**35 931**	**35 488**	**34 017**	**32 546**
B-9	**Total assets**	**50 500**	**84 611**	**87 931**	**103 988**	**86 517**	**104 046**
B-10							
B-11	**LIABILITIES**						
B-12	Total loans	91 300	172 031	242 556	268 443	322 573	342 475
B-13	Accounts payable - hardware	0	10 000	0	22 500	0	30 000
B-14	Accounts payable - software	0	3 591	3 591	8 274	8 274	12 253
B-15	Accruals (staff pensions)	417	833	1 250	1 667	2 083	2 500
B-16	**Total liabilities**	**91 717**	**186 455**	**247 397**	**300 884**	**332 931**	**387 228**
B-17							
B-18	**CAPITAL & RESERVES**						
B-19	Share capital	1 000	1 000	1 000	1 000	1 000	1 000
B-20	Unremitted P&L	−42 217	−102 844	−160 467	−197 896	−247 414	−284 182
B-21	**Total capital and reserves**	**−41 217**	**−101 844**	**−159 467**	**−196 896**	**−246 414**	**−283 182**
B-22							
B-23	**Total liabilities and equity**	**50 500**	**84 611**	**87 931**	**103 988**	**86 517**	**104 046**

Current assets that could quickly be converted into cash are very low in relation to current liabilities. If the loans were short-term and could be called in tomorrow this business would be in a critical cash flow squeeze. No worries really because it is a new venture and in practice it would have more share capital (and less debt) than shown here – I hope.

Balance sheet with cash flow surplus

	May	Jun	Jul	Aug	Sep
Balance sheet, *end month*					
Assets: Cash at bank	0	100 000	210 000	310 000	390 000
Profit and loss account, *whole month*					
Net profit		...	...	...	...
Cash flow, *whole month*					
Net profit brought forward		...	...	...	...
Adjustments		...	...	...	...
Net cash flow in month		+100 000	+110 000	+100 000	+80 000
Cumulative cash flow	0	+100 000	+210 000	+310 000	+390 000

Balance sheet with cash flow deficit

	May	Jun	Jul	Aug	Sep
Balance sheet, *end month*					
Assets: cash at bank		5000	5000	5000	5000
Liabilities: borrowing		−105,000	−215,000	−315,000	−400,000
Profit and loss account, *whole month*					
Net profit	...	...	...	...	
Cash flow, *whole month*					
Net profit brought forward	...	...	...	...	
Adjustments	...	...	...	...	
Net cash flow in month		−100,000	−110,000	−100,000	−80,000
Working balances		−5000	0	0	0
Net cash flow requirement		−105,000	−110,000	−100,000	−80,000
Cumulative cash flow, end month		−105,000	−215,000	−315,000	−400,000

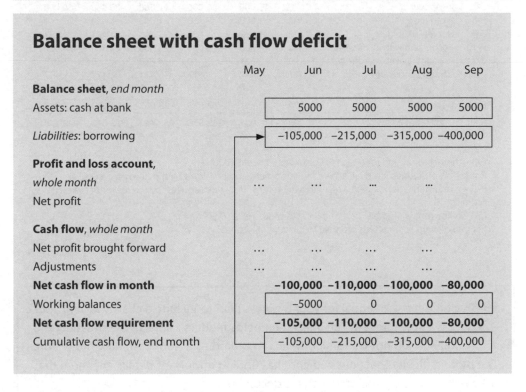

Your maximum funding requirement (or maximum cash surplus) is the point where your cumulative cash flow reaches a trough (or peak) and changes direction. Remember that the figures you have calculated are for end-period. For your worst months, you might have to do a day-by-day check to make sure that the payments and receipts fall in the correct order. If you have to pay your bills on the first of the month but do not receive sales income until the last day, the month is fine on average but you have a nasty overdraft for 29 days. The contingency reserve that you built into your profit and loss account (Chapter 9) will help to cover this. You might want to reconsider whether it is adequate.

Figure 10.3 Cash flow details from the back of the business plan

TETRYLUS Inc Financial plan

Cash flow, first six months
Dollars

		Month 1	Month 2	Month 3	Month 4	Month 5	Month 6
F-1	Net profit	−42 217	−60 627	−57 622	−37 430	−49 518	−36 768
F-2	Adjustments for changes in:						
F-3	Cash at bank	−1 000	0	0	0	0	0
F-4	Accounts receivable	0	−20 000	20 000	−40 000	40 000	−50 000
F-5	Deposits paid	−2 000	0	0	0	0	0
F-6	Prepayments (rents)	−11 000	1 000	1 000	1 000	1 000	1 000
F-7	Inventory	0	−15 000	−25 000	22 500	−25 000	30 000
F-8	Fixed assets	−36 500	−1 500	−750	−1 000	0	0
F-9	Depreciation	0	1 389	1 431	1 443	1 471	1 471
F-10	Accounts payable - hardware	0	10 000	−10 000	22 500	−22 500	30 000
F-11	Accounts payable - software	0	3 591	0	4 683	0	3 979
F-12	Accrued pensions	417	417	417	417	417	417
F-13	Equity	1 000	0	0	0	0	0
F-14	**Cash flow**	**−91 300**	**−80 731**	**−70 525**	**−25 887**	**−54 130**	**−19 902**
F-15	Cumulative cash flow	−91 300	−172 031	−242 556	−268 443	−322 573	−342 475

Notes:
F-3 – there is provision for a working bank balance of $1000.
F-4 & F-10 – 30 days' credit is allowed to customers and provided by the hardware supplier.
F-5 – a returnable deposit equivalent to two months' rent was required by the lessor of the office premises.
F-6 – office rent is payable 12 months in advance.
F-11 – software licence fees are paid to the supplier annually.

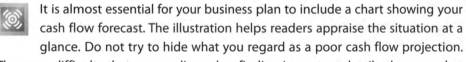

It is almost essential for your business plan to include a chart showing your cash flow forecast. The illustration helps readers appraise the situation at a glance. Do not try to hide what you regard as a poor cash flow projection. The more difficulty that your audience has finding important details, the more that they will become exasperated with the document.

Don't forget interest

If you are being funded by borrowing, or if you expect to leave a surplus sitting on deposit at the bank, you need to allow for interest payments. For the moment, assume that you are paying interest monthly. For month 1 in Figure 10.3:

- The approximate average balance for month 1 is $0 + $91,300 divided by 2 = $45,650.

- At 1% per month the interest would be $45,650 × 1/100 = $457.

- The revised cumulative cash flow (including interest) at the end of month 1 is $91,300 + $457 = $91,757.

- The revised loss (including interest) at the end of month 1 is $42,217 + $457 =$42,674.

You can add a few lines to your spreadsheet to perform these calculations (for the average balance, the interest rate, the interest amount, the revised cash flow and the revised profit and loss account).

HOW MUCH CASH DO YOU NEED?

Your cash flow forecast identifies precisely how much additional funding (if any) you need to keep your business above water. It's reasonably safe to assume that you need additional funding, because this is usually the case in the start-up, growth, recovery, and even maturity phases of business. And your business plan is ambitious. Right?

A chart such as the one in Figure 10.4 shows graphically how your cash flow looks. This one is based on a new project and for simplicity the curve is unrealistically smooth. Yours will bump up and down reflecting seasonal pressures and other leads and lags between action and results.

Figure 10.4 Graphic cash requirements

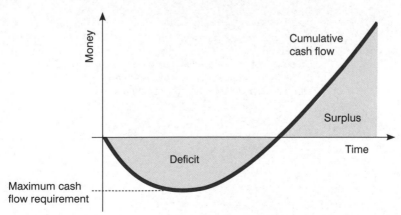

Figure 10.5 Financials from the business plan

The real grit was in the sales projections, and cost structure. Now this is brought together to reveal the bottom line. You need a sensible summary highlighting key points (think about it from the perspective of your audience).

This is starting to illustrate value to prospective backers.

This is the hole that you are asking backers to jump into ...

... and here is their reward when they climb out.

FINANCIAL ANALYSIS, continued

Profit and loss account

The revenues and costs described above are brought together in the profit and loss account in Table 12 (full details are in Annex A). The $1.4m net loss in year 1 reduces to $0.2m in year 2 and turns to a net profit of $3.8m by year 3. Sales could ...

Balance sheet

A summarised balance sheet is shown in Table 13 (full details are in Annex A). By year 5, retained earnings exceed $12m and net asset value is ...

Cash flow and funding requirements

The following chart illustrates our cumulative cash flow projection (detailed figures are in Annex A). Monthly cash inflows start to exceed outflows by month 14 and we move into a surplus by month 30. Our maximum funding requirement is $1.25 million ...

Cumulative cash flow projection

...

Valuation

On a modest price earnings multiple of 10, the implied market value of the equity capital will be nearly $40m by year 3 ... This would represent a potential return on investment of ...

Using a surplus

There are two ways of looking at a cash flow surplus. If you are drawing up a business plan for part of a larger organisation, your surplus might go to fund another part of the strategy. A worthy use. If you are looking at the entire enterprise, you have a problem. Why? Any surplus that remains after paying dividends or funding withdrawals from a partnership or sole trader's business will claw down your return on investment (ROI) – unless you invest it wisely. As we discuss later, the largest ROI should come from minding your own business. If ultimately you can earn more by putting the money in a bank, you might as well sell the business and sit on a beach. It is time to revisit your strategy and put the surplus to good use. Take another look at Chapter 6.

Getting it funded

If your plan is for internal use, you will probably know whether the cash flow is acceptable. If you do not know, you should start asking questions now. You want the plan to be feasible when you come to presenting it for approval – even if you still have to fight for that extra bit of funding. If there is absolutely no chance of funding your strategy, you need to revise it now and work back through the numbers until you arrive at an acceptable cash flow projection.

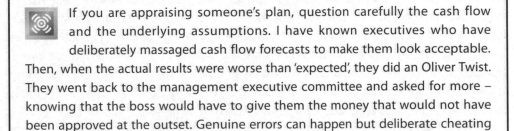

If you are appraising someone's plan, question carefully the cash flow and the underlying assumptions. I have known executives who have deliberately massaged cash flow forecasts to make them look acceptable. Then, when the actual results were worse than 'expected', they did an Oliver Twist. They went back to the management executive committee and asked for more – knowing that the boss would have to give them the money that would not have been approved at the outset. Genuine errors can happen but deliberate cheating such as this suggests incompetence on both sides that usually ends in tears.

If you are going outside for funding, you have to look at the amount of cash that you need and decide whether it is realistic in relation to the potential return expected by your backer and the associated risk that you are asking them to undertake. Let's take a look.

Debt or equity?

Along the way, I have assumed that you will use trade credit as and when it is available. Your choice for your excess cash requirement is to fund it by borrowing or by increasing the owners' capital. The owners might be a sole proprietor, partners or shareholders. The jargon varies, so from now on I will refer to loan capital as *debt* and to owners' capital as *equity*. With that out of the way, what difference does it make whether the funding comes from debt or equity?

COMPARING DEBT AND EQUITY

Debt is repayable

Lenders are very demanding. They are concerned mainly with security and cash flow. They usually lend to you only if you *own* more than you *owe* (so that they can seize your assets if you default on repayment) and if you can prove that you can definitely afford to pay it back. The main cost to you is the interest charge.

Equity is not repayable

Shareholders recover their capital in one of two ways. Either the business goes to the wall and shareholders take the final pickings after all other creditors have been settled. Or the shareholders unlock value by selling their shares to another investor. We should assume that you do not want to close your business. The alternative then is to run a successful company so that the amount that people are prepared to pay for your shares increases. Shareholders can then sell their shares at a premium. You usually have to keep them happy along the way by giving them dividends (sharing out a bit of annual profit as pseudo interest payments). As shareholders are the owners of the company, those with a high proportion of the shares usually want a say in how it is run. A shareholder – or group of shareholders – with a dominant stake can force majority decisions. The cost, then, is mainly an obligation to be good managers and a loss of ownership and control.

I said that lenders are very demanding. It sounds as if shareholders are worse. The big difference is in the cash flow.

Debt is a burden – repayments of principle and interest drain your cash flow. Equity does not necessarily involve parting with any cash – even the dividends can be deferred until better cash flow days. Moreover, equity investors accept higher risk in exchange for better returns in the future. This means that you can persuade backers to swap their cash for your shares when the bankers are sucking in their breath and shaking their heads. But while the cash flow effect of equity is far less painful, the overall cost is actually greater than that of debt.

Why is the cost of equity greater than the cost of debt? Follow through these simple arguments.

1 Your investors are looking for a *return on equity* that is greater than the rate of interest that they could earn on a lower-risk investment.

2 Your debt is secured against assets and cash flow, so your debt must be a lower risk than your equity.

3 Therefore, logically, your equity must produce a higher return than the interest rate that you pay on your debt. If it did not, shareholders would desert you.

Put another way, you increase the *return on equity* by *leveraging* it and using it to help you borrow at a lower cost.

 When you increase the proportion of your debt (relative to your equity), your overall cost of capital falls. If you earn the same profits for a lower amount of equity capital, the return on equity (profit divided by equity) must increase.

I do not know about you, but sometimes I find that simple logic can be very demanding. It gets easier now.

CHOOSING DEBT FROM EQUITY

The relative merits of debt and equity are compared below. To a large extent, the choice is dictated by circumstances. Figure 10.6 provides a simplistic decision chart. If you have a good track record, security for a loan, adequate cash flow, and a not-undue burden of existing debt you might be able to borrow more. Otherwise, you might be forced to look for equity – especially if you are in a start-up situation with few assets and a higher-risk venture.

Of course, you may also decide that your particular circumstances make equity preferable even if you could justify increasing your debt. In particular, if you sell some of your own shares you can unlock some of the value that you have created in the business and treat yourself to a vacation or a new executive jet.

Figure 10.6 Choosing debt from equity

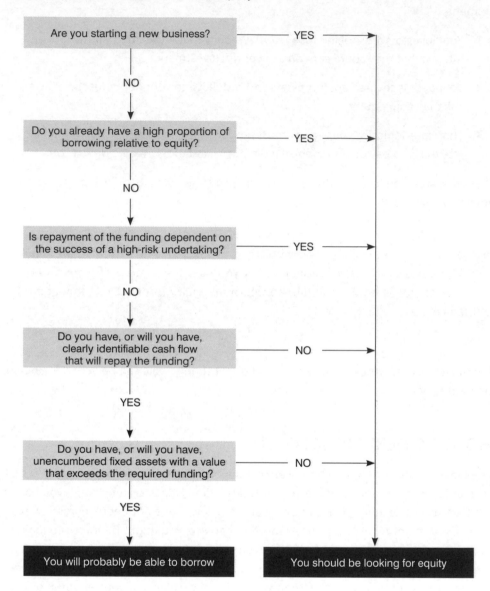

Debt and equity compared

Debt	Equity
Lenders are risk averse	Equity investors accept higher risk
No loss of ownership	Involves giving up some ownership
No explicit loss of control	May reduce control
Has to be repaid	Does not have to be repaid
Increases demands on cash flow	Exerts smaller demands on cash flow
Reduces cost of capital	Increases cost of capital
Increases return on equity	Reduces return on equity

FINDING FUNDING

Having decided whether you need debt or equity funding, where do you look for it? Figure 10.7 shows common sources with a crude indication of the likelihood of extracting the required funds from each, depending on your stage of development. These stages – start-up, early operations, growth, maturity and recovery from crisis – equate very loosely with the amount of risk for the provider of funds. The earlier and late stages tend to be riskier. The table also has an even more tongue-in-cheek identification of the associated quality of assets – start-ups tend to have fewer tangible assets than mature companies.

Start-up equity

The indications of the likelihood of receiving backing from these sources are also tainted by my cynicism – based on experience.

- For example, **venture capital providers** are supposed to exist to pour equity into start-up situations, but their definition of start-up seems to be 'a well-developed product and full order book'.

- **Business partners** – including big companies that would benefit from your invention – are also remarkably inept at grasping opportunities.

- In my opinion, you are more likely to find pure **start-up capital from working partners and angels**. Angels (sometimes known as the Three Fs – family, friends and fools) are people you can persuade to invest their spare cash in your business. The term 'Angels' comes from the original sponsors of Broadway shows.

Figure 10.7 Sources of funds

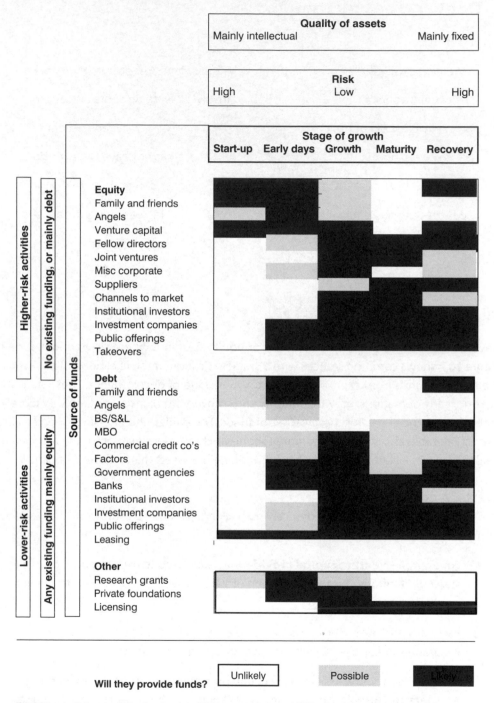

BS/S&L = building societies/savings and loans associations; MBO = management buyouts

Later equity

● When your business is gaining a foothold, after a few months or years, **working relationships** are good places to look for equity. With an attractive win-win proposition (boosting both businesses), you might persuade *suppliers*, your *channels to market* (re-sellers, independent service providers), or other *joint-venture partners* to buy some of your equity.

● **Investment companies** specialising in corporate finance and *institutional investors* (pension and life assurance funds with cash to invest) are generally looking for lower-risk investments with a stronger promise making good returns. **Public offerings** – stock market listings – generally require a great deal of planning and a three-year track record.

Debt

● You can look to the same sources for debt (family and friends may be good for short-term loans).

● The most obvious additions to the list are **banks** (not just for straight loans – some start-ups have been financed using credit cards). Note that merchant/investment banks often provide creative loan finance.

● **Factors** – possibly banks but also specialised businesses – will buy your *accounts receivables* at a discount from the book value and use their specialist debt collectors to call in the money. This *can* be a useful way to convert an asset into cash.

● **Leasing** has already been discussed as another way of easing cash flow pressures when you acquire assets (or a way of unlocking existing balance sheet value). Again check the banks as well as established leasing companies and equipment suppliers.

● **Building societies/savings and loans associations** will sometimes lend against real estate. Some are even turning into banks – don't necessarily believe what their name suggests.

Other

● Do not forget to explore the assistance that you might be able to receive from central **government**, federal, state and local authorities **and non-government agencies** such as the European Union or the Asian Development Bank. This can take the form of loans, research or development grants or – very occasionally – equity investment.

- **Private foundations** sometimes make grants, especially for environmental, developmental, cultural and arts-related activities.

- Finally, if you have a good business proposition or intellectual property (special technology, a unique way of doing something, a good brand image) you might be able to **license or franchise** its use to other companies, perhaps overseas or in a market that does not interest you – often for large amounts of money.

Variations, hybrids

We have talked as if your choice is exclusively debt or equity. There are interesting variations and hybrids that can make your proposition look more attractive.

- Investors sometimes try to limit their risks and increase their options by providing you with a loan (*debt* – perhaps with a floating charge over your trading assets) that commits you to repaying the interest and principal but also gives them the *opportunity to convert some of the loan into equity or buy equity* at some pre-agreed price when they see how things are going.

- **Management buyouts** (MBOs) often include a similar mix of debt and equity – sometimes known as *mezzanine finance*.

- **Preference shares** rank before ordinary shares in the event of liquidation, and offer a slightly better guarantee to investors. **Cumulative** preference shares promise the same, plus a guaranteed dividend that can be deferred, rolled up (cumulated) and paid when cash flow permits.

 We'd rather risk being trampled by you

Amazon.com is now the world's largest online retailer and the world's largest book store, with profits of over US $1 billion in 2010. Yet in 1994 founder Jeff Bezos failed to obtain backing from anyone in the book trade. The obvious sources of finance – existing corporations that could gain from (or later be trampled by) your vision – are almost always not interested. Amazing but true. (See also *Test marketing* Chapter 8 and the many anecdotes in Chapter 12.) What do your people say when someone brings them a new idea?

What do you want it for?

Seed, venture, start-up, adventure, risk or injection capital are various names for the cash needed to get a business off the ground.
Working capital is money used to pay for inventory, salaries and other production/operating costs.
Fixed capital is money locked up in fixed assets such as buildings and equipment.
Growth capital is cash targeted specifically to fund expansion.

What's the deal?

If you are going cap-in-hand to your bankers, you will be telling them that you want a $10,000 increase in working capital … or a $25 million loan for the specific purpose of acquiring the following assets, with repayment proposed … They will mumble some incantations and arrive at an interest rate that they want to charge you. (But do not accept it – negotiate.) It is not quite so simple if you are looking for equity funding.

In theory, you value the business (we will do this in a moment), see what proportion you will raise, and allocate a chunk of shares accordingly. The business is worth $10 million today, you are raising $1 million; therefore, you will swap 10% of the equity capital for the cash. Sometimes it works in much this way, especially for an established business with a known price for existing shares. Of course, you have to take perceptions of risk and reward into account.

Frequently, you will work backwards. You place a value of $10 million on the company (stock market listing or trade sale) at the likely exit point, say, three years hence. You need $2 million now, your investors' required overall return is 100%. This means that the investor wants $4 million back in three years' time, equivalent to 40% of the equity at that point. So you issue 40% equity today in return for $2 million.

Sometimes, it is entirely down to supply and demand. You need restructuring capital. There is only one offer. Take it or leave it. As a point of interest, 40% is a magic figure. I have shown potential backers varying profits and cash flow projections with the same business proposal, and they have all tried to negotiate for 40% equity. Maybe it sounds to them as if it is the largest proportion that they can get away with? It is not always like this. Capital providers will come in for anything between 1% and 100% depending on the proposition.

Does this sound all very hit and miss? It is not really. It is all a case of understanding the value of what you are offering, and the return required by the investor. It is time to value your business.

Putting a price on success

Valuing a business is similar to valuing a project (see Chapter 11) only a little more vague. The principle is simple. You buy a business not for today's profit, but for the value of the future stream of income that the business will produce.

For example, if you were generating a profit of $1 million a year and interest rates were 10%, an investor would have to put $10 million in the bank to produce the same flow of income. So a wily backer would happily pay you $10 million – especially since it is expected that your business will grow and the annual return will increase (this *is* what your business plan promises, isn't it?).

The practice is confused by the fact that everyone's view of the future – and risk – differs. However, there are two very simple rules of thumb that do the job nicely. You can use them to cross-check each other.

The accountant's approach
One way is to project your net profit for, say, the next 10 or 20 years and work out the net present value at an appropriate discount (i.e. interest) rate. Net present value is discussed in Chapter 11.

What the markets do
A more simple approach is to look at similar industries and see how they are valued in the financial markets. You can then use a similar basis for your own business. The key is the *price earnings ratio* or *multiple* (PE or P/E), which is no more than the price someone would pay for the company expressed as a multiple of profits. Technically, for a company with shares traded on the stock market the price earnings ratio is the share price divided by *earnings per share* (see page 299). For example, if a company with 1 million shares earns a net profit of $2 million, earnings per share are $2. If that company's share price is $20, the price earnings multiple is 10. It sounds complicated, but it is actually simple enough. In this example investors are prepared to pay $20 million (1 million shares at $20 each) to acquire a stream of earnings worth $2 million a year – a multiple of 10. If they were prepared to pay $40 million, the multiple would be 20. This is very similar to the 'interest on a bank deposit' example just discussed. Investors might pay higher multiples for a company if they expect profits to increase in future years. Generally, price earnings multiples of 10 to 20 are the norm. On average, corporate acquisitions have tended to take place at multiples of around 20. Generally, the higher the price–earnings multiple, the more investors

expect profits to increase in future years. Favoured companies might enjoy multiples of over 50. Anything much more than this appears to be unsustainable. At the peak of the *dotcom boom* in 2000, some technology companies traded at multiples of over 600. They came crashing down.

A quick digression. If there is no hope of a stream of income, if the business is totally on the rocks, then forget this. It's a case of settling the creditors and seeing what is left to sell – and how much you can get for it.

Does it all hold together?

Hold on. I was just talking about funding as if your financial forecasting exercise was finished. By and large, it is. But you need to sit back and look at the work that you have done so far. In this chapter, you used your earlier work to draw up balance sheet and cash flow projections. You identified your surplus or funding requirements. You valued your business. And you decided how to fund any deficit. Now you should review the risks and rewards and decide if everything holds together, or rework any parts of your strategy and operating plans if necessary. Chapter 11 takes a look at this.

Managing risks

Each problem has hidden in it an opportunity so powerful that it literally dwarfs the problem. The greatest success stories were created by people who recognised a problem and turned it into an opportunity. JOSEPH SUGARMAN

- Identify risks and improve planning
- It's normally like this
- How many coconuts do you need to sell?
- Marginal likelihood of shutting down?
- What you need, when you need it
- Will it pay off?
- What if?
- The economy
- If the worst comes to the worst …
- Grand finale

I f this chapter makes you think carefully enough about risks, it has done its job. There are four key steps.

1 *Think* – identify the risks that could affect you.

2 *Assess* – use the techniques presented here to help.

3 *Plan and position* – incorporate them in your strategy, position yourself accordingly.

4 *Monitor* – keep constant watch for expected and unexpected batterings, and react immediately.

Identify risks and improve planning

As you worked through your assessment of your business (Chapters 4 and 5), you built up a list that included weaknesses and threats. When you developed your strategy (Chapter 6) you attempted to deal with these and even position yourself to take advantage of them. No doubt when you worked through the financials (Chapters 7–10) you noted a whole new set of uncertainties and risks. Twenty to think about are listed on pages 225 to 256. They are selected at random and in no particular order. You should be able to add your own. Each variable will have a different relative importance for your business.

At the end of the day, there is no alternative to good management – which includes the ability to identify and negotiate hazards using a wide range of skills and experiences. I suggest that you make a list of the major risks that affect your business and arrange them in order of likeliness. Then ask how well your strategy handles them.

The more carefully that you identify the risks, the better your planning. Take a simple example. If you do not give thought to crisis management, you will not have a disaster recovery plan. Perhaps by focusing your attention, this chapter has proved its worth already.

TECHNIQUES FOR HANDLING RISK

There are procedures that you can follow and things that you can do to identify and minimise your exposure. I urge you to look back at *Nine steps to successful project planning* on page 132. You will recall that this encourages you to break problems into small, manageable parts; attempt to dispose of the riskiest activities first; proceed in small, reversible steps; set targets for each step; and establish a culture that reacts immediately to variances.

Scattered throughout this book there are other suggestions for handling risks. This chapter introduces a few more techniques. It divides into three parts.

1. Some common techniques for quantifying and assessing risks.

2. Ways that you can use simple financial analysis to prioritise options and choose between them.

3. Pulling it together for *what-if* and *worst-case* analysis, and checking that you have a really solid strategy.

There is a risk – even a certainty – that after reading the next few pages you will either hate me or love me. I am about to take you on a voyage through a simple topic that *some people* (see below) have tried to make obscure and tedious with unfamiliar terminology and boring tabulations. However, to me it is one of the most interesting manifestations of the obvious, with great value in business and enormous benefit when drawing up business plans. It is called the *normal distribution*, because if you *distribute* a bucket of numbers this is how they *normally* look. Now I have given the game away. The *some people* I referred to just now are statisticians. I avoided using the word too soon, because I did not want to put you off. Now you know. Take a look. You will love it. If it is new to you, you might gain insights that you have never thought of before.

The fast track to managing risks

1. Think hard, identify risks in advance.

2. Quantify risks.

3. Use suitable techniques and procedures to handle risks (do not worry if these sound scary, they are simple in practice):

   - Look back at page 132 – which shows how projects succeed.

   - Use the normal curve to quantify risks, probabilities and confidence.

   - Use other quantitative techniques, including break even analysis, marginal analysis, capacity planning and inventory control.

   - Use net present value and hurdle rates to assess projects.

   - Use what-if analysis.

   - Review alternative scenarios.

   - Develop a worst-case forecast and strategies for coping with it.

4. Develop risk-handling strategies, plans, policies and procedures.

5. Position yourself accordingly.

6. Monitor and react.

Special mission – limiting factors

In previous chapters you undertook special assignments – watching for core competencies, competitive advantages, etc. In Chapter 6 you identified your critical success factors. From these, and other things that you come across in this chapter, make a list of your *limiting* factors – maybe constraints on capacity, staffing levels, funding and so on. Understanding these will help you to identify and manage risks.

Risks to consider

1 **Industry.** What are your competitors dreaming up?

2 **Market.** How is it changing? How will this affect your sales?

3 **Your product.** Watch out for quality problems, cost overruns, declining demand.

4 **Sales.** Poor sales cut profits; high sales squeeze capacity.

5 **R&D.** Make sure that you do not pour money into a black hole (expect perhaps if you are NASA).

6 **Quality assurance.** Poor quality costs money at the production line.

7 **Quality control.** Poor quality control damages your reputation and sales.

8 **Resource constraints.** Watch for lack or excess of skills, facilities, materials …

9 **Productivity.** Poor productivity pushes up product costs.

10 **Capacity.** Excess (idle) capacity costs money. Capacity constraints cost sales.

11 **Inventory.** Not enough kills sales. Too much drains cash flow.

12 **Investment.** Insufficient investment in marketing, machinery, training, career development or research can leave you unable to compete.

13 **Information technology.** Are you prepared for system disasters? Corrupt backups? Obsolescent systems? Inadequate processing capability? Insufficient management information?

14 **Administrative blockages.** The sheer volume of order- or cheque-processing can bring an unprepared business to its knees.

15 **Business management.** Poor management hurts morale and profits. Failure to notice external threats can leave you holding a bankruptcy notice.

16 **Corporate politics.** Infighting depletes energy, strangles efficiency and can seriously affect your company's reputation if it reaches the outside world.

It's normally like this

If statisticians have added anything to human knowledge, it is their insight about what you *normally* find when you look into a bucket of numbers. In case you are unfamiliar with this, I will elaborate. It is a masterpiece of observation. But do not dismiss it lightly. It provides a great tool for understanding present and future events that affect your business.

It allows you to say with confidence, *I am 95% certain that sales will be between $80,000 and $100,000. There is only a 12% chance that R&D will fail to deliver* (you must have excellent boffins). *There is an 80% likelihood that profits will exceed $5 million.* And so on. You can use this tool to qualify any such statement. First, the mechanics. Remember, this is all painfully obvious logic.

SYMMETRICAL OR SKEWED?

Take any measurement that is affected by a large number of independent influences. This could be heights of mature trees lazing in a sunny forest, diameters of ball bearings rolling off a production line, teenage girls' spending on cosmetics. The measurements are always clustered evenly on either side of the average.

If you plotted a chart showing these observations, you would have a *bell-shape curve*. (See Figure 11.1.) It is called the *normal curve* because it is what you normally find in such situations.

A digression. Sometimes observed values are not distributed so neatly. For example, a chart of annual salaries would be *skewed* with a hump on the left – comparatively few lucky tycoons earn big money. However, any set of data can be described with just three statistics.

1   **The average** (a measure of the middle or most usual value).

2   **The spread** (the range, between the smallest and the largest).

3   **The shape** of the distribution (*normal, skewed*).

If you are a number-cruncher and someone tells you these three facts about any set of numbers, you can instantly visualise the data and make all manner of wise pronouncements. It is not dissimilar to looking at dice and knowing how they will roll. Sounds useful?

Most of us spend our lives comparing ourselves with averages (average income, weight, height) and we know well enough what they are. You will have gathered that I am focusing on the *normal* shape. This just leaves measures of spread, which I will talk about for a moment because the terminology is less well known.

MEASURING SPREAD

There is a neat measure of spread with a horrible name – *standard deviation*. Do not be put off. This is just a way of presenting a range as a standardised average. It is calculated very simply. You will probably never need to do it manually, but the calculation is shown on page 259.

If you work out this standardised average range (i.e. standard deviation) for any *normally* distributed data it is **always** the case that:

- 68.3% of all values are within one standard deviation of the mean;

- 95.4% of all values are within two standard deviations of the mean;

- 99.7% of all values are within three standard deviations of the mean.

This is incredibly useful. Turning it into English. If the average height of trees in a hill-top copse is 10 metres and the standard deviation of tree heights is 1 metre:

- just over two-thirds of trees are 10±1 metres high – that is, between 9–11 metres;

- 95% are 30±2 metres high, or between 8–12 metres;

- nearly all trees (99.7%) are 10±3 metres high, or between 7–13 metres.

 Blinding insight

If measurements are distributed normally, and if you know their average and standard deviation, you have the key to unlocking everything there is to know about them. Turn this upside down. If you make a central and a worst-case forecast, and if you attach a probability to the worst-case, you can predict the probability of every other outcome. (Your central, or most likely, forecast is the 'average'.) Your bank manager ought to be impressed.

Figure 11.1 It normally looks like this

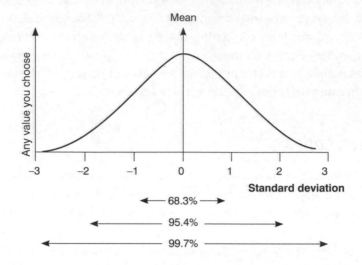

BE CERTAIN ABOUT HOW UNCERTAIN YOU ARE

With outline knowledge about this appallingly named *normal*, you can add amazing rigour to your business judgements. Take a simple example.

Suppose that your central forecast is that next year's sales will be $10 million, but you estimate that there is a 15% chance of your nightmare scenario of sales being just $9 million or less. Using the *normal* you can say that there is a:

● 67% probability that sales will be between $9 million and $11 million;

● 95% probability that sales will be in the $8 million to $12 million range;

● greater than 99% probability that sales will be above $7 million.

You might see a stunning similarity with the trees described above. Both examples use the same numbers with different labels. This is all that there is to the *normal*. It is identical logic applied to different situations. Moreover, you are not restricted to these three observations. You can read anything from the chart of the *normal* curve. In fact, to make it easier for you, I have already put the numbers into a little table, which I will describe next.

Calculating standard deviation

If you ever need to calculate standard deviation, you will use a calculator or a computer spreadsheet. However, if you really want to know how it is done, this is the procedure. To calculate the average (4) and standard deviation (1.63) of the three numbers: 2, 4 and 6:

1	Find *arithmetic mean* (a statisticians' name for this particular *average*)	$(2 + 4 + 6) \div 3 =$	4
2	Find the deviations from the mean	$2 - 4 =$	−2
		$4 - 4 =$	0
		$6 - 4 =$	+2
3	The deviations would (obviously) sum to zero, so you square the deviations	$-2^2 =$	+4
		$0^2 =$	0
		$+2^2 =$	+4
4	Add the results	$4 + 0 + 4 =$	8
5	Divide by the number of observations	$8 \div 3 =$	2.67
6	Take the square root of the result	$\sqrt{2.67} =$	**1.63**

SEE THE WOOD FROM THE TREES

A simple table that helps you handle normal situations is included as Figure 11.2. The bewildering mass of figures in it is actually simple. Take it step by step.

- Column A is the *number of standard deviations* measured along the horizontal scale of the chart in Figure 11.1. Statisticians get everything wrong when they name things. The *number of standard deviations* is called a *z score* – which I suppose is their best shot so far.

- Column B is the data that creates the bell curve in Figure 11.1.

The z score for the trees and sales examples above happens to be 1. If you find 1 in column A, and read the matching value in column B, you get the answer 15.87% – call it 16%. Bear with me. This is the amount of the distribution to the right of 1 on the chart. In other words, just 16% of trees are 1 m or more taller than the average. There is a 16% chance that sales will be $1 million or more above the *expected central value*.

You can pick any number in column A. For example, take 0.5. The corresponding value in column B is about 30%. So, 30% of trees exceed the average by half a metre or more. There is a 30% likelihood that sales will exceed $10.5 million.

The distribution of values is symmetrical. So for the previous example, you can also say that 70% of trees are shorter than 10.5 metres. You can turn it upside down also. Thirty per cent are shorter than 9.5 metres; 70% are taller than 9.5 metres. Just in case you are not too fond of subtracting from 100, column C does it for you. Put another way, column B + column C = 100%.

Columns B and C look at *one* side of the picture. They reveal how much of a normal distribution lies on either side of a specific point. Columns D and E relate to *both* sides of the middle. Go back to the $1 million example. Against 1 in column A, column E indicates that there is a 68% probability that sales will be within (i.e. plus or minus) $1 million of expected value – between $9 million and $11 million. Column D says that there is a 32% chance that they won't be. Clearly, columns D and E must also add to 100%.

IN THE REAL WORLD

I do not know about you, but I am seriously weary of all these numbers. Hang in there a little longer, there is only one more step and it is the most interesting one. This is how you apply all this to real-world situations.

1 Make a realistic (be honest) central observation, estimate or forecast.

2 Make a realistic second observation, estimate or forecast.

3 Attach a probability to the value in step 2.

4 Find the standard deviation implied by step 3.

5 Use this to estimate other values.

Box A opposite takes you step by step through the process of finding standard deviation. For example, if you estimate that a machine can produce 150 widgets, but there is a 10% chance that it will stamp out only 126, you can establish that the standard deviation for this situation is 20.

Armed with the standard deviation you can do one of the following.

1 Choose any other value, find the z score and read off the percentage likelihood of that value (see Box B on page 262). For example, if you chose 126 you would find that there is a 10% chance of making this many or fewer widgets.

2 Choose any percentage, read off the z score, and convert it into a useful value. (See Box C on page 262.) For example, there is a 90% likelihood of producing 176 or fewer widgets.

As with most worthwhile things in life, this is harder to describe than to do. Once you are familiar with the principles, it is really very useful. In the next few pages, I will look at some practical applications.

> You have just read about a wonderful tool. Used correctly it adds rigour to your analysis and credibility to your business plan. There are two traps. First, beware of assuming that your set of possible outcomes is bell shaped. If it is skewed or jagged the *normal* does not work. Second, do not allow this tool to give your estimates and forecasts a spurious sense of meaning and accuracy. The only thing that is certain about the future is uncertainty.

Box A: Seven steps to deviation

(Using Figure 11.2)

Procedure	Example	Your own calculations
1 Make your most likely forecast or estimate	Say, 150 units of your product	
2 Make a second forecast or estimate – perhaps a worst-case scenario	Say, 124	
3 Estimate the probability of the second situation arising	Say, 10%	
4 Find a figure in column B or C that is closest to your answer to step 3	9.68%	
5 Read off the corresponding z score from column A.	z score = 1.3	
6 Find the difference between your answers to steps 1 and 2	150 − 124 = 26	
7 Divide the answer to step 6 by the answer to step 5	26 ÷ 1.3 = 20	
The answer to step 7 is your standard deviation	**Standard deviation = 20**	

Box B: Four steps to a score

Procedure	Example	Your own calculations
1 Identify your average or most likely forecast or estimate	Say, 150 units of your product	
2 Select the value that you want to convert to a z score	Say, 124	
3 Subtract step 2 from step 1	150 − 124 = 26	
4 Divide step 4 by the standard deviation	26 ÷ 20 = 1.3	
The answer to step 4 is your z score	**z score = 1.3**	

Box C: Five steps from likelihood to outcome

(Using Figure 11.2)

Procedure	Example	Your own calculations
1 Think of a percentage	Say, 90% on one side of the centre	
2 Find a figure in column B or C that is closest to your answer in step 1	90.32	
3 Read off the associated z score	z score = 1.3	
4 Multiply step 2 by the standard deviation	1.3 x 20 = 26	
5 The result of step 3 is the *distance from the central* value	150 + 26 = 176 and 150 − 26 = 124	
Use common sense to interpret the result	**90% of values are 176 or lower** and **90% of values are 124 or above**	

Figure 11.2 Z scores

Showing percentage of distribution in the shaded areas

Column A	Column B	Column C	Column D	Column E
	Your focus is on one side		Your focus is on the middle or both ends	
z score	% in tail	% before tail	% in tails	% in middle
0.0	**50.00**	**50.00**	**100.00**	**0.00**
0.1	46.02	53.98	92.04	7.96
0.2	42.07	57.93	84.14	15.86
0.3	38.21	61.79	76.42	23.58
0.4	34.46	65.54	68.92	31.08
0.5	**30.85**	**69.15**	**61.70**	**38.30**
0.6	27.43	72.57	54.86	45.14
0.7	24.20	75.80	48.40	51.60
0.8	21.19	78.81	42.38	57.62
0.9	18.41	81.59	36.82	63.18
1.0	**15.87**	**84.13**	**31.74**	**68.26**
1.1	13.57	86.43	27.14	72.86
1.2	11.51	88.49	23.02	76.98
1.3	9.68	90.32	19.36	80.64
1.4	8.08	91.92	16.16	83.84
1.5	**6.68**	**93.32**	**13.36**	**86.64**
1.6	5.48	94.52	10.96	89.04
1.7	4.46	95.54	8.92	91.08
1.8	3.59	96.41	7.18	92.82
1.9	2.87	97.13	5.74	94.26
2.0	**2.28**	**97.72**	**4.56**	**95.44**
2.1	1.79	98.21	3.58	96.42
2.2	1.39	98.61	2.78	97.22
2.3	1.07	98.93	2.14	97.86
2.4	0.82	99.18	1.64	98.36
2.5	**0.62**	**99.38**	**1.24**	**98.76**
2.6	0.47	99.53	0.94	99.06
2.7	0.35	99.65	0.70	99.30
2.8	0.26	99.74	0.52	99.48
2.9	0.19	99.81	0.38	99.62
3.0	**0.14**	**99.86**	**0.28**	**99.72**
3.1	0.10	99.90	0.20	99.80

For any value 'value' from a set of values with a given mean and standard deviation:

$$z = (value - mean) \div \text{standard deviation}$$
$$\text{Value} = (z \times \text{standard deviation}) + mean$$
$$\text{Mean} = value - (z \times \text{standard deviation})$$
$$\text{Standard deviation} = (value - mean) \div z$$

How many coconuts do you need to sell?

After the stress of reading about unfamiliar statistical terms, our discussion now becomes really easy again. Every reader of your business plan wants to know how much you have to sell to break even. You break even when you just cover the costs of buying or making the product *and* other operating expenses (*indirect costs* such as office rental, administration fees and so on).

Here is a real-life example. Suppose that you sell coconuts at the roadside. You buy them for one peso each and sell them for five pesos. Your gross profit is four pesos a coconut. You have to sell 20 to break even – to cover the 80 peso operating costs of renting the stall each day. The 21st coconut starts earning you net profit.

> The number of units that you have to sell to break even is *operating costs* divided by *gross profit per unit*.

Remember that operating costs do not include those items that go into cost of sales – otherwise you would be double counting, or perhaps I should say double dividing.

A PICTURE IS WORTH A THOUSAND WORDS

There is a neat little chart that illustrates break even and adds great value to your business plan. It provides a usefully *graphic* indicator of how much you have to sell to make it worth being in business.

If you examine how gross sales revenue increases as your sales increase, you will find a curve similar to that shown in Figure 11.3. The more you sell, the more you earn. The curve flattens off because usually sales taper away as the market becomes saturated. There comes a point when people just will not pay as much as five pesos for a coconut.

You can also show how costs increase with quantity. This curve starts above zero because you have an underlying level of fixed expenses that you have to meet even if you are not doing anything (your coconut stall). The curve then slopes more gently than sales, reflecting the fact (I hope) that your prices exceed product costs. However, I would expect the curve to turn upwards at higher volumes due to the quaintly named *law of diminishing returns* – you have to start employing coconut sales assistants who become more and more difficult to manage, and so on.

The point where the two curves cross indicates your break even sales revenue and quantity. You uncovered all the costs and prices associated with your own business in Chapters 8 and 9. You could easily draw this chart yourself. I am willing to bet that it will have two straight lines. This is how it is shown in simple introductory books, and it is how most people project costs and revenues. It does not matter too much – straight lines work well enough over a limited range of production and sales. But I wanted to draw your attention to it to help you review your analysis and decide if you could improve your techniques.

One message is that rather than identifying break even as a precise figure, it is better to consider it as a range (19–21 coconuts). Add a bit on each side to give you a margin for error because it is rarely as simple as the example given.

If you can refine your figures enough, you might be able to identify the optimum production level. Notice how profits are revealed by the gap between sales and costs on the right-hand side of Figure 11.3. Profit is maximised where the two lines are furthest apart. As noted, many simple texts show two straight lines that continue to diverge indefinitely – implying that the more you sell the more money you make. In practice, profits and costs sometimes change direction and start to converge again as shown here. In such instances, profit is maximised where the two lines are furthest apart – before they start moving back together. Selling too much can be counterproductive. There is a limit to how many coconuts your customers can consume.

BREAK EVEN AND CAPACITY PLANNING

If you consider the scale along the bottom of Figure 11.3 to run from 0–100% of capacity, then the break even quantity indicates the minimum capacity level at which you can operate. The difference between this and 100% indicates your room for manoeuvre.

Figure 11.3 Plotting to break even

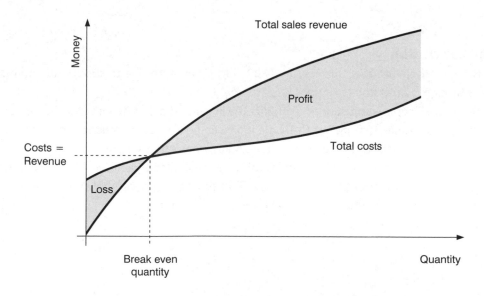

THE CHANCES OF BREAKING EVEN

Knowing how many coconuts you have to sell to break even is helpful. Knowing the likelihood of actually breaking even would be better still. You have probably guessed that I am going to refer to the *normal* again. Let me take a different example. A re-seller has established that she can source about 100,000 telephones, but there is a 10% chance that deliveries will be 10% lower than this. She needs to sell 85,000 to break even. What is the probability of failure?

The facts

- Expected supply: 100,000 telephones.

- Alternative scenario: 10% possibility that supply will be 90,000 or fewer telephones.

- Model: the telephones are supplied by a large number of manufacturers who in turn source their components from many different companies and countries – it is therefore considered appropriate to assume that supplies are *distributed normally*.

The arithmetic

- Take the above figures, work through the seven steps to deviation (page 261), and you will find that the standard deviation is approximately 7700.

- Next, from the four steps to a score (page 262), the z score associated with 15,000 (100,000 less 85,000) is 1.9.

- Finally, from Figure 11.2, the percentage associated with a z score of 1.9 is 2.8% – call it 3%.

The conclusion

There is a 3% chance that this venture will fail to break even due to supply constraints. The situation is illustrated in Figure 11.4.

The normal curve was just used to predict the likelihood of a re-seller being able or failing to source adequate supplies. The same logic can be applied to production – and also to the sales side of the break even equation (and to many other situations).

You need to check your break even point/range and the likelihood that it will be achieved and then bettered. If the risks of falling short are unacceptable you have to go back to revise your strategy and plan as described in Chapter 6.

Figure 11.4 Not enough telephones?

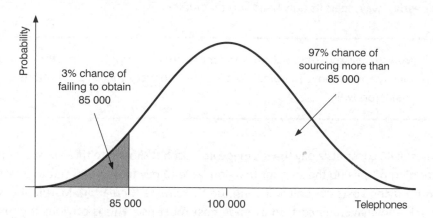

3% chance of failing to obtain 85 000

97% chance of sourcing more than 85 000

Probability

85 000   100 000   Telephones

 Break even in your business plan

Most readers will check your business plan for your break even analysis. I have taken you a little beyond the usual 'straight-line analysis' to give you a head start in the hard world of business planning and funding. However, even if you just draw two straight lines and identify where they cross you will have aided understanding of your business case. Expand on this by assigning probabilities and you will boost your credibility and your perceived ability to manage.

Marginal likelihood of shutting down?

Would you sell your product for less than it cost? Does this sound likely? Obviously, you should sell one more coconut only if the revenue from that sale exceeds its cost to you. But what, exactly, is the cost?

Think about the problem. Let's talk coconuts again. Recall that you buy coconuts for one peso each and sell them for five pesos and you have operating expenditure of 80 pesos a day for renting the stall.

If you sell just one coconut in a day, your *total, average* and *marginal costs* were 81 pesos. If you sell two nuts, *total costs* edge up to 82 pesos, *average total cost per nut* slips to 42 pesos and *marginal cost per husk* plummets to one peso.

Marginal cost is the expense associated with selling one more item. In this example, the total cost will rise steadily, the average cost will continue falling, and the marginal cost of every nut after the first one will remain fixed at one peso. Except that it won't. At some point the marginal cost will start rising due to limited supply of coconuts or the additional costs of employing staff, renting more stalls, trucking more nuts – the *law of diminishing returns* nearly always rears its ugly head sooner or later.

 Always, always sell coconuts for more than one peso – in other words, always price above marginal cost – except for very special promotions or to gain goodwill.

At sales of 40 coconuts a day the *average total cost* has slipped to three pesos. Suppose that rationing pushes up the amount that you have to pay for the 41st nut to four pesos (and your buying costs per unit will continue to increase thereafter). Marginal cost has gone back above average cost, so average cost must rise. This is obvious if you think about the way that an average is calculated.

If you were to plot these trends, you would see a chart similar to Figure 11.5. I have cheated by making the curves smoother than the coconut example implies. Corporate life is somewhat more complex than selling nuts at the roadside and there are rather more factors at play. However, if you follow through this analysis, you will spot two key figures from Figure 11.5.

Figure 11.5 Shut down or expand?

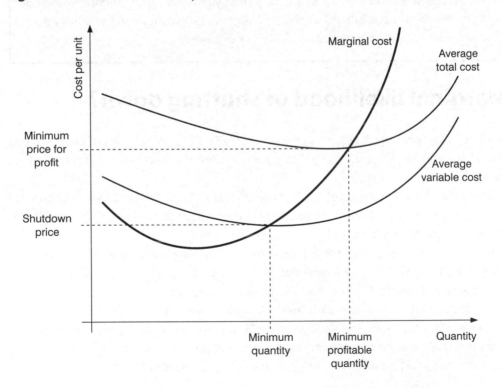

1 **Shutdown price.** If your income per unit is less than minimum *average variable cost* per unit (less than the point where *marginal cost = average variable cost*) you are not covering your variable costs. In other words, if gross revenue per coconut is less than one peso, you might as well close the stall and spend your days on the beach.

2 **Minimum economic price.** If your income per unit is less than the lowest point in your average total cost curve (where *average total cost = marginal cost*) you are not covering fixed and variable costs. If you sell coconuts for less than three pesos, you will make a net loss.

If you are selling between your shutdown and minimum economic prices, you are covering the variable costs of the product, but not your fixed costs. You are making a loss, but at least you are earning more than if you did nothing. For example, if you are selling coconuts for between one and three pesos and have paid for your stall rental today, you are recovering some of the rental. You need to develop a sales strategy in order to move to full profitability.

 Stall holders at hot dusty bazaars in the Middle East know all about marginal analysis. Their haggling will go all the way down to just above their shutdown price. They would rather make a sale at just above average variable costs – never mind their fixed costs – than see you buy from their neighbour. Small retailers in smart shopping malls sometimes sit idle, without recognising this, while lost custom drifts past.

MARGINS AND THE NORMAL

As you will have spotted already, you can apply the *normal* to marginal analysis and calculate the likelihood of various outcomes. It is exactly the same as all the other examples of using the *normal* – so I won't labour this one. An interesting exercise, if you feel so inclined, is to assume that costs are distributed normally around the central expectation and establish a *range* of probable outcomes.

Marginal notes for your business plan

You certainly want to think about marginal analysis when you plan and run your business. The calculations are usually more complex than the example here, but the conclusions will hit you like a coconut falling from the palm tree. Remember that average costs are not static. Watch for them to jump about when the stall owner suddenly increases the rent. It is a rare – and advanced – business plan that includes much marginal analysis. Nevertheless, you may find it useful to say a word or two about marginal costs, not least to demonstrate that you understand costs and prices – and that you have them well under control.

What you need, when you need it

Too much inventory costs you money. It ties up cash in stock that can, of course, become obsolete or damaged. At the other extreme, not enough inventory tests customer loyalty and leads to lost or delayed sales. Remember how you reacted last time that you were told that something you wanted was out of stock?

You know your minimum inventory levels (established in Chapter 8). Obviously this is not necessarily the optimum level, but it can be identified using some simple arithmetic. Consider that the only things that vary are:

● **Ordering costs** – the costs of processing purchase orders, taking delivery and/or tooling up for a production run, and so on. Ordering costs per unit decline as volumes increase due to economies of scale.

● **Carrying costs** – including premises, insurance and funding costs. These increase steadily with volume.

Figure 11.6 shows these costs separately and combined. The optimum inventory level is where ordering and carrying costs are minimised, which is where they equal each other. In other words, in any one period, the quantity of inventory that you should order is the quantity where:

$$total\ ordering\ costs = total\ carrying\ cost$$

$$or$$

$$number\ of\ orders \times cost\ per\ day = average\ inventory \times carry\ cost\ per\ unit$$

Figure 11.6 Optimum inventory level

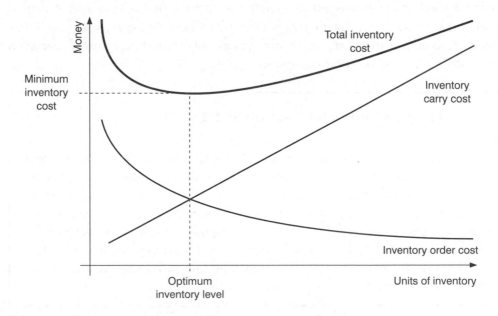

For *just-in-time* inventory management, the reorder point is triggered when inventory falls to a level equivalent to daily demand × delivery time in days. This presupposes that demand is steady and delivery is always on time. Maybe you want to carry a buffer stock!

IT'S NORMALLY IN STOCK

So, you know how to minimise the costs of carrying inventory. But how do you achieve an acceptable chance of having the right products in stock? Yes, the *normal* can be applied to inventory control. Consider a transport café. The owner knows from experience that he usually sells 400 meat pies a week and the *standard deviation* of demand is 20 pies. He will accept a 15% risk of being out of stock. How many pies should he buy in his weekly order each Monday afternoon?

If you look back at Figure 11.2, you will see that 15% *in one tail* of the normal distribution happens to be about one z score, and therefore one standard deviation. (By the way, you can probably see that 15% is a useful percentage to pick because it equates to one z score and one standard deviation.)

One conclusion is that the pie man should order 400 plus 20, in other words, 420 pies. Another conclusion is that you probably do not want to buy a pie from him on a Monday morning.

'Ready money can buy whatever is in stock.'

CHINESE PROVERB

Will it pay off?

If your boffins want to spend a large amount of money on a new coconut processing plant, how do you assess the financial viability of the proposed project? You are constantly forced to choose between alternatives when planning and drawing up business plans. There is always a danger that you will make the wrong choice. Take a quick meander through some techniques for assessing activities and choosing between them.

By the way, in this context *project* means anything on which you spend money with the expectation of generating a future stream of income. This includes R&D, exploration, buildings, plant, machinery, equipment, marketing, takeovers and other ventures. You have to value these streams of income and assess the comparative risks before you can decide which are viable and, of those, which you should undertake. The box on page 272 shows some key considerations. They are very straightforward when you are familiar with them. We can work through them in four steps.

Points to consider before saying yes

1 Forecast the expected cash flow from each project.

2 Choose an appraisal method – net present value or internal rate of return (which are explained in a moment).

3 Identify your cost of capital (how much it costs you to fund the project).

4 Assess the returns from the project (financial and other gains such as prestige or experience).

5 Assess the risk of the project.

6 Identify the hurdles that this project should clear to be considered acceptable.

7 Review comparative risks and returns on alternative projects.

8 Assess the opportunity costs of not using these resources for something else.

STEP 1: MAKE YOUR CASH FLOW FORECASTS

The first step is to draw up a cash flow forecast for each project. This will be easy after your work in Chapters 7–10. The box below shows the type of summary that you might produce showing the *after-tax* cash flow. Next, you have to value the projected stream of income.

Forecasting a stream of income

Project *Watchman*

Cash flow projection

Euros, millions

	Year 2	Year 3	Year 4	...
Outlays	−10,000	−8,000	−5,000	...
Income	11,000	15,000	25,000	...
Net income, before tax	**1,000**	**7,000**	**20,000**	...
100% *less* tax rate	75%	75%	75%	...
Income after tax				
(excl depreciation allowance)	**750**	**5,250**	**15,000**	...
Add back depreciation × tax rate	1,000	1,000	1,000	...
Net cash flow after tax	**1,750**	**6,250**	**16,000**	...

Inflation

Some companies run projections in constant price terms (ignoring inflation). However, given that our real-world experiences relate to cash values that include the effects of inflation, it is probably more realistic to work in expected real-world prices. This makes observation and measurement easier.

The UK government used to project and approve spending plans in constant price terms. As a result, nobody really knew what was going on because prices were changing all the time. For example, big pay increases were sneaked through because they did not change the approved volume figures (number of employees).

The only thing that you have to remember is to ensure that all your figures, including the cost of capital discussed here, are in money terms.

'And the trouble is, if you don't risk anything, you risk even more.'

ERICA YONG

STEP 2: CHOOSE YOUR VALUATION TECHNIQUE

Present value

The *present value* of any future stream of income is equivalent to the amount of money that you would need to put in a bank deposit today to generate the identified future stream of income.

Take an example. I offer to give you £1000 at some time in the future. What is this pledge worth to you today?

● If you will have £1000 in your hand in 12 months' time, this is exactly equivalent to investing about £910 today at 10% interest.

● To have £1000 paid to you ten years from now would require an investment today of only £385 (with interest at 10% per annum compounded once a year).

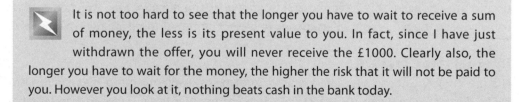

It is not too hard to see that the longer you have to wait to receive a sum of money, the less is its present value to you. In fact, since I have just withdrawn the offer, you will never receive the £1000. Clearly also, the longer you have to wait for the money, the higher the risk that it will not be paid to you. However you look at it, nothing beats cash in the bank today.

If you project the pattern of income that a project will generate, calculate the present value of each future cash amount and sum the results, you arrive at the overall *net present value* (NPV) of a project. Simplistically, the project with the highest value gets your money.

You will be happy to know that calculators and computer spreadsheets do this calculation for you painlessly – see Figure 11.7. As you can see from the example, you can have payments and receipts dotted around a project. It does not have to be one outlay and a series of regular income. Watch, though, that at different interest rates, different projects become more attractive because of the varying valuations of future income and payments.

Figure 11.7 Let computer spreadsheets do the work

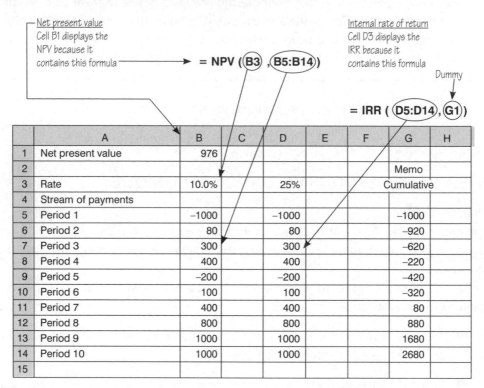

One decision that you do have to make is the correct interest rate to use. Actually, in relation to present value this is more correctly known as the *discount rate*, which in turn is usually called the *hurdle rate* when applied to project appraisal. More on this in a moment.

Internal rate of return

Net present value has an alternative which is known as the *internal rate of return (IRR)*, also called *discounted cash flow (DCF)* and *yield*. Some companies use it, so we had better take a quick look at how it works.

The *internal rate of return* is simply the compound interest rate that links the present and future. Think of it as the interest rate that a bank would have to charge if it were to make you a loan (the project cost) that was going to generate the projected future stream of repayments (the returns).

Calculators and computer spreadsheets make it a breeze to find the IRR. This is also shown in Figure 11.7 – note that if the rate in cell B3 had been set equivalent to the internal rate of return of 25%, the NPV in cell B1 would be zero.

So, you line up the projects and see which one gives the best return? Yes, and no. It is rarely quite so simple in real life. The table below shows why. It illustrates two projects, code-named Alpha and Beta, returning 20% and 15% respectively. It happens that Project Alpha wins hands down. It requires an outlay of only $1000 and returns 20%, whereas Beta requires double the outlay but returns only 15%. However, what if it was not so clear-cut? Then you do your analysis at the margin.

Projects on the margin

You can consider Project Beta to be made up of two sub-projects: Project Alpha and Project Charlie. This new project Charlie is simply the difference between the other two projects – cash flow in Project Alpha subtracted from cash flow in Project Beta. Thus, your choice is actually undertaking:

- option one – Project Alpha; *or*

- option two – a project with returns equivalent to Alpha *and* Charlie.

All you have to do is assess the returns from Charlie to decide if it adds to or subtracts from Project Alpha. In this case Charlie doesn't look too good, so Beta would probably be junked. Alpha comes first again.

IT'S AS SIMPLE AS *ALPHA BETA CHARLIE*			
	ALPHA	**BETA**	**CHARLIE**
Outlay	1000	2000	1000
Return	1200	2300	1100
Yield	20%	15%	10%

Choosing between twins

You can probably see that net present value and internal rate of return are the same thing approached from different angles. Internal rate of return produces a familiar percentage figure that feels friendly. However, there are occasions when IRR is impossible to calculate (you might find this if you switch from negative to positive cash flows several times). Moreover, with internal rate of return the reinvestment rate is the calculated IRR, whereas with net present value the reinvestment rate is the discount rate that you specify – which is superior.

Your choice might be dictated by company policy. If not, you pay your money and take your choice. You can probably see that I lean towards net present value.

 Pay-back

It is common to hear executives talk about pay-back. I do not mean getting even with political opponents. I am thinking about the amount of money that a project pays out and the speed with which it happens. *This project pays back $10,000 in 12 months*. By itself, this is not a very useful statement. However, a company with cash flow problems might become concerned primarily with making a fast return. This is one situation where pay-back might take precedence over value.

STEP 3: IDENTIFY THE HURDLE RATE

The hurdle rate is a yardstick by which you judge a project proposal. If the proposal clears the hurdle, you can give it further consideration. In essence, each project has its own hurdle rate. These are based on the cost of capital, plus an allowance for non-profit-making projects, plus a risk premium. If you are preparing a business plan to raise funding, you might find it enlightening to consider whether your promised return will meet your potential backer's hurdle rate. This is discussed in Chapter 12.

Cost of capital

You know how much a loan costs – its price is the rate of interest. What is the cost of equity? Basically, it is the rate of return that shareholders expect after corporate taxes have been paid. How much is this? It is generally considered to be:

● a *risk-free rate of return* (use the interest rate on government securities as a proxy); plus

● the *risk premium* required by people bold enough to hold your shares.

If you are in a publicly quoted business, it is likely that someone has calculated the risk factor associated with your equity. You will find this published by one of the big investment houses as your *beta*. Multiply this by the average stock market rate of return to arrive at the risk premium.

For example, if the market is paying 5% more than government securities and your beta is 1.6, your risk premium is 8% (5 × 1.6). If the coupon on government securities is 7%, the required rate of return on your equity is 7% + 8% = 15%. This is the rate of return *on equity* that you have to produce *after* corporate taxes to keep your investors sweet.

If you are not listed on a public stock exchange there is a lot of guesswork in assessing where your investors are coming from. You could try asking them. One venture capital provider told me that he looks for a 40% per annum return on investment. This is generally at the high end of expectations. Or you could compare yourself with similar public companies and other investments.

Your overall cost of capital reflects your gearing – your mix of loans and equity. For example, if 80% of your capital is equity, you pay 12% on your loans and your required rate of return on equity is 15%, your cost of capital is as follows.

Loans	*20% of 12%*	*=*	*2.4%*
Equity	*80% of 15%*	*=*	*12.0%*
Total (weighted average)		**= 14.4%**	

Non-profitable projects

In principle, any project has to return at least the cost of capital to be worthwhile. Sound high? What if you undertake projects that do not add to your profits – such as that new executive restaurant or your ever-popular environmental programme – you need to earn more on the profitable projects.

Developing the example above, if just 85% of your spending is on profit-earning projects, they have to earn you at least 14.4% ÷ 85% = 17%. But even this is not the figure that the bank manager will be looking for. The hurdle is probably even higher than this.

Accounting for risk

Almost there. There is one more step. You cannot use the same hurdle rate for every project, because different projects have differing risks. Key factors are:

- **Gearing** – risks increase as the proportion of variable cash flows (e.g. sales) rises relative to more certain cash flow (e.g. the initial investment).

- **Revenue sensitivity** – risks are higher when projected cash flows are more volatile.

- **Timing** – the longer that it will take to produce revenue, the greater the risk.

This is where a touch of subjectivity comes in. You can assign different *betas* or different risk factors to various projects or classes of projects. For example, for low-risk activities you might add 3% to the 17% in the above example, to arrive at a hurdle rate of 20%. For high-risk undertakings, you might pump up the hurdle rate to 30% or 40%.

We have finally arrived at the hurdle rate. It is:

● the cost of capital;

● *plus* an adjustment for non-earning projects;

● *plus* a risk premium for the specific project (or project class).

Some companies draw up a matrix of risk premiums that they apply to various classes of project. You might like to do this to help classify projects according to risk, and to help achieve consistency now and in the future.

 Don't let your upside idle away its time

When I was a school governor, I once asked a headteacher about the school's facilities for children with special needs. After a short discussion, it became clear that the head assumed that special needs related only to learning disabilities. Children who were exceptionally bright were required to idle away their time at the back of the class. Risks are sometimes treated a bit like this. Do not focus entirely on the downside. Remember that risks relate to the upside also. Do not waste the upside potential by letting an opportunity idle away its time at the back of the class.

'If you don't enter the tiger's den, how can you get the cub?'

CHINESE PROVERB

STEP 4: MAKE THE DECISION

You are now ready to line up the projects and make a decision. The following table shows six projects ranked according to their net present values at their respective hurdle rates. The hurdle rates reveal the degree of risk attached to each project – the lower the rate the safer the perception of the project.

In terms of net present value, project 104 appears to be the most attractive; project 101 the least. If there were capital constraints that allowed spending of $250,000 only, probably the first five would be approved while project 101 would be axed.

Of course, this is not the end of the story. First, you will consider the extent to which projects and finance can be matched. You will also take into account the opportunity costs of these projects, intangible benefits such as prestige, and other factors including liquidity. But the methodology shown here is a good starting point for rigorous analysis – before you apply your management judgement which is, after all, what you are paid for.

SIX PROJECTS RANKED

PROJECT ID	COSTS	HURDLE RATE (%)	NET PRESENT VALUE	CUMULATIVE COSTS
104	40 000	19	90 000	40 000
100	50 000	15	80 000	90 000
105	100 000	40	70 000	190 000
102	10 000	22	50 000	200 000
103	30 000	36	40 000	230 000
101	100 000	25	30 000	330 000

What if?

Isn't it always the simplest techniques that are the best? If you followed the steps outlined in Chapters 7–10, you will have built a series of inter-linked spreadsheets. If you amend one of the basic inputs or assumptions, the changes ripple through and you see immediately the net effect on profits and cash flow. You can use this to build a table such as that shown in Figure 11.8. This is easy to do and boosts understanding significantly – for you and for your readers.

In practice, you need to check that the relationships built into your forecast hold good under the new conditions. A 1% change probably will not make too much difference. However, a 10% fall in market share would prompt you to revisit your strategy – and then you might have to rework the early part of your forecast. The mechanical steps from profit and loss to cash flow will remain unchanged.

Figure 11.8 Avoiding risks in the business plan

This section will demonstrate that you have given due consideration to risks. Given its importance (will I get my money back?) it might run to two or three or more pages.

RISK ASSESSMENT PART ONE – Major Risks

Introduction
We have endeavoured to identify all possible risks and position ourselves appropriately. Major risks that we have considered and attempted to eliminate or minimise include the following.

Tetrylus is showing that it has thought about and tried to eliminate glitches in production. It draws attention honestly to an external factor and, I hope, explains the possible effects.

Production. *Tetrylus ONE* has been successfully prototyped and the feasibility and cost of the manufacturing process is known. The manufacturing is undertaken by a company with quality procedures that meet ISO 9002 standards, and we will conduct our own quality control sampling at their premises … The one remaining uncontrollable factor is the availability and price of silicon on the world market which …

Sales. We pass breakdown when we sell more than 124 *Tetrylus ONE* packages at a minimum price of $95 000 each, as shown in the following chart:

You may decide to include here your list of limiting factors, critical success factors, and/or SWOT (strengths, weaknesses, opportunities and threats).

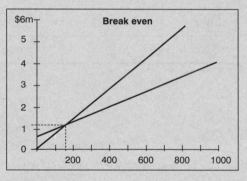

A careful choice of scales has made this look better than it is!

You could also have located this chart with your sales forecast and financials.

The likelihood of failing to break even is … because we have …

Replace ROE (return on equity) with ROCE/ROTA (return on capital employed/total assets) if the plan is not written to raise equity capital (see Chapter 12).

Sensitivity analysis
The following table shows our assessment of the effects of a 1% increase in key variables. A 1% decline will have approximately the opposite effect:

Your what-if table will include other factors related to your own set of risks.

A 1% increase in	Net profit $000	Will change these by borrowing $000	ROE %
Sales volume	+167	−83	+3.3
Sales price	+134	−57	+2.7
Marketing expenditure	+15	−8	+0.3
Raw material prices	−59	+30	−1.2
Labour costs	−23	+12	−0.5
Other costs	−12	+5	−0.2

The economy

Business people know only too well how recession can suddenly wipe out demand – and suppliers or business partners. Remember to include an assessment of the effects of economic developments in your business plan. If you are currently operating in a healthy environment, demonstrate how your strategy will protect you when there is an economic downturn. If you are struggling through depression, show how it is affecting your industry and how you are positioned for the next boom. The whole point of the business plan might be to obtain the funding that will get you through the bad times.

ARE BANKERS USEFUL AFTER ALL?

How vulnerable are you to changes in exchange rates or interest rates? Should you be hedging? By this, I don't mean avoiding the issue when in the bank manager's office. I am thinking of covering your bets if you trade overseas. For example, you have just signed a contract for which you will be paid in Bangladeshi Taka or Kyrgyzstanian Som in three months' time. (No, I didn't invent those names.) What will happen if those currencies go through the floor in the tense intervening period? You can cover your risks by selling the currencies *forward*. Your bankers will guarantee to buy a fixed amount from you at today's exchange rate plus a margin. The margin is essentially the difference between domestic interest rates and those in Bangladesh or Kyrgyzstan – plus a handsome fee for the bank. This replaces risk with certainty – so long as you really do get paid.

This is where export and import guarantees come in. You can arrange for your bankers to act as intermediaries, guaranteeing that payment will be made on delivery of goods. It is important to remember, however, that you can only hedge major currencies – there is not a market in the more obscure ones.

If the worst comes to the worst …

A coconut falls off the tree. Will it hit you on the head and break, or will you sell it for another five pesos? On your journey to the current point in this book, you have probably found ways to turn many problems into advantages. You have built up a deeper understanding of the risks that assail your business and identified strategies to prepare for and handle the worst. And perhaps most important, you will have quantified the likely impact of being hit by curved balls. Your *what-if* summarised these in a neat little table.

Readers of your business plan also expect to see a worst-case forecast that shows what would be the end result if all the worst possible things that could happen did happen. I suggest that you make a copy of your central forecast, re-label one 'worst-case' and then amend the assumptions to reflect your view of the gloomiest scenario. This will be a combination of events – e.g. R&D is six months late with the product update, sales are 20% below expectations, and interest rates rise three points.

 Nine times out of ten, the people approving your plan will want to know about the likely effects of delayed production and lower-than-expected sales.

When you have changed the inputs to your forecast, and confirmed that the strategy reflected in the forecast holds good under these new conditions, you will have a new bottom line. It is usually enough to explain the basis for this scenario and include a brief summary of the end results in your business plan. You will want a short, reassuring commentary. And, of course, an indication of the likelihood of the worst case happening. I have already shown you how to use the *normal* to do this (see page 256).

 By the way, what will happen to your profits if your main competitor announces that they have taken over that upstart company that has a great product but was too small to threaten you?

Grand finale

The aim of this chapter is to help you think about and assess risks. Unfortunately, or perhaps fortunately, your analysis might have taken you back to revise your strategy and operating plans. This is what the business planning process is all about: finding the best path to the future. When you have gone around this loop enough times to maximise your strategy while controlling and minimising risks, you have completed your business planning process. You can then write a few pages demonstrating to readers of your plan that everything is under control. Remember, you want to try to anticipate their concerns.

Congratulations. Now all that remains is the satisfying task of pulling it all together, tidying up your plan and getting it approved. The 'grand finale' is in sight.

Getting it approved

Victory comes to the most persevering. NAPOLEON

- Pulling it all together
- Focus
- What readers of the plan will look for
- Those financials again
- Final check on the plan
- They don't know what's coming to them
- Preparing for the meeting
- At last, the first meeting
- Meeting post-mortems
- Follow up
- Back to the drawing board
- Due diligence
- The contract
- Cash in the bank

At last, you have everything that you need to complete your business plan. We have covered many topics to arrive here, and for good reason – the more effectively you do your groundwork, the more easily you will gain approval for your business plan.

Frankly you should find it very easy to win internal corporate approval for your plan, unless you have made some fundamental error or you have been particularly creative with the facts. You have enough information in this book to produce an impressive plan and if you have read this far I know that you also have the drive to see it through. That said, the corridors of power sometimes conceal menaces waiting to knock down an excellent plan. I have one or two suggestions to help you through this.

If you are looking for external approval for funding, I have to warn you not to underestimate the obstacles that might still be in your path. It can sometimes be very frustrating trying to persuade a banker or backer to share your vision. Not to worry. Share my experiences, persevere, and you will make it through the labyrinth.

Pulling it all together

The hard work is over. Or is it? As you worked through this book, you developed an appraisal of your current situation, looking both inwards and out to the world at large. You built a strategy, turned it into a plan, costed it and forecast the end result in terms of profits, assets, cash flow and funding requirements. You assessed risks and produced variations on your plan. You now have a bullet-proof operating plan and budget to work with.

All you need is a rubber stamp or perhaps a more-considered approval. Either way, you want to get on with the business. The approval process is not always as straightforward as you might expect. And even if it is, you still want to make the best possible job of presenting your plan. Let me share my experiences.

 Definitions

To avoid long complex sentences the terms *internal plan* and *external plan* are used here.

- An **internal plan** is for use within an enterprise – such as a small firm, a company, a charity, a government department, or any of the above forming part of a larger undertaking.

- An **external plan** is one that is going outside for funding.

The fast track to approval

1 Take a short vacation. Visit the health club. Play golf. Go fishing. Do anything to make sure that you are in good shape and ready for a fight.

2 Mentally revisit your intended readers. Make sure that you really understand what they want to read.

3 Make sure that your plan answers the right questions – as completely and concisely as possible.

4 *Plan* carefully before delivering the plan.

5 Prepare thoroughly for the first and subsequent meetings.

6 Give as much assistance as possible to help your readers understand what is in the plan.

7 Follow up promptly with additional information. Make revisions to the plan if necessary and learn for the future. Help recipients through their *due diligence*.

8 Do your own due diligence. Do not sign anything without checking it carefully.

9 Persevere. Be prepared for delays, disappointments and set-backs.

10 Once the cash is in the bank, go straight to Chapter 13.

Focus

The German, American and Englishman introduced on page 3 each had differing plans for different readers. I hope that the reason has become clear. Before you start sharing your plan with all and sundry, check to see that it really will meet their needs and answer positively their questions. Many pages ago, you set off by identifying your potential readers. As already discussed, you are seeking:

● **internal approval** for the strategy and plan (perhaps in competition with another department) – which tends to imply automatic funding; or

● **external funding** – you have already looked at who you might approach (see Chapter 10).

The two are of course very similar, but there is a slight difference of emphasis. Picture in your imagination the people who will be reviewing and approving the plan. Will it give them the information that they want? The list of business plan reviewers on page 289 shows how emphasis might vary among different readers.

'I think there is a world market for maybe five computers.'

THOMAS WATSON, CHAIRMAN IBM, 1943

 ## Venturing forth

If you are looking for start-up funding (or maybe even growth equity) – and I am sorry to have to be the bearer of bad news – this is not going to be much fun. It can be a full-time job, lasting several months, sapping your energy and shattering your morale. I am not trying to deter you. Quite the opposite. It would be a waste of all our hard work producing such an exemplary business plan if you gave up. I hope that you are the exception and have a smooth ride. Just in case you do not, be prepared. You must find the grit and tenacity to see this through, to keep fighting. It really is worth it at the end of the day.

You have to remember that you have the vision, you know that you can turn your ideas into a hugely successful business, or take an existing business to new heights. The people you talk to do not share that vision. Otherwise they would not be sitting in ivory towers reviewing business plans. They would be out there doing what you are doing.

Remember the countless venture capital providers, no doubt clever and knowledgeable people, who nevertheless time after time turned down breathtaking opportunities such as the jet engine, the hovercraft, the bagless vacuum cleaner, and many others. How many hundreds of stories have you read of brilliant inventors or entrepreneurs who were turned away from countless offices for being *too new, too advanced* or *too revolutionary*. The worst rejection of all: *We can't see a need for this product or idea, no one will ever buy it.*

This said, it is possible. It can be done. If you refuse to give up, sheer perseverance will bring you success. Take comfort in the corporate finance officers' most-used defence about opportunities that they turned down, ventures that were financed elsewhere and went on to be huge successes. *I did not back it because when it was offered to me the market was not ready for it.* Right. Another month made all the difference, I suppose.

Table 12.1 The easiest countries in which to do business in 2010

THE BEST	RANK
Singapore	1
Hong Kong SAR	2
New Zealand	3
United Kingdom	4
United States	5
Denmark	6
Canada	7
Norway	8
Ireland	9
Australia	10
Saudi Arabia	11
Georgia	12
... and the worst	
Central African Republic	182
Chad	183

A high rank means that the regulatory environment is conducive to business operation. A rank of 1 is best.

Note that China ranked 79th and India came in at 134.

Source: © 2011 The World Bank

What readers of the plan will look for

Assuming that you know who is going to receive your plan, your first challenge is ensuring that it is read. This is why the presentation and executive summary have to be good. It is highly unlikely that anyone will read the plan from cover to cover between you giving it to them and the next time that you meet – no matter how much time separates the two events.

Ten business plan reviewers – and what they think about when they read your plan

1   **Board of directors.** Have you correctly identified the corporate objectives and developed a winning competitive strategy? Will it enhance the board's prestige?

2   **The CEO or other internal managers.** Is the strategy good and the operational plan feasible? Is it in line with their style of management? Will they see it as a threat to their empire or alternatively as an opportunity to increase their prestige?

3   **Government agencies.** Are you meeting their objectives; providing education and training, creating jobs, helping revitalise depressed areas, boosting exports? If you are, make sure you say so. Will it help them look good in the media? Can they and you gain good publicity?

4   **Bankers.** Do you have the security and cash flow to repay your loans? Does the plan minimise the risks for the approving officer?

5   **Business partners.** Do your skills and resources complement theirs? How will you add value to their business? Have you displayed your reliability and dependability?

6   **Friends, angels.** Will they get their money back?

7   **Venture capital providers.** Is the management up to it? Is the business proposition unique? Will you follow through effectively?

8   **Investment companies.** What makes this business special? How will the business grow?

9   **Institutional investors.** Is this a solid business? Will it outperform the market in the longer term?

10 **Investment advisers.** Have you met the formal requirements for listing or private placement?

INTERNAL PLANS

You can be reasonably confident that plans for use within a closed organisation will be given some attention. You can also be fairly certain that they will not be read in their entirety. The best that you can hope for is that readers will grasp some good points from the plan before the next meeting in the boardroom or in the chief executive's office. You do not want casual readers to find things that they can readily pick on and criticise. Think about the people who will be sitting around that highly polished table – see page 290.

You might think that I am getting ahead of myself. We haven't even finalised the plan yet and I am already talking about the first meeting. However, I want you to try to see your plan from every perspective. Obviously, you want a sensible review when the time comes and your plan will benefit from valid input. But you do not want to be shot down by pointless sniper fire.

With the personalities in your organisation in mind, read your plan again and try to see where your opponents, the point-scorers and the vetoers might find ammunition. Consider if you have mistakenly overemphasised a weakness or an uncertainty, or whether you have made assumptions that can be torn apart. If possible, discuss the plan with your mentor to see where he or she finds weaknesses and where you can look for support. You might want to rewrite these parts, removing or defending weaknesses and emphasising strengths.

If you are fighting in a tough political atmosphere, do not let your plan be discussed too freely in advance. Too much idle chatter gives your opponents time to formulate strategies. Do not show everyone your hand or your best ideas will turn up on the boss's desk in some else's memo two days before you can present your brilliant business plan.

Seven groups at the conference table

1 **The decision-maker.** Even if the chairman or chief executive makes the decision, it might be based wholly or partly on feedback or recommendations from others. Do not focus on the head of the table to the exclusion of all others.

2 **The influencer.** Frequently, there is a wise sage or muse who exerts strong influence on the decision-maker. Win the influencer's support and you might win the battle.

3 **Your mentor/coach.** If you are younger, or new to a situation, you might find that an older, longer-serving, generally respected executive becomes your mentor and coach. You can usually expect a constructive attitude from this person and you are strong if he or she is the key influencer.

4 **One of the 'Big Five' with power of veto.** Sometimes one person has the ability to kill a proposal, regardless of how well it is received overall. The spoilsport might be the bean counter who says that your figures are unworkable, the lawyer who questions the legality, or the boffin who doubts the feasibility. (The term comes from the five nations with power of veto in the UN Security Council.)

5 **Your opponents.** It is likely that you will have some opponents. They might be motivated by personal grudges against you, personality disorders, ambition, or maybe their divorce is making them grouchy. Whatever the cause, they will pick up on anything negative in the business plan.

> 6 **The nasty point-scorers.** There are invariably a few people knocking around your enterprise who spend their time looking for an opportunity to look good in front of the boss or otherwise score points – even if this means wrecking a perfectly reasonable plan just because *it was not invented here*.
>
> 7 **Your supporters.** Finally, fellow contributors, executives likely to gain from the plan, and (if the plan is sound) your boardroom chums are likely to be generally positive. But watch out for unexpected *point-scorers* and those with hidden agendas. Do not rely on goodwill or friendship for votes, prefer facts and good arguments.

EXTERNAL FUNDING

Business plans going outside your enterprise are even less likely to be read. Around six out of ten plans are junked before the recipients have read even the first page fully. If your mail contained ten business plans a day or a week, you could not read them all. How would you discriminate between them?

I have already mentioned the case where a plan produced by a top-grade bank was binned by a top-rank finance house because the executive summary contained one almost irrelevant factual error.

Ten reasons given by investors for discarding business plans are listed on page 292. Obviously, these do not apply to all readers and all plans. I know of capital providers who have backed a brilliant idea that was presented in possibly the world's scruffiest plan. And there are certainly instances where professional advisers have produced plans that have been financed. But there are some useful – and obvious – warning lights in the illustrations. I regularly hear the following comments.

● If the management has not taken trouble in producing a decent plan, how can we expect them to run the business properly?

● If a key fact is missing – such as market size, selling skills, capital required – we have to assume that the managers don't know this important information or do not have required skills in areas that are glossed over.

I know that you are not going to make such basic errors, because if you were you would not have taken the trouble to read this book. So assuming that you make it past this broad level of discrimination, what are the next stumbling blocks?

'Everything that can be invented has been invented.'
CHARLES H. DUELL, COMMISSIONER, US OFFICE OF PATENTS, 1899

The key questions that potential financiers are going to ask as they work through your business plan are listed in Figure 12.1. They are trying to measure:

● the validity of business ideas;

● the quality of the management team;

● the commercial viability of the business;

● how much money you need, what you need it for, and how you are going to pay it back.

Every reader will want to see that you are presenting an attractive business. For an existing organisation, the track record is of overwhelming importance. For a new business proposal, the perceived quality of the management weighs heavily. At one extreme, banks are very unlikely to lend to a brand new venture. They are less impressed with new ideas and are more enthusiastic about established businesses. At the other limit, equity investors usually want to see something unique – more so in a start-up situation.

With specific regard to the finance, bankers are more concerned with security and cash flow. As you know, they lend to you only if you can prove that you do not really need the money and you can definitely afford to pay it back. Equity stakeholders are more interested in the size of the return that they might make. The bigger the better. But do not make the mistake of thinking that just because *shareholders' funds* are sometimes called *risk capital*, shareholders enjoy risk. As a crowd, they are every bit as conservative as bankers. We need to look in more detail at how readers will assess your financials.

Ten reasons business plans fail at first glance

1 The presentation is too scruffy or too slick – it feels amateur or false.

2 The text is too long, with too many generalisations, too much waffle.

3 The text is too short, too weak and vague.

4 Whatever the length, there are not enough hard facts and details.

5 There are errors of fact (a major sin).

6 Specific omissions suggest that vital skills, resources or knowledge are lacking.

7 There is not enough what-if analysis? (What if sales drop 10%? Increase 10%? If interest rates rise one percentage point?)

8 The financial projections are unreasonably optimistic, especially if sales or cash flow improve unrealistically smoothly – without seasonal variation or downward blips.

9 The plans are obviously produced to raise finance, not for running the business.

10 The plan was produced by professional consultants, raising doubt about the management's own skills.

Why plans fail after passing the first glance

If business plans are rejected after passing the first glance, it is usually because they do not answer the questions in Figures 12.1 and 12.3. The most common omission is failing to reassure the reader that marketing and sales *will* bring home the silver. The second most frequent problem is lack of operational detail – *how* it will happen. Both of these boil down to a weakness in (explaining) the strategy. Beyond these factual details, the major hurdle for new ventures is conveying your vision – as shown by the quotations scattered throughout this chapter.

Those financials again

Remember how you looked out of the window and compared yourself with other companies in your industry (see Chapter 5). Recall how you valued capital projects and assessed your rate of return (see Chapter 11). This is exactly how others – bosses, bankers and backers – will crawl over the financials in your business plan. You know how you did the analysis so it should not be too hard to visualise how others will do it to you. They will:

- review your break even position to ensure you have comfortable safety margins;

- look at the state of your profit and loss account and compare costs and revenues;

- analyse your balance sheet, checking for liquidity and valuable assets;

- examine your cash flow to ensure that it is healthy;

- compare you against other companies in similar industries.

None of this should hold any terrors for you – you have already worked through these details. However, as promised earlier, now is a good time to run through the measurements that are taken during your health check.

If you go to a doctor for a medical check-up, you will be measured exhaustively. A nurse will check your age, height, weight, blood pressure, pulse, take a blood sample and so on. Interesting stuff, but so what if your red blood count is 4 million/ml? This is meaningless unless explained and compared against some measure. You do not want to be in good shape for a 60-year-old if you are only 32. This is exactly how it is with many of your financials.

Figure 12.1 The things that they want to know!

Everybody

1 Can the management adequately describe their ideas? Do they have good communication skills?
2 If it is an existing business, how has it been managed up to now?
3 What is the quality of the management?
4 Do they understand their business? Do they have a penetrating understanding of critical factors such as costs per item, break even, sales per product?
5 Do they understand the market? Who will buy? Why?
6 Do they understand the competition? Who are the key competitors? What is their market share?
7 Where is the action plan? How will theory be turned into action?

Fussy equity investors

Funding requirements
8 How much funding is required?
9 What will the money be used for?
10 What will we be buying – in terms of fixed assets, intellectual property, dreams?

The history
11 How much money has gone in already?
12 How much came from the existing owners?*
13 Where else did it come from?
14 How was it used?
15 With what results?

The future
16 How will further expansion be funded?
17 How will our investment grow and how will it be diluted by further share issues?

The deal
18 What percentage of the company is on offer?
19 At what price?
20 What sort of shareholders are required? Passive or active. With specific skills, expertise, contacts?
21 How will investors unlock future value?
22 What will be the return on equity?
23 What are the risks of losing the investment?

Easy-to-please bankers!

8 Is there adequate security for loans?

9 Will there be adequate cash flow to pay interest and repay principal?

* Yes, I know that the owners, logically, own 100% of the issued capital. However, a founder presenting a plan might have spent his entire savings and mortgaged his house in return for 10% of the equity, or he might have risked almost nothing in return for 90%. A big difference in *perceived* commitment.

Take an obvious example. A high proportion of overdue *accounts receivable* might be normal for a company selling household appliances on credit, but it would be very odd for a clothing retailer with a cash-based business.

There is a message here. I can show you some of the figures that bankers and other investors will look at, but you have to use your own knowledge of your industry to know whether yours look good, bad or indifferent.

Of course, you have to compare like with like. If you assemble computers from components sourced overseas, your balance sheet will look very different from another computer company that itself manufactures the main boards. They will use more machinery and equipment than you. They probably have more fixed assets – and this means that the ratio of their sales to assets will be smaller than yours if you have the same market share.

> If you look poor against an industry average, but good against a specific competitor, make sure that you are compared with the company not the average. You could make specific reference to this by identifying the best comparison, or by including some helpful figures that do the work. Take care to explain it well, or a naïve reader stumbling upon the poor comparison might think that you had deliberately tried to mislead.

What will readers look at? Some key indicators are shown on the following pages. You will find that the names, constituent parts and arithmetic vary from country to country – and indeed from analyst to analyst. For example, the *receivables turnover ratio* – sales divided by accounts receivable – in the US is turned upside down in the UK and called the *trade debtors to sales multiple* – trade debtors (that is, accounts receivable) divided by sales.

Different name. Different way of expressing the relationship. Same message. Incidentally, try to use the terms familiar to your readers.

However, from the information given, you should be able to cope with the indicators whatever guise they are wearing when you meet them. I have written the commentary as if you were the one interpreting the indicators, because this is how I want you to look at your business plan right now. You do not need to worry too much about the arithmetic – just look at what is being compared with what. When you have glanced through these examples, I will show you a delightful relationship that will help clarify the meaning of it all.

> Do you need a summarised plan? Sometimes commentators suggest sending the executive summary only to your targets, and following up with the full plan in due course. I am not enthusiastic about this. If you decide that you do need a summary, extract the appropriate information from your full plan to create a short version (with its own executive summary). Make it lighter – closer to magazine format – and indicate that a detailed plan is available.

What do I get for my money?

Where possible, include in your business plan a table showing how you will use the funds. If you can demonstrate *increasing value* at the same time you will make your backers feel much more comfortable.

The following schedule shows how the funds will be applied. By the end of July, total outlays of $500,000 will have secured assets and inventory with a book value of $485,000 (value will be added by manufacturing process). We will also have an exclusive sales licence for Africa which we value at. …

Date	Item	Amound payable	Running total	Comment
1 June	Deposit for machine	10,000	10,000	Refundable
15 June	Legal fees	15,000	25,000	Exclusivity for Africa
25 June	Deposit for prototype	25,000	50,000	Refundable
1 July	Machine delivered	90,000	140,000	100% increase in capacity
12 July	Inventory delivered	200,000	340,000	Basic inputs for production
18 July	…			

Indicators of liquidity

Liquidity ratios indicate whether the business is likely to be able to meet its financial obligations as they fall due.

Indicator	Comment
Current ratio Current assets *divided by* Current liabilities	If the answer to this simple sum is less than 1, current liabilities exceed current assets. It looks as if you cannot meet your daily commitments. A figure of 2 used to be a safe rule of thumb (current assets are twice current liabilities) but 1.5 is often acceptable.
Acid test (quick ratio) Cash, marketable securities and accounts receivable *divided by* Current liabilities	This is similar to the current ratio but it excludes inventory and other current assets that are likely to be difficult to turn into cash. It is a better measure of current liquidity. A result of 1 is a useful rule of thumb – but businesses that buy on credit and sell for cash (e.g. food retailing) may have acid test ratios as low as 0.2. This shows how careful you have to be interpreting ratios.

Debt indicators

Indicators of debt reveal whether a business is borrowing too much (in which case it might have to look to equity for additional funding), or whether the company could borrow more.

Indicator	Comment
Leverage (US) or gearing (UK) **Debt** (liabilities) *Divided by* Equity	This indicates the extent to which a company is dependent on debt or equity. Low leverage (low gearing) indicates a low reliance on debt – finance is mainly equity – which suggests less risk of a cash flow crisis and a greater likelihood of borrowing if required.
Debt to net worth Total debt (liabilities) *divided by* Tangible net worth (owners' equity less intangible assets)	This compares what is owned with what is owed. A high ratio (e.g. if it was 2 then liabilities would be twice tangible net worth) indicates that creditors' claims exceed those of the owners. In this case a business is *borrowed up* and its ability to raise more debt is in question – equity might be the only way to go.
Debt-service coverage Cash flow from operations (profit before interest and tax) *divided by* Annual interest payments	This is a measure of a company's ability to meet its interest on borrowings. The higher the ratio the more likely it is that the business will be able to pay interest on (i.e. *service*) its debt. A figure of at least 3 is usually considered safe, and would be a good sign for a company wanting to borrow more. A figure of below 1 indicates a high risk of default or bankruptcy.
Contingent liabilities Contingent liabilities *divided by* Owners' equity	Recall from Chapter 10 that contingent liabilities are probable or possible liabilities that do not show as actual liabilities on the balance sheet. Contingent liabilities that are large in relation to equity could seriously undermine financial stability if they materialised into payments due.

'This "telephone" has too many shortcomings to be seriously considered as a means of communication. The device is inherently of no value to us.'

WESTERN UNION INTERNAL MEMORANDUM, 1876

'We don't like their sound and guitar music is on the way out.'

DECCA RECORDING COMPANY, REJECTING THE BEATLES IN 1962

Indicators of profitability and operating efficiency

Indicator

Comment

Profit margin
Trading profit
(before tax, interest, etc.)
divided by
Sales

This indicates the profit per unit of currency of sales. A low figure is not necessarily bad – for supermarkets it can fall to 1% – check against inventory and receivables turnover, asset value, gross profit margins, etc. and the industry average. A figure below the industry average might indicate low prices and/or high costs.
A high figure might attract competitors.

Return on total assets (return on capital employed)
Trading profit
(before interest and tax)
divided by
Total assets
OR
(Assets less current liabilities)

This is clearly important as a measure of the company's operating efficiency. A low return on assets or capital employed (very similar, given the relationship between balance sheet entries) suggests a candidate for disposal – or bankruptcy in the next economic downturn. If the return is below the cost of loans, additional borrowing will reduce earnings per share. This measure provides a good yardstick for assessing new ventures – if their return is below it, it will be clawed down.

Turnover of (working) capital
Sales
divided by
Capital employed
OR
Working capital (current assets less current liabilities)

This measures sales per unit of capital. It shows how efficiently capital is being used to generate sales. A low ratio (sales are low relative to capital) tends to suggest that capital is not being used profitably. At the other extreme, a very high ratio of sales to working capital warns of *overtrading* – inadequate working capital which could put creditors at risk. Watch also that a growing ratio might indicate that plant and machinery is not being kept up to date (depreciation is reducing the capital base and making the ratio look better).

Receivables turnover (trade debtors to sales)
Accounts receivable
divided by
Sales

This shows credit allowed to customers. If payment is collected by the end of the month following delivery, receivables will run at about 12% of sales. A high figure might indicate sloppy financial control. A reduction might suggest better control – or reflect a desperate need for cash. Factoring (selling) debts also reduces the figure.

Payables turnover (trade creditors to sales) Accounts payable *divided by* Sales	This indicates the amount of trade credit that a company is allowed by its suppliers. Watch trends over time – an increase might indicate a rise in trade credit necessitated by cash flow problems. Other measures used include: – Payables to inventory – which shows what proportion of stocks is financed by suppliers (exceeds 100% in food retailing). – Debtors to receivables – where sudden big changes can also give early warning of cash flow pressures.
Inventory/stock turnover Cost of goods sold *divided by* Average inventory (half opening plus closing stock)	This shows how fast inventory is moving through the business. A high turnover indicates healthy, saleable and liquid inventory with lower demands on cash flow (or maybe there are stock shortages!). A low average turnover suggests overstocking and dated merchandise (or stockpiling to meet seasonal demand). Calculating the average from only two days a period is highly dangerous if those are not representative days. I am sure that you would not manage your inventory levels to influence this ratio.

Investment indicators

Indicator	Comment
Return on equity Profit (after tax) *divided by* Owners' equity	Alternative measures of return (return on assets and return on capital employed) are significant for the *business manager*. But this one, return on equity, is critical to *shareholders*. It is their bottom line. By the way, contrast this with bankers – whose bottom line is interest and security.
Earnings per share (EPS) Profit *divided by* Number of ordinary shares	The profit attributable to each ordinary share (i.e. after tax, etc.) is one statistic that you cannot compare between companies directly – it depends on the number of shares issued. But the trend over time is often regarded as critical – for many companies, steady long-term growth in earnings per share is *the* central objective.

**Price earning (ratio/
multiple) – PE/PER**
Share price
divided by
Earnings per share

The price earnings ratio indicates the number of years' earnings acquired when you buy one share. It reflects the market's expectation of future earnings growth – and it is a crucial measure of the value of a company (see Chapter 10). It is the carrot to dangle in front of investors, because it indicates the way that they will be able to leverage their share value on the way out.

**Dividend cover
(payout ratio when
inverted)**
Earnings per share
divided by
Net dividend per share

Dividend cover indicates how many times the dividend is covered by profits. A high cover (low payout ratio) suggests that profits are being reinvested for future growth – and that there is sufficient margin to ensure that dividends will remain stable. The opposite suggests that dividends might disappear in a downturn.

Net asset value
(Ordinary) shareholders'
equity
divided by
Net dividend per share

Net asset value indicates the proportion of the share price that is represented by assets (albeit at book value) – the other portion of the price therefore reflecting expectations about profits. The alternative is market capitalisation to book value (how much it would cost you to buy all the

Market to book
(see comments)

Company's shares – and how much you would get back if you sold all the assets and settled all liabilities). These indicators reveal exactly what the market thinks about the value of the company's future income stream.

Economic value added (Note: EVA is based on the work of Professors Franco Modigliani and Merton H. Miller, extended and trade marked by Stern, Stewart & Company; EVA momentum is a further development by Stewart.)

Indicator

Comment

Economic value added
Net operating profit *less*
taxes *less* cost of capital.

A measure of value and performance. When profits exceed the cost of doing business and the cost of capital, the firm creates wealth for the shareholders. Here, capital includes cash, inventory and receivables (working capital), plus equipment, computers and real estate. The cost of capital is the rate of return required by the shareholders and lenders to finance the operations of the business.

EVA momentum
This year's EVA minus last
year's EVA *all divided* by last
year's sales revenue

A measure of the EVA growth rate, scaled to the sales size of the business, and therefore directly comparable across businesses of differing sizes and in differing industries.

IT DEPENDS WHAT YOU MEAN BY RETURN?

Everyone wants to know what *return on investment* (ROI) they will earn – how much will they get back in return for their outlays?

- For **lenders**, the ROI is the interest that you pay them on the money loaned.

- **Equity investors'** ROI is measured by *return on equity* (ROE) – since, of course, their investment is your equity capital.

- For you, as the **business manager**, the ROI that you are interested in is *return on capital employed* (ROCE) or *return on assets* (ROA).

This is straightforward. If someone enquires about ROI, just ask *who wants to know?* ROE is important to equity investors, so we should look at how they will extract its likely *outturn* from your financials.

> *'Who the hell wants to hear actors talk?'*
>
> H. M. WARNER, WARNER BROTHERS, 1927 ON THE
> INTRODUCTION OF SOUND IN MOVING PICTURES

KEY INFLUENCES ON RETURN ON EQUITY

The way that the objectives of company management and of investors hang together is illustrated in Figure 12.2. The connection between the two sides of the diagram is self-evident. Vary one number in the profit and loss account or balance sheet, and this must result in a change in the return on equity. It does not take a genius to see this. However, if you follow the logic through the centre – and remember that assets = liabilities (debt) plus equity – you can see how the following classic relationship holds true:

$$\frac{Profit}{Sales} \times \frac{Sales}{Assets} \times \frac{Assets}{Equity} = \frac{Profit}{Equity}$$

Or, essentially:

$$Profit\ margin \times Asset\ turnover \times Leverage = ROE$$

Thus, increase any one of the terms on the left (profit margin, asset turnover or leverage) and you increase return on equity. Some companies actually manage these indicators specifically. You can see why equity investors enjoy them.

> *'Airplanes are interesting toys but of no military value.'*
> MARSHALL FERDINAND FOCH, PROFESSOR OF STRATEGY, ECOLE SUPERIEURE DE GUERRE

Figure 12.2 How it all fits together

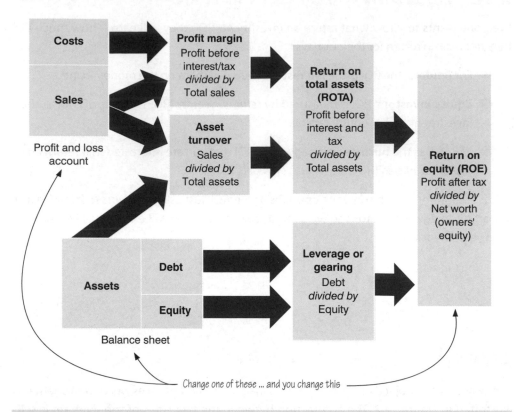

 # Health warning: watch all the gauges

The nice people with money are going to be very interested in the potential return on their investment. But beware of the perils of monitoring the health of your business using too few indicators.

Here's why. In 2008 Lehman Brothers collapsed. Overnight it went from being the fourth largest US investment bank, to the world's largest bankruptcy case – with US$619 billion (yes, billion) in debt. Why? Executive pay was linked to return on equity (ROE). Borrow more, ROE increases; get paid more; never mind the firm's burgeoning debt.

Measuring performance using one indicator is similar to driving a car using only the speedometer. All well and good but if you don't notice the engine temperature rising, oil pressure falling, or revs going off the scale, the engine will seize and you won't be going anywhere anymore.

Post-Lehman, commentators are showing interest in a comparatively new indicator called EVA momentum (see page 300) that takes a broader view of corporate performance. EVA momentum rankings for top US companies are now being published in journals such as *Fortune* and *Forbes*. See this book's website for more information.

Final check on the plan

You have now reviewed your business plan from the perspective of a potential reader. Does the plan answer satisfactorily their likely questions? From this perspective, Figure 12.3 illustrates the six most important pages in your plan.

- **For the business proposition**, check that your strategy has unique attributes, that you do not appear unduly reliant on one supplier, one product or one customer and that you do not look vulnerable to attack by a big competitor. These should not be problems given your journey through this book.

- **For the finances**, check that you have highlighted sufficiently the prospective cash flow. Corporate bosses and bankers will be interested in return on capital employed or (almost the same thing) return on total assets. If you are looking for shareholders, emphasise the potentially excellent return on equity.

- **For a non-profit plan**, check that you have highlighted potential attainment required objectives – social welfare, development assistance, *customer service*, prestige, etc.

When you are comfortable that your business plan will do its job, go back to the executive summary and conclusion (Chapter 3) and rewrite them. Make sure that they read well and highlight the key facts. In this connection, take a look at Figure 12.3.

At last, you are ready to launch the plan. But do not act too hastily. Please read the next section first.

They don't know what's coming to them

 Never deliver a copy of your business plan to someone unless they request it specifically.

But I was going to send it to those venture capital people in the new business park? Don't. You have to make them ask for a copy. Then you have shifted the focus. It is no longer the case that you are sending the plan to an unwitting recipient. They have asked to see it, are expecting it, and are more likely to give it consideration.

> 'There is no reason anyone would want a computer in their home.'
> KEN OLSEN, PRESIDENT, CHAIRMAN AND FOUNDER, DIGITAL EQUIPMENT CORP, 1977

Figure 12.3 Six key pages in your business plan

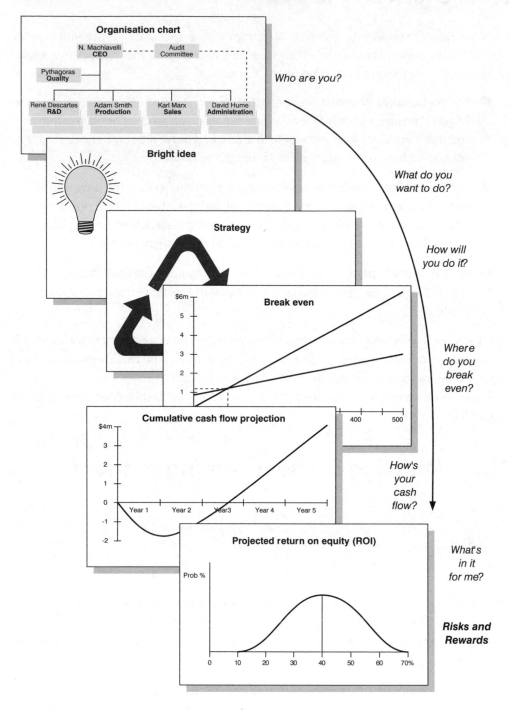

The first thing that you need to know is the name of the right person. The general rule is to go in at the top, or as far up the ladder as possible. Sometimes it might be better to approach a specialist somewhere down the ladder, especially if you know that they will be sympathetic to your cause. If you have a biotech business, you might telephone *those venture capital people*, and ask the receptionist for the name of their biotechnology expert. Never allow the telephone call to be connected unless you know the name of the person to whom you want to speak. But you probably do not want to be connected right now.

 These are my preferred techniques for contacting your target, with the best at the top of the list.

1   Have a respected mutual acquaintance introduce you, preferably at a social gathering.

2   Contrive to meet the intended recipient by 'chance' at a business or social function.

3   Telephone, introduce yourself, and try to arrange a meeting.

4   Write introducing yourself and asking for a meeting.

Do not say too much or hand over the business plan yet.

You want the target to confirm that they do make the required type of investments. Then you make a one-line reference to your proposition, and hold your breath. With any luck they will pick up on your comment. If they do not, you might have to ask directly. Tell them as succinctly as possible:

● **Why they should be interested in you** – *I have invented* …

● **What you have** – … a safety device that saves companies thousands a week …

● **What you want** – … and I need additional funding to expand the market.

Notice the example. One sentence. A statement of benefits – no specific mention of the product. An indication that you need funding for a purpose, but again no specifics. Some people might go further than this and say that they are looking for an *investor* (customers do not spend, they invest) *to help finance a specific project with guaranteed returns*. Try not to be drawn into great detail yet, but remember that you want to establish a working relationship with them. Your sole objective is to have them ask you for a business plan. If you are unlucky, if you get a flat no, ask for a referral to another potential investor. Then you have a head start when you speak to that person. *Joe Smith told me that you might be interested in* …

You probably want to start making notes, documenting telephone conversations, delivery dates and so on. Keep good records and you will not be caught out. In particular, note which version of the business plan you will hand over. Otherwise, later on, after knocking on a hundred doors looking for start-up capital, you will be so tired that you will not remember what you gave to, or followed up with, whom.

 Overheard at the golf club

'George, I'd like you to meet Joe.'
'Nice to meet you, did you have a good game. ...'
After a few moments general chat:
'George, Maggie told me that you are a banker.'
'Yes, I've just taken over the corporate finance department.'
'That's interesting, I'm looking for funding to expand my marketing company.'
'It might be of interest to us, do you have a business plan?'
'Of course. Maybe I could bring it round to your office next week?'
'Check with my secretary. I'm probably free on Wednesday afternoon.'

DELIVERY

Once a plan has been requested, write a suitable covering letter and deliver it in person if possible. Try to hand it directly to the reader so that there is a clearly identifiable connection between your plan and you. Just in case you are called upon to explain the content, prepare for the first meeting properly as described below before making the delivery.

I'M NOT SIGNING THAT

If you are protective of the information in your business plan – and remember it contains your strategy, your secrets – you are fully entitled to ask readers to sign a confidentiality agreement before delivery. Some plan owners are embarrassed about doing this. There is no need to be. Some financiers get uppity. They are entirely in the wrong. Professional bankers and investors understand that you are entrusting them with trade secrets and will sign without hesitation. Well, after one hesitation. They could well want their legal adviser to review the agreement first. Be ready to accept their own form of words, a simplified agreement, or tolerate a slight delay.

CHASING IT

No matter how often you check your mail, there is nothing from the bank. No matter how hard you stare at the telephone, it does not ring. When will your nerve break? When will you chase the target? Circumstances might guide you. If not, a telephone call after about two weeks will probably nudge things along. Invariably, when this is necessary it means that your plan was sitting still unread in an in-tray. As I keep saying, it is really difficult to persuade people to find the time to read your plan. This is one of the reasons why you want to make it *flickable* and include photographs and charts to pull in the potential reader. Presentation is everything right now.

Preparing for the meeting

Usually your first meeting is a round-table discussion, a general chat. You are more likely to make a formal presentation at internal corporate reviews. Sometimes this is requested at second or third meetings with external sources of funding – but I have seen or made formal presentations at probably only 1 in 100 outside business plan meetings.

Nevertheless, it is important to be ready to give a formal or semi-formal presentation of the plan. Whether or not you expect to make a presentation, it is a good idea to prepare enough slides or handouts to take you through the key points. Again, the key is remembering what the audience wants to hear and telling it to them.

Try to find out who will be at the meeting and how they will fit into the decision -making process (see *Seven groups at the conference table*, page 290). For example, if a lawyer will be there, you might expect questions about your copyright or patents, while an accountant is more likely to quiz you on financial details.

You know almost for certain that when you arrive at the meeting, you will be the only person who has read the plan from cover to cover. You might want to think about how you will explain the contents. If you have done your homework properly, you can use the list of contents as your (informal) agenda.

> Whatever the occasion, you should probably prepare some hand-outs. If it is my plan, I usually print a few of the charts, each one as large as possible in colour on a single sheet of crisp A4 or letter paper. Make sure that you have enough copies so that you can give one to each person in the meeting. Then, if the discussion turns to an appropriate topic – such as break even, sales, or cash flow – you can produce a picture to illustrate your point. Include a cross-reference to the business plan so listeners can later find and read the associated commentary.

PERSONAL PRESENTATION

The day has finally come. It's terrible weather so you wear a track suit and put your copy of the business plan in a plastic bag to keep it dry. Your car breaks down. The train is cancelled. You arrive late, soaked through by the rain, and looking thoroughly dishevelled. What impression have you made?

No one would be this careless? This would not happen, I hear you say. Wrong. I have seen people arrive at meetings in *exactly* this way. Forget self-importance. Make sure that you are early. Be dressed appropriately and well groomed, and for goodness sake find a decent folder or briefcase to hold your papers.

> *'The concept is interesting and well formed, but in order to earn better than a C the idea must be feasible.'*
> YALE UNIVERSITY MANAGEMENT PROFESSOR RESPONDING TO A PROPOSAL FOR A RELIABLE OVERNIGHT DELIVERY SERVICE PRESENTED BY FRED SMITH WHO WENT ON TO FOUND FEDERAL EXPRESS CORP.

Think about what your audience is expecting and try not to create any surprises. You do not want to get snagged on someone's personal prejudices. This is not the day to make a stand over the right to dress as you wish. In particular, wear your smartest *business uniform*. Corporate executives are usually attired in formal business suits. Fashion designers present themselves in the latest style of semi-formal day-wear – probably their own creation. Artists are allowed to be a touch creative in their dress sense. The one exception is if you are an economist, computer programmer or playwright then leave the carpet slippers and cardigan behind. You want to give the impression that you are part of your industry and you are a competent businessperson. Almost anywhere in the world, dark suits help convey an impression of business competence – unless you usually wear a dishdasha, toga or barong to the office. Whatever it is, make sure that it is immaculate.

At last, the first meeting

When you finally sit down to talk to the nice people with the money, whoever they are, you will find that their focus is on *what-how-money* in exactly this order.

1   **What** – what is your business proposition?

2   **How** – how will you achieve the intended results?

3   **Money** – how will the funds be applied and what do your financials look like?

They want to get a clear idea about the business before they look at the numbers. Of course, you might begin with two minutes on the amount and terms that you are looking for – otherwise you could all be wasting your time. There is little point in talking to a leasing company about factoring (selling them) your trade debts.

If the ball is thrown to you immediately, I suggest that you start by telling them about yourself. If you have gone along to the meeting with colleagues, introduce them also. Explain who you are and why you are there. Give yourself credibility by mentioning relevant experiences and successes. *I am a research chemist with 20 years' experience in the petroleum industry … .*

As already indicated, assume that you are the only person in the room who has read the business plan. Never show exasperation when others do not know the most basic of details. Explain it to them carefully and gently, avoiding jargon. Use anecdotes to introduce complex topics.

SELL TO THE QUEEN BEE

Remember to sell to everyone present, and especially to the person who will make the decision (again, see *Seven groups at the conference table*, page 290). The person showing most interest or asking many questions may be trying to impress the boss, but might not have any influence in the decision-making process. Of course, your answers and the respect you show to everyone are critical, especially if the thoughtful observer who says nothing and leaves early turns out to be in charge of hand-outs from the honey pot.

COPING WITH QUESTIONS

The most common error that I observe at meetings is that people actually answer the questions that are asked. The worst offenders are technical experts called in for the day who are eager to please.

Do not answer until you know what it is that the questioner wants to find out. Sometimes queries are badly phrased. Remember that the people you are meeting are probably not experts in your business and they might make errors when using jargon or when making assumptions. You might find it useful to restate the enquiry so that it is clear what question you are answering.

When you know what the question is, always ask yourself – and perhaps the questioner – *why do they want to know?* This is easiest to illustrate in a sales situation.

Invariably, technical staff do not realise that they have made these mistakes and the prospective customers remain disappointed (and prospective). Much better to determine what the customers want to hear and make them happy. This is exactly how it is when presenting business plans. Tell them what they want to hear – of course, within the bounds of honesty – not what you think they want to hear.

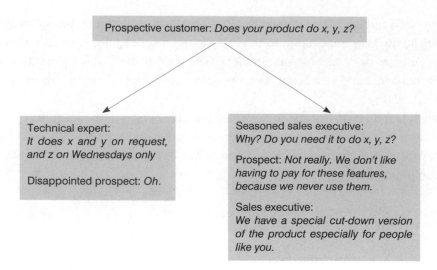

Prospective customer: *Does your product do x, y, z?*

Technical expert:
*It does x and y on request,
and z on Wednesdays only*

Disappointed prospect: *Oh.*

Seasoned sales executive:
Why? Do you need it to do x, y, z?

Prospect: *Not really. We don't like
having to pay for these features,
because we never use them.*

Sales executive:
*We have a special cut-down version
of the product especially for people
like you.*

BODY LANGUAGE

Body language is hugely important. Yours and theirs. It is terrible listening to people talking about their business plan if they are slumped in their seat and mumbling. If you are bored with your business, how can you expect someone else to be enthusiastic? In fact, executives tend to take more notice of business plans when they are presented with enthusiasm. *She is certainly excited by her plan, let's take a closer look* is the sort of comment that I have heard frequently after these meetings.

By the same token, if you notice signs of boredom in your audience, you need to liven up your presentation, change tack, or otherwise create some excitement. Directing a question to the disinterested person might help bring them back into the conversation. Watch your audience carefully. Listen aggressively. Pick up on interests *and* concerns.

PLAN FOR ACTION

As the meeting draws to a close, try to establish a clear point of contact, agreed actions and a key date.

More important perhaps, you want to know who is responsible for assessing your plan and how long they will take. Try to establish agreement that you will work closely with this person. Immediately schedule a meeting for just after they have conducted their preliminary review so that you can answer the questions that will arise. When you have agreement to this, and as you leave, suggest that you will call them the next morning to see if they need anything else from you.

While you are focusing on the lead analyst, do not overlook the most senior person present. Suggest that you telephone that person *maybe in a couple of weeks* to obtain his or her latest views on your proposition. You now have a plan for follow up.

Meeting post-mortems

While the meeting is still fresh in your mind, replay it mentally and consider if your business plan did its job. Make notes for reference and list the topics to cover at the next meeting. Were there questions that the plan does not answer? Did you identify the decision-makers? Were there prejudices or concerns that conflict with the plan? Were you asked for further information that could have been in the plan? You might want to revise the document, especially if you expect to be showing it to other people.

When you are in a repetitive cycle, you will certainly want to make sure that next year's plan covers these points.

Follow up

A short thank-you note is always a good idea after a meeting. If you were asked for further information that will take a few days to compile, write immediately confirming that the information will be forthcoming. Then provide it as promptly and accurately as possible. Do not forget to keep your own notes and diary up to date. You do not want to forget a vital deadline at this stage.

Telephone as promised. Build a relationship with the analyst and help him or her see things from your point of view. You want to aim for understanding, support and absolutely no hostility. Being asked for extra information (aside from suggesting that things might be missing from the plan) is generally a sign of progress.

I find that complex business proposals tend to spawn a series of related reports. For example, a request for technical information can be answered by a short technical appraisal written for the non-specialist. Aside from this, the most commonly used additional documents are a detailed market appraisal/marketing plan, and an FAQ – a list of *frequently asked questions* with answers. The Internet seems to have encouraged their use. I find them a very effective way of explaining concepts.

You might also bring together a set of information that helps backers with their *due diligence* – see page 313.

> 'A cookie store is a bad idea. Besides, the market research reports show that America likes crispy cookies, not the soft and chewy cookies like you make.'
> RESPONSE TO DEBBI FIELDS' IDEA OF STARTING MRS FIELDS COOKIES

CHASING AGAIN

Generally, you do not have to chase good news. If all goes quiet and you do not hear anything for a long time, it probably means that you are not going to get funding from that source. Of course, this is not necessarily the case. You should certainly never assume defeat. Always follow up positively. The agreement to telephone the most senior person at your first meeting provides an opportunity to do so without appearing to pester.

Interestingly, investors are remarkably bad at saying no. As a group, they prefer to let matters drift until the message sinks in, rather than helpfully saying 'sorry, not for us'. Bankers are better at this, having attended training courses dedicated to helping them say no.

> 'Most people give up just when they're about to achieve success. They quit on the one-yard line. They give up at the last minute of the game one foot from the winning touch.'
>
> H. ROSS PEROT

Back to the drawing board

If you are rejected, the best consolation that you can have is knowing why you failed. Always ask. At worst, you might learn something that will improve your business plan or next presentation. Or better, there might be a simple gap that you can close. *We like your proposal but we have decided not to invest unless we have. ...*

If you are getting nowhere, you need to consider redrafting some or all of your business plan, or maybe revisiting the strategy. I was once involved with a business plan for a unique invention. I cannot tell you about it specifically because it is still under wraps. The point is that there was absolutely no competition for this amazing item. But it soon became clear that saying this was counter-productive. Recipients of the business plan had to analyse the situation within their established framework – which includes competitive analysis. Once I had documented some theoretical competition – other things that consumers might spend their money on – the plan was much better received. It is partly this collection of experiences that has shaped this book's suggestions about 'what you put in a business plan'.

If you are looking for outside funding, use the first couple of meetings to build experience. Start opening up additional avenues as soon as possible. It can take three months (or three days) for someone to appraise your plan. If you have to approach ten sources of capital, you want them to be concurrent. Otherwise, if they were end-to-end you might spend three years raising the cash.

Due diligence

When your bosses or prospective financiers go ahead in principle with your proposal, they will start their review process described earlier. They will also make other investigations to confirm that you are legal, decent and honest. This is quite simple for internal plans, more complex for external business plans. Whoever approves your plan will want evidence on file that they have exercised *due diligence* in deciding to provide you with backing.

> Indeed, the business plan is a key document. Sometimes its main purpose seems to be to go on file as protection for the decision-maker. It must be a fair and truthful assessment of the situation. Users will do their painstaking best to confirm that it is, but whatever happens it is you who will be held responsible at the end of the day.

External financiers will want to see the organisation's memorandum and articles of association, by-laws or charter and its certificate of incorporation, licence, etc. These prove legal existence and confirm that you can do what you are proposing. You will probably need a board resolution or a secretary's certificate authorising a share issue, borrowing, legal charge over assets and any other major undertaking. Depending on the situation, investors will want to see existing partnership or shareholders' agreements, loan agreements and security charges, franchise and licence agreement, etc.

For external funding, an auditors' report will be required if the business is already trading. The cynical say that the audit fee is hush money that obtains acceptance of your accounting principles. I have seen *start-ups* with an auditors' report confirming share capital of $1 and a bank balance of $1. This doesn't really prove anything, except perhaps a relationship with a respectable professional adviser.

Evidence of relationships with other professionals such as accountants, tax advisers and lawyers might be requested and may be investigated. Expect backers to ask for bankers' references for the directors and for the business and to check for criminal records and outstanding legal claims. Other checks that financiers make in pursuit of their *due diligence* will include character and employers' references for you and for other senior directors.

Eventually, someone might even check to see if your product really exists and does what you say it does.

LIFE IS A TWO-WAY STREET

You would not buy a Rolex watch from a plausible stranger in a bar because it still works after he dropped it in a glass of beer and he swears that it is legitimate. So do not assume a slick investor with a big office, a smooth story and a glossy sell is a safe source for your funding.

Remember that life is a two-way street and you have to exercise due diligence before accepting money from a stranger. Make sure that you do not unwittingly help to launder drug money or other illegally obtained funds. Unless you are dealing with a well-known and reputable company, you should take up your own references and keep them safely on file. You do not want funding at *any* cost. This goes for extortionate funding as well, which brings us to the contract.

The contract

Experienced and professional lenders and investors will want to use their own legal agreements setting out the terms of the funding, security and repayment if appropriate, and obligations on both parties.

Newcomers to the game – including but not limited to family, friends and angels – usually go over the top. Often, they retain a lawyer who has not done this before either, who attempts to earn a fat fee by drafting the world's longest agreement. Try to keep it short and simple (as well as professional and legally effective).

Make absolutely sure that you review any agreement before signing. Check that the terms and conditions are acceptable. Almost certainly have a trained corporate-finance lawyer make sure that there are no traps. Just occasionally, unscrupulous investors deliberately strangle a company's cash flow to force non-compliance with deadlines, and then wrest ownership from the people who did all the work. Do not be caught in this way. Never be bamboozled into signing. I have heard *sign now on these terms or we walk away*. No legitimate and honest financier or investor would ask this. I have also seen entrepreneurs desperate enough to sign anything because they were so exhausted by the funding process. Hang on to your business prowess and common sense.

Once signed, the agreement will quietly fade to yellow in a filing cabinet somewhere. You will only refer to it after signing if there is some conflict. If your relationship with your creditor or investor has sunk to the point where you need to rely on the small print, you can be sure that things will get nasty. Make sure that it is acceptable today, before you sign, while you are all good friends.

Talking about good friends, if you are working with partners in any new venture make sure you know them well. In fact, right at the outset before you write your business plan and start to look for finance, draw up some sort of partnership agreement between you. The stress of getting funding or the temptation of a large amount of money finally in the bank can make people do strange things. I've seen desperate men siphon off seed capital for personal use, crooks run off with a business plan and start their own business, and boardroom coups aimed at obtaining a bigger share of the pie for the perpetrators. And it's not just the money. The second largest area of dispute is *intellectual property*: which partner actually owns the ideas, trade names, logos and website domain names.

Cash in the bank

Finally, your plan is approved. Your balance sheet has changed. The total of *debt* or *equity* has increased and *cash at bank* has been boosted by a similar amount. This cash will soon run down as you convert the new-found liquidity into fixed assets, inventory and operating costs. The challenge is to move it through your profit and loss account and back on to a growing balance sheet as cash or investments on the assets side and a matching increase in retained earnings on the other side. The business plan's job is not done yet. It is time to take a look at how you use the plan to run a successful business. You have to prove that your plan will work. Chapter 13 takes you through that process.

Now make it happen

Great thoughts reduced to practice become great acts. HAZLITT

The journey through the business plan is now complete. You have a sparkling new plan with all the required approvals and funding. So where is it that you have arrived? Only at the starting point. You are embarking on a new era. You have a new or revitalised business to run. I am envious. I wish I was in your shoes at this moment. There is so much to do and it is all new and exciting.

In exactly the same way that I took you mechanically through the process of preparing a business plan, I will now run through the logical steps that turn a plan into reality. I think you will agree that these are simple and obvious. But please do not become obsessed with them. They are tools only. Your other management skills are much more important.

When you have completed this chapter, you will be armed with an excellent plan and a solid method of executing it. Then it is down to your personal and unique business acumen and skills. I know that you can make it happen. Good luck.

Time for a break?

You have produced a superb business plan. It has been approved by your shareholders, board of directors, bank manager, the boss or whoever. You have the required funding sitting in the bank. You know what has to be done. I guess that it is time to stick the business plan in a drawer, enjoy the honeymoon period and worry about getting results later.

This is the worst possible step to take. Start turning the plan into reality while it is still fresh. Extend it into policies and procedures, objectives and budgets. This is easy after all the hard work that you have done up to this point. Make it permeate every nook and cranny of the business. Monitor the results and the environment – watch the economy and especially your competitors, business partners and customers. Keep the plan up to date. Most important, revise the strategy and plan if new information so requires. Do anything other than put the plan away in a drawer.

From plan to reality

There is a simple relationship between a business plan and all those ring binders and papers on your shelves. This is illustrated in Figure 13.1. The business plan is the basis for creating:

- job descriptions;
- policies, rules and procedures;
- operational limits;
- budgets;
- employee objectives.

These are the things that get your people pulling together to make your business a success. We will run through them one by one. First, though, think about communicating your aims throughout your enterprise.

 Avoid bureaucracy

Please keep remembering that good management is the key. The mechanisms described in this chapter are just that – tools – but no more. Do not become bogged down in paperwork. Keep everything simple and efficient.

 The fast track to making it happen

1   Communicate the plan. Make sure that you have the widest possible understanding and commitment throughout your enterprise.

2   Develop policies, rules and procedures that extend the plan right to the very edges of your business.

3   Develop job descriptions and allocate responsibilities.

4   Set objectives for every employee.

5   Set spending and decision-making limits at the functional level (e.g. Head of R&D, accounts clerk grade 3) and the personal level (the Head Boffin, Bobby Bookkeeper).

6   Distribute budgets.

7   Monitor the objectives, budgets and the world.

8   Reward success.

9   Take confirmatory or corrective action as necessary. Revise the strategy and plan if necessary.

10   Feed back outcomes into the planning exercise and make a start developing the next business plan.

'He that is over-cautious will accomplish little.'

SCHILLER, *WILLIAM TELL*

Figure 13.1 Business plan to action and back

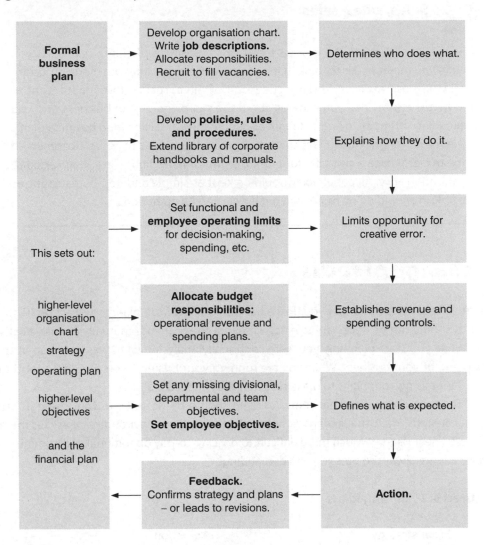

'First, make yourself a reputation for being a creative genius. Second, surround yourself with partners who are better than you are. Third, leave them to get on with it.'

DAVID OGILVY

Sales, sales, sales

This chapter describes the process that turns a business plan into reality. As you read it, you might begin to think that processes and procedures are more important than your business itself. This is just a result of the particular focus that I want to give here. I assume that you know all about the sharp end of your business, and you are reading this book to find out more about creating and executing business plans.

Never lose sight of the fact that all organisations exist to serve *customers* in some guise. Service – and sales for profit-making organisations – are what keep the organisation alive. All paperwork should be kept as simple and non-bureaucratic as possible. It should do no more than enable successful operations.

A change of focus

It hardly needs to be said that your focus has now shifted from planning to action (Figure 13.2). It should not be necessary to emphasise that these are not mutually exclusive activities. While you were planning, you were continually analysing what was going on at the sharp end of your business. While you are running your business you should be continually re-appraising your plans to make sure that they are still realistic.

All the new information that comes to hand should be slotted into your strategic and tactical analysis. You can react and adapt to changes in your environment. Easy for me to suggest, I hear you say. Much more difficult to do. Day-to-day operational and administrative issues are always so pressing and demanding.

Figure 13.2 Shifting focus

From strategy

- Positioning for the future
- Intellectual exercise
- Focus on effectiveness
- Analysis and intuition
- Fewer participants

To action

- Reacting as the future unfolds
- Operational undertaking
- Focus on efficiency
- Motivational/management skills
- Larger number of participants

However, you have a head start this time, because you developed a plan that is all yours – you sweated over it, lived and breathed it, burned the midnight oil possibly for several weeks developing it, fine tuning it, and now it is neatly bound and sitting on your desk.

You understand what it is trying to achieve and why. You know all its blind alleys, winding lanes and expressways that will eventually take you to success. You are much less likely to ignore *this* plan.

But what about that bright young technician in research and development, the enthusiastic new employee in marketing, the faithful old accounts manager who has been with you for years? Do they feel the same? In fact, do they even know that there is a plan? Or what is in the plan? Or why?

 This is the crux. The first thing that you have to do is communicate the plan to all those who could not be involved in its development. Help everyone understand and support the plan and get them working towards its success.

Of course, some elements of your plan might be trade secret. This is, after all, your intellectual property, your unique formula for success. You cannot patent a business plan (although a US federal appellate court ruled in late 1998 that an accounting method was eligible for a patent – possibly opening the door for better legal protection of business strategies in the future). You must, therefore, identify any elements of your strategy and plan that have to be restricted in their circulation. These are usually parts of the *strategy*. Once you start doing something *operationally*, the cat is at least peeping out of the bag.

I apologise for creating a little obstacle for you already. If, say, parts of your strategy are under wraps, how can anyone else understand the associated operating plans? Well, you have to adopt a sensible approach, maybe even stretch the truth. You can probably find logical reasons that explain the activities and motivate the troops while camouflaging the true objective from the enemy.

Communicating the plan

Motivation has to come from the top. I really do think that the ideal situation is for the big boss to hold a meeting with the largest practical number of employees to introduce the plan – not necessarily at a great level of detail. Lieutenants at that meeting can then hold separate briefing meetings at the next level of detail, and so on. Overlap helps (see Figure 13.3). If you are not right at the top, you might want to encourage your chief executive to kick off this process. If you have difficult labour relations or a highly unionised workforce, do not forget to keep union or staff representatives involved all along the way. Sometimes, it pays to let others think that they contributed and tacitly approved what you were going to do anyway.

Figure 13.3 Cascading meetings

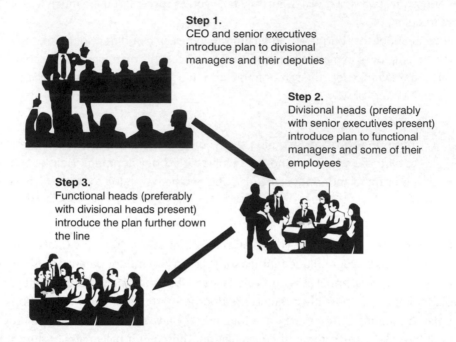

Step 1.
CEO and senior executives introduce plan to divisional managers and their deputies

Step 2.
Divisional heads (preferably with senior executives present) introduce plan to functional managers and some of their employees

Step 3.
Functional heads (preferably with divisional heads present) introduce the plan further down the line

Where do you draw the line?

Blowing your business-plan trumpet is fine. But you have to follow up rapidly with actions. This is going to sound familiar. A long time ago, back in Chapter 6, you set strategy and strategic objectives in an iterative process. You followed this through by developing operating plans and operating objectives in another set of intertwined activities. Yes, you guessed – you can now pick up from where you left off and do this at yet a finer level of detail.

The logical flow from strategy to action is shown in Figure 13.4. If you tried to document everything in your business plan, you would never get anything done. You have to draw a line somewhere – and this is where you stop adding detail to your business plan and move on to other things.

Take a look at Figure 13.5. This is very similar to the previous example. It shows how strategy thrusts (or trickles, depending on your management) down through your organisation. When operational plans are executed they result in single and repetitive processes that are guided by policies, rules and mini-plans. In developing these, you are extending your planning and control right through your business.

Figure 13.4 Drawing the line

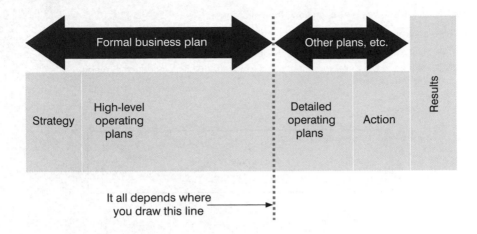

Policies, rules and procedures

All of us follow certain set rules and procedures. You put on your shoes *before* you tie your laces (theoretically, anyway). You buy a ticket *before* travelling on the underground, subway, metro, whatever you call it. Many of these things we learn by rote with coaching from a patient parent. Other routines we pick up deliberately or unconsciously from experience.

It is just the same in business. In your office, the last one to leave at night probably carries out the following procedure.

1 Checks that windows and secondary exit doors are secure.

2 Checks that everything that should be locked away is locked away (confidential papers, cookies and biscuits).

3 Checks that everything that should be switched on is on (fax and telephone answering machine).

4 Checks that everything that should be switched off is off (coffee machine, lights).

5 Sets the security alarm.

6 Exits and locks the door.

This is an example of a *standard operating procedure*. It might be undocumented. Or you might have made it into a little check-list and pasted it on to the wall by the door or put it into a big ring binder of procedures.

Figure 13.5 Getting to the action

This illustration shows how action flows from strategy.

The blue background represents policies and rules:

– Policies evolve from strategy, planning and activity.
– Policies lead to the development of rules, which themselves influence strategy, planning and action.

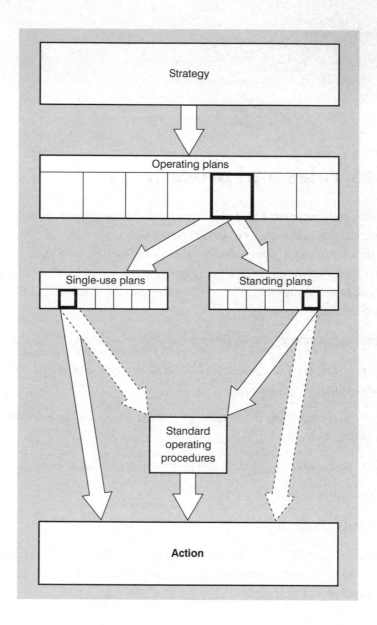

Procedures develop from your business plan in the following way.

1   Set *policies* that guide activities – someone has to lock up at night.

2   *Develop rules* – the last person to leave *will* set the alarm.

3   *Create procedures* – such as shown in the six steps above.

You will document all of these in varying degrees – keep them simple. Manifestations of policies, rules and procedures that are possibly already on your company bookshelves are listed opposite. You might want to make a list of handbooks and manuals that would guide decision-making and activities in your business. It might be much shorter than the list shown. Or it might be much more complex. (You could develop a *plan* for creating these documents.)

A warning:

> 'A person who is devoted to paperwork has lost the initiative. He is dealing with things that are brought to his notice, having ceased to notice anything for himself. He has been essentially defeated in his job.'
>
> PROFESSOR C. NORTHCOTE PARKINSON

It is a delight to be able to generate standard policies and procedures. In particular, get the procedure right, do it the same way every time, and the result is always consistent and as expected. This applies equally to processing customer orders, setting up manufacturing equipment, approving credit applications, etc.

Procedures make it easier for the next person, simplify staff training, are the basis for quality systems (such as promoted by the international standards organisation ISO) and – most important – help you please the customer. They do not, as human-resources-Luddites might suggest, take away employee dignity or creativity. Quite the opposite, procedures are the underlying framework that free resources for better things and – as it happens – create stability and consistency as a basis for standards and the ultimate reputation of your business.

We do not need to discuss this much further. You have probably spotted where I am heading. The finest business plan would be one that could be taken to the point where instructions it contains are phrased in terms of *follow procedure A, B, C*, etc. You really could play golf all day if your business was this well planned. Or at least, you could once you had decided who would execute the procedures.

Fifteen of the handbooks and manuals that should be on your shelves

1 **Quality Systems Manual** – perhaps the central reference that directs users to all other policies and procedures.

2 **Employee Handbook** – terms and conditions of employment, employee rights, health and safety.

3 **Employee Induction Handbook** – an introduction to the company, its mission and values, and basic rules and procedures.

4 **Employee Training Manual** – the application of policies and procedures to specific situations.

5 **Finance Manual** – policies and procedures to smooth and control the flow of payments and receipts.

6 **Legal Manual** – rules for contract administration, displaying copyright notices, etc.

7 **Purchasing Procedures** – how you buy supplies and where from, approved suppliers.

8 **Inventory Control Procedures** – the basics of stock control.

9 **Process Manuals** – how to do whatever it is you do: operate machinery, manufacture whatsits, cook and serve pizzas, produce software, write consultants' reports.

10 **Product Technical Manual** – the nuts and bolts of your product.

11 **Product User Manual** – instructions for using your product.

12 **Product Service Manual** – how your product is kept in tip-top order.

13 **Marketing and Sales Manual** – policies and procedures for adding to the bottom line.

14 **Customer Service Handbook** – policies and procedures to keep your customers happy.

15 **Business Continuity Plan** – who contacts whom and does what in the event of a disaster.

Who does what?

You are now ready to allocate responsibilities and activities from the plan to individual job titles – and, therefore, to individuals.

While you were developing your business plan, you designed an organisation structure that would make it work. If this was high-level, you should extend it to identify every employee. Finally you pull this out into job specifications and job descriptions. (You already know from your resource plans where you need to recruit.) Now all you have to do is communicate the responsibilities to the individuals concerned. The best way is in an employee objective-setting exercise.

Employee objectives

Almost the final step in turning a business plan into action is making sure that everyone knows what they should be doing. In the same way that strategy turns into action, so strategic objectives result in objectives for each employee. Figure 13.5 earlier could almost be re-labelled top-to-bottom with the words *objectives, targets* and *milestones*.

In fact, I have illustrated the way that objectives cascade downwards in Figure 13.6. The broadest strategic objectives are set at the corporate level. Managers at the first level – general managers – have specific, mainly strategic objectives framed around the corporate objectives. And as you move down through your line management structure, objectives become more precise, more operational, and more urgent.

Figure 13.6 Cascading objectives

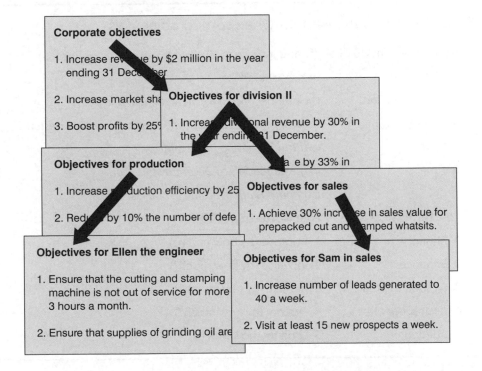

I use the word *urgent* in a time-related sense. I would expect a general manager to have objectives with a longer horizon – *achieve this in the next 12 months*. I expect clerks and computer programmers to have objectives measured almost in hours – *do this in the next two days*. Maybe I am being a little extreme, but I am sure that you can catch my drift.

> *'Everybody knew what Walt wanted. Everybody had objectives. Both were communicated all the way down the line. The management layer was flat and responsibilities were clearly defined. We had a good self-image and the company ran well.'*
> EX-WALT DISNEY EXECUTIVE (WHEN THERE WERE 2000 EMPLOYEES)

MANAGEMENT BY OBJECTIVES

You can see where I am heading. Develop personal objectives for each employee based on the overall business plan, send them off to do their bit, and everyone will be pulling in the same direction. They use your policies, rules and procedures in pursuit of their objectives, and your plan is executed exactly as you intended.

You can also measure employee performance against target. You then have an employee appraisal system – *management by objectives*. As at the corporate level, employee objectives should be defined concisely with clearly measurable targets. Here are some things to think about.

Fifteen words to think about when setting objectives

Five measurements to quantify and include in all objectives

1 Change	*Increase by 25% …*
2 Entity or action	*the number of cold (i.e. new, uninvited) calls …*
3 Quality	*to prospective customers confirmed as potential investors …*
4 Cost	*without increasing headcount …*
5 Time	*in the period July to December this year*
	(compared with the same period last year).

Five terms to avoid	**Five words to qualify**
1 Minimise (maximise)	**1** Improve (by how much?)
2 Enhance	**2** Increase (by how much?)
3 As soon as possible	**3** Reduce (by how much?)
4 As appropriate	**4** Restrict (by how much?)
5 Adequate	**5** Limit (by how much?)

Unfortunately, it never works quite as smoothly in practice as this simple exposition suggests. But the logic is compelling and intellectually satisfying. I will look at some stumbling blocks in a moment. First, we should complete the mechanics by looking at how the financial part of your business plan is brought into play.

How much freedom?

You want your employees to try to achieve their objectives while operating within your plans, policies, rules and procedures. It is common to set limits on the amount of discretion permitted – at both the functional and the personal level. This might be related to general decision-making (*the Chief Executive is authorised to operate the business within the business plan as approved providing that the following exceptional items are pre-approved by the Board of Directors on a case by case basis …*). Or limits might be financial.

For example, department heads might be permitted to spend up to $10,000 in one month or on any one item, but your head of R&D has had his knuckles rapped for buying pointless electronic gadgets and his personal limit is just $5000. This spending usually, of course, has to be within guidelines already identified in their *budgets*.

Financial objectives

There is one more set of objectives that you need to take into account: budgets – which is another name for financial objectives. They are yardsticks against which you can measure actual performance. People tend to get rather hung up about budgets. They are actually straightforward. Keep an open mind as you read the next few paragraphs.

You do not have any more work to do at the outset. In the financial section (Chapters 7–10) we agreed that you would use your central – most likely – forecast as an operating budget for the first year of your plan.

As you progress through the year, your accounting people will prepare monthly statements of actual revenue and spending. You might sit behind the accounting desk from time to time yourself and do this if you are running your own business and the finances are simple.

Once a month, as close to the end of the previous month as possible, compare actual spending and revenue against the budget. I do not suggest waiting for the end of the quarter. Three months is too long if things are going off track.

 Don't forget to watch all the gauges, see page 302.

COMPARING THE REALITY WITH THE PLAN

Numbers tend to look scary when they gather together in large groups. My grandfather always used to say *avoid any gathering of large numbers*. With hindsight, I am not sure if he was warning about crowds of football spectators or the monthly budget review. In fact, although this might look dull and complex, it's actually simple and revealing. It can provide valuable insight.

Figure 13.7 shows extracts from three spreadsheets that you might use.

1   The first is your original budget – this is what you planned.

2   The second shows the actual transactions (the *outturn*) – this is what you did.

3   The third brings the first two together in a common summary format – this shows where the reality diverged from the plan.

Look carefully at the third spreadsheet. It shows planned and actual spending in the month, together with the actual and percentage *variance* between the two. It also does the same for the year to date – the first six months in this example.

The three examples, salaries, travel and total spending, are illustrated graphically in Figures 13.8–13.10. With such pictures, it is easy to spot what is happening. You can read the same information from the budget report (the lower spreadsheet).

Taking each graph in turn, the following information is revealed.

SALARIES

Salaries were close to budget each month until June. Over the first six months they were just 2.3% above plan and even in June itself they were within what might be regarded as a reasonable margin of error – 10%. However, the sudden jump in June suggests an unexpected event – perhaps across-the-board pay awards or recruitment of an extra member of staff. This merits investigation.

TRAVEL

The percentage variances show that travel spending is running seriously over budget and needs investigation. Looking back at the raw data (illustrated in Figure 13.9) there is persistent overspending that should have been questioned already.

Figure 13.7 Sample monthly budget health check

	A	B	C	D	E	F	G	H
1	ZXTY International							
2	Marketing Department							
3	Budget for calendar year 20xx							
4	Local currency							Year to
5		Jan	Feb	Mar	Apr	May	Jun	end June
6	Salaries	10 000	10 000	10 000	10 000	10 000	10 000	60 000
...	...		...	...	...	...	...	...
24	Travel	5 000	5 500	4 000	4 500	4 750	5 000	28 750
...	...		...	...	...	...	...	...
51	Total actual	400 050	410 150	385 450	433 000	453 200	399 750	2 481 600
52	Contingency	40 005	41 015	38 545	43 300	45 320	39 975	248 160
53	Total spending	440 055	451 165	423 995	476 300	498 520	439 725	2 729 760
54	Cumulative	440 055	891 220	1 315 215	1 791 515	2 290 035	2 729 760	
56								

	A	B	C	D	E	F	G	H
1	Marketing Department							
2	Outturn for January to June 20xx							
3	Local currency							
4								Year to
5		Jan	Feb	Mar	Apr	May	Jun	end June
6	Salaries	9 986	9 986	10 125	10 125	10 125	11 004	61 351
...	...		...	...	...	...	...	...
24	Travel	5 120	5 977	5 450	5 569	5 420	5 995	33 531
...	...		...	...	...	...	...	...
51	Total actual	399 457	420 435	399 499	451 397	490 364	458 204	2 619 356
52	Unused contingency	40 598	30 730	24 496	24 903	8 156	–18 479	110 404
53	Total budget	440 055	451 165	423 995	476 300	498 520	439 725	2 729 760
54	Cumulative, actual	399 457	819 892	1 219 391	1 670 788	2 161 152	2 619 356	
56								

	A	B	C	D	E	B	C	D	E
1	Marketing Department								
2	Budget report June 20xx								
3	Local currency								
4		Month of June				Year to end June			
5		Actual	Budget	Variance	Var, %	Actual	Budget	Variance	Var, %
6	Salaries	11 004	10 000	1,004	10.0	61 351	60 000	1 351	2.3
...	...	...	...	...	...	...	...	...	...
24	Travel	5 995	5 000	995	19.9	33 531	28 750	4 781	16.6
...	...	...	...	...	...	...	...	...	...
51	Total spending	458 204	399 750	58 454	14.6	2 619 356	2 481 600	137 756	5.6
52	Contingency used	58 454	39 975	18 479	46.2	137 756	248 160	–110 404	–44.5
53	Total spending	458 204	439 725	18 479	4.2	2 619 356	2 729 760	–110 404	–4.0

Salaries within acceptable % variance but check if Marketing recruited above headcount budget in June or conceded big pay increases

Total spending was high in June. Contingency for month was exceeded by 46% (worrying) BUT less than half the contingency for Jan–June was consumed (good) and overall spending is 4% below the total provision

Travel is running over budget. Check and control or revise budget

Figure 13.8 Salaries, planned and actual

This shows that spending was close to plan every month until June (note that to magnify
the pattern, the left-hand scale does not start at zero)

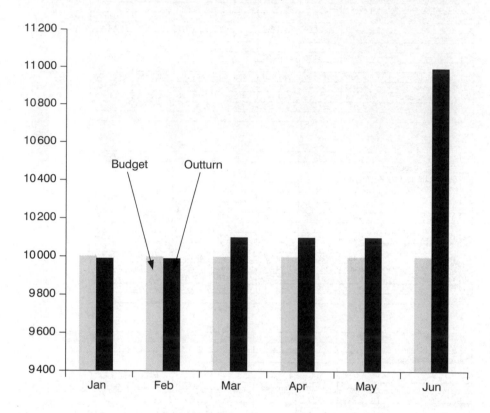

TOTAL SPENDING

The summary shows that total expenditure in the year to June was 5.6% over the level
of *identified* planned spending, but still within the overall plan including the 10% contingency. Spending in the month of June was over target.

What does all this tell us? It indicates that percentages are more revealing than raw
numbers. It shows that many questions can be raised by a quick perusal of the budget
report. It highlights the fact that more information is needed. It is, incidentally, valuable
to include volume figures – such as planned and actual headcount, number of units produced or sold, volume of inventory, number of contracts completed.

 Most important, you cannot make any decision without looking at both the
spending and the revenue side of the equation.

Figure 13.9 Travel spending, planned and actual

This shows clearly that spending was above plan every month

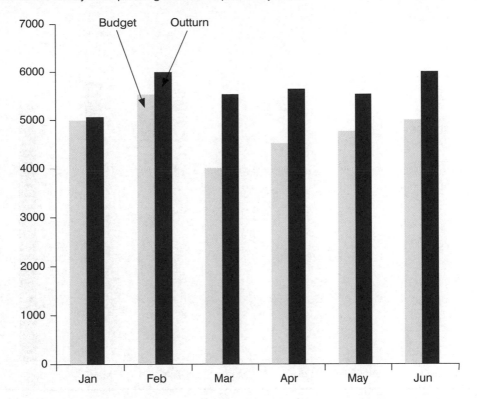

If the extra spending is going into generating more sales it might be entirely acceptable and welcome. However, recall from Chapter 11 (risks) that it can sometimes be counter-productive if sales exceed their optimum level.

EXTRACTING VALUE FROM A BUDGET REPORT

There is perhaps nothing more common or more irritating than a manager or director who is hung up on spending figures. The budget is only a forecast. The reality is more important. And this is not usually measured by whether you are or should be spending $100 or $200 on telephone calls. It is usually measured by whether you are achieving your objectives. So, as already indicated, take spending with revenue – and look at this in the light of your overall objectives and constraints.

When it comes to producing or reviewing monthly budget reports, it is clearly necessary to have an understanding of why the *outturns* are above, in line with or below plan. This understanding is usually conveyed in a written commentary. Ten warnings are listed on page 336 – things to explain in the commentary or to watch for when reviewing budget reports. Remember that the originator always knows better than the recipients the details and where to hide things. In this connection, you might also wish to look back to page 210, *Areas where managers massage costs.*

Figure 13.10 Total spending, planned and actual

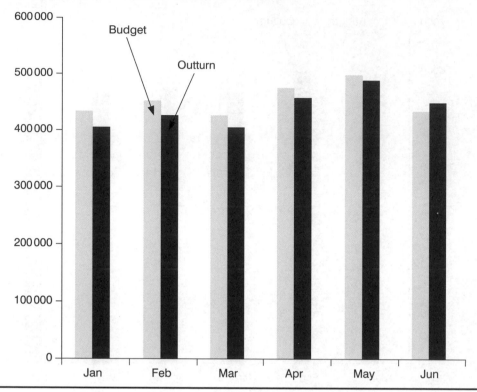

Total spending was below plan every month – until June

Ten items in budget reports that might conceal threats

1 Spending is on target, sales are not (or vice versa).

2 Variances that are, say, more than 10% above or below plan.

3 Sudden, large changes.

4 Single items of expenditure that exceed corporate, departmental, personal or other spending limits.

5 Outlays on rental and leases that could be circumventing controls over capital spending and/or creating long-term liabilities.

6 Unhealthy increases in accounts receivable (credit to customers).

7 Ageing accounts receivable – debts not being collected in a timely manner.

8 An increasing proportion of uncollected debts hidden within accounts receivable.

9 Other changes in balance sheet entries that do not relate directly to the expenditure reports (accruals and prepayments).

10 Commission, cost of sales, and other headings concealing payments ostensibly to agents or third parties – I have witnessed some very devious practices here.

Finally, make sure that you do more than just go through the motions. Make sure that you always ask, what does this tell me about my business plan? Are the strategy and plan working, or should they be revised? Or if they are working, should the financial projections or any other objectives be revised to bring them back into line with reality? A plan is only a plan. The outturn is much more important.

Monitoring other objectives

The monthly budget report is a regular mechanism for tracking performance against financial objectives. You can set up similar procedures for non-financial objectives. Most companies have regular reporting of sales, complaints, production output, staff turnover, a whole host of interesting information. These should include progress against objectives. The more solidly that they are quantified, the easier they are to track. *Production is 3% above plan* is more useful than *we are very busy in the production department*.

You will recall from Chapter 6 that my preference is for exception reporting. *Tell me when it's going wrong, not when it's going right*. Regular meetings tend to turn into dull affairs where small problems are glossed over and attention is shifted to the insignificant. Dominant personalities do this on purpose. Wafflers do it by accident.

If you are at board meetings, watch for the Maxwell style of chairmanship. *Any other business … no … right … I have important things to do*. This reduces the meeting to a pointless rubber-stamping exercise.

Ten reasons why business plans that look good on paper fail in practice

1 **Poor specification.** Ineffective strategy, plans or objectives.

2 **Conflicting objectives.** Watch for budgets that restrict action.

3 **Stifling heat.** Poorly set or an excessive number of objectives deplete energy and enthusiasm, and stifle creativity and innovation.

4 **Weak employee management.** Make sure that employee objectives-setting, appraisal and counselling are effective; encourage good leadership.

5 **Not invented here.** Resistance to change arises when employees are not sufficiently involved with a plan and do not buy into it – *we've always done it this way*.

6 **Poor integration.** Marketing does not understand why production cannot deliver enough products; sales promises things that R&D cannot deliver.

7 **Authoritarian regime.** Domineering management usually prevents employees from pursuing their objectives.

▶

Monitoring the world

As discussed in Chapter 5, all your people should be constantly gathering information about your competitors and their products, actual and prospective customers, and so on. Build this feedback into your monitoring process. Make sure that your external assessment is up to date. Exchange information at formal and informal meetings – keep brain-storming your strategy in the light of the latest news about rivals' products, advertising, sales activities, R&D, industry mergers and takeover activity, world news and so on.

> '*Strategic leadership requires one other skill. It is a readiness to look personally foolish; a readiness to discuss half-baked ideas, since most fully baked ideas start out in that form; a total honesty, a readiness to admit you got it wrong.*'
>
> SIR JOHN HOSKYNS

Confirming and revising strategy and plans

Picture this. You are in Nepal. You step out of the cold, noisy streets into a crowded coffee house. The heat from the wood-burning stove slaps you like a hot towel. But if you sit in a cool room that is gradually warmed, you tend to be much less aware of the change. Remember the last conference that you attended, where you gradually became comfortable, warm – and dozed off (I hope that I wasn't speaking).

It is the same with all this monitoring of budgets, corporate and employee objectives and the world at large. Small changes go unnoticed but build up into major discrepancies. Little trickles turn into breached dykes. This is why I am so enthusiastic about ticking off regular and measurable milestones. Of course, you still have to use sensible judgement to decide whether variances merit revisiting the strategy and/or plan. But at least you are more likely to spot gradual changes in temperature – or adverse cash flow that is going to wash away your sea defences.

 Put a recurring reminder in your diary, to-do list, or your mobile phone's calendar. Once every three months take time out to look very hard (very, very hard) at your financials (year to date, and projections) and key strategic objectives (are you really achieving them, should they be revised in the light of developments?). On that day, do something you do not normally do. Go bungee jumping, watch a movie, take your kids to the zoo. This will really help your thought process.

Don't forget the carrots

Not many people work for your business for love. We are all in it for specific reasons – success, personal achievement, financial gain. You can encourage your employees to work towards your common objectives by using appropriate carrots as incentives and rewards.

Such incentives are often linked to the achievement of one or more of corporate, divisional, departmental, team and personal objectives. Common rewards are salary increases and bonuses. Share hand-outs and stock options are frequently attractive – and can help limit your cash outlays when your business is short on cash flow. Other recognition should go without saying. Never forget to say thank you. Even simple acknowledgements help, such as a letter from the boss, a certificate of appreciation or a thank-you dinner. By the way – have you shown suitable appreciation to those who helped you prepare the business plan?

Take care not to shoot yourself in the foot. Many chief executives have been known to take big profit-related bonuses and run – before the short-term gains and long-term downside of their recent strategies became apparent.

'The man who is denied the opportunity of taking decisions of importance begins to regard as important the decisions he is allowed to take. He becomes fussy about filing, keen on seeing pencils are sharpened, eager to ensure that the windows are opened (or shut) and apt to use two or three different coloured pencils.'

PROFESSOR C. NORTHCOTE PARKINSON

And into the next business plan

At an appropriate point in your operating cycle, you have to start developing the next plan. This should be easy. Your execution of the current plan includes continual monitoring of all the internal and external influences that affect strategy. You need to make sure that you isolate yourself from day-to-day pressures, cast off your blinkers, and re-appraise this feedback in as unbiased a way as possible.

This time the work will be easier. You have laid the groundwork, established planning procedures. You will be able to delegate more. Share the work and halve the burden. The essence of business. So if you will be kind enough to turn back to Chapter 3, we can start all over again …

'If you don't know where you are going, you will probably end up somewhere else.'

DR LAURENCE J. PETER

Trying to catch the tail

Business planning is similar to a dog chasing its tail. The end is always in sight but you never arrive there. A new business-planning cycle always starts before the old one is over. Targets are continually shifting in this ever-changing world. Plans are always being revised. You never quite know whether your original plan was accurate. You always think that it was, because you measure the present against the latest modification to the plan, not the original plan which is invalid now anyway.

Once in a while, grab the tail and see what you can learn from the current divergences from the very first plan. Congratulate yourself if you have successfully steered a course through the changing environment.

> The plan is where you start from. Its objectives are your destination. What happens in the middle is down to your good captaincy – with the aid of your crew. Without a good lookout you might founder on the rocks. I think that this sums it up quite well. Bon voyage et bon chance.

Appendix:
Tetrylus Inc business plan

This appendix contains pages from a sample business plan. Your plan may have different headings and may be arranged in a different order, as discussed in the book. Each page below is cross-referenced to the appropriate chapter of this book and, if applicable, to the closest matching figure in that chapter. To receive the address of the supporting website which contains this sample business plan, send a blank email to defbizplan@ business-minds.com

1. Cover *See Chapter 2, p.32*

Tetrylus Inc

BUSINESS PLAN

2012 to 2014

[a sample framework for a business plan]

Introducing *Tetrylus ONE*

A radio frequency tracking system

for remotely tracking and safeguarding

employees in hazardous working environments

Tetrylus ONE

2. Contents *See Chapter 3, p.46*

Contents

3. Preliminaries *See Chapter 2, p.36*

Contacts

For further information please contact
Niccolò Machiavelli
Group CEO, Tetrylus Inc
Mega House, 2010 Boston Road,
Guesswhere 32266
Tel: 0161 224 3270
Fax: 0161 224 3275
Email: inquiries@tetrylus.com

Professional Advisers

Bankers   First Second Bank, City Branch, address....
Lawyers   West Central Attorneys, address....
Auditors   Arthur & Sons, address....

Definitions

....
Interrogator   A control device which....
RFID   Radio frequency identification
....

Document Control		Within ISO 9002 control: NO	
Owner	Niccolò Machiavelli		
Date	Originated February 2012		
Copy	Issued to	Format	Notes
1	File	Original	
2	Niccolò Machiavelli	DOC	
3	René Descartes	PDF	
4	Adam Smith	PDF	
5			
6			
7			
8			
9			
10			

4. Executive Summary *See Chapter 3, p.48*

Executive Summary

Tetrylus is offering 40% of its authorized share capital for $1.25m. This is the amount of additional funding that we need to meet orders for our unique industrial computer system and generate net profits of $6m a year by 2013. We are positioning *Tetrylus* for an initial public offering in that year at an expected market capitalization of $60m. This Business Plan sets out our strategic, operating and financial ...

The Company

Tetrylus was incorporated in February 2010 with issued share capital of $10,000. The founder, Niccolò Machiavelli, is well known for his strategic management. He is supported by René Descartes as Head of Technology. René is famous for his powers of reasoning and he brings important experience from his previous post as Head of ...

The Product

Tetrylus ONE is a package of computer hardware and software that reduces accidents in dangerous working environments and cuts the cost of complying with health and safety regulations. Our first users include major petroleum, mining and construction companies. They recover their full investment in the system within ten months ...

Corporate strategy

Pilot sales confirm that our strategy will be successful. There are five key elements to our strategy ...

Financial projections

Net profit is projected at ... Cash flow will turn positive by month 15 and the potential surplus will reach ... Funding requirements peak at ... On a realistic appraisal ... pushing the potential return on equity to ...

5. Current situation *See Chapter 4, p.64*

Basic corporate data
Name of Company: *Tetrylus Inc*
Status: International business company
           Incorporated in the British
           Virgin Islands (BVI) on 29
           February 2010.
Capital   Authorized: 10,000 ordinary $1 shares.
           Issued: One $1 share to Niccolò
           Machiavelli
Registered Office: Frond Chambers, Tortola, BVI.
Company no: IBC--3471231
Head Office: 2010 Boston Road, Guesswhere

Vision

Tetrylus is dedicated to becoming the world-leader in industrial health and safety equipment ...

Mission

Tetrylus mission is to provide excellent industrial health-and-safety computer systems in Asia-Pacific. We aim to establish a 5% market share within the next three years, taking sales to over $15 million a year, and net profits to more than $6 million. We will list on NASDAQ by year five. During this time period, we will comply with ISO 13000 environmental standards, provide first-class career development for employees, reduce the maximum customer-response time to one hour, and work closely with our shareholders to meet their other objectives.

Company values

We will operate within strict legal and ethical guidelines ... We will not test our product on animals ... We will nurture our employee-team and will introduce measures to promote job satisfaction ...

Brief history and current status

Tetrylus is in a start-up situation. We have successfully completed one pilot project that ...

Current financial data

The summary below shows that ... Financial forecasts are included in the Financial analysis on pages 11 and full historical and forecast data are at Annex A.

6. Current situation (continued)
See Chapter 4, p.75

Organisation and management

The management team comprises six professionals with appropriate qualifications, solid experience, and complementary skills. They have worked together previously and demonstrated their ability to ... Short résumés are below and detailed biographies are at Annex B.

Organization chart for Tetrylus Inc

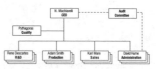

Production

Our Production Department is headed by Adam Smith. He was one of the first experts to identify the benefits of specialisation and can produce pins (for identification badges) better than anyone else ...

Sales

Karl Marx is in charge of Sales. His recognized ability to identify and satisfy customers' needs provides us with a significant competitive advantage. His deputy, Karl Popper, has shown that sales forecasts cannot be proved to be accurate but can be disproved ...

Infrastructure

Tetrylus is currently operating from the founders' garage. We have negotiated a lease for office premises in the Millennium Industrial Park. We will relocate in the first month of our start-up phase. The office is ideally situated close to suppliers, customers and the airport ...

Products

Our launch product is *Tetrylus ONE* – an automated tracking system for remotely tracking employees in hazardous working environments. The system comprises a computer software application, radio-frequency network cards and identification badges with built-in transmitters ...

The software is licensed from Arthur Andy and Son, a major international consulting house. The software is running ... The identification badges are modified versions of badges currently produced by ...

Core competencies

A review of the current situation analysis shows that we have developed core competencies in the following areas ...

7. Market analysis *See Chapter 5, p.106*

Market Analysis

The industry
The product class is industrial health and safety monitoring and compliance equipment (HSMCE). There are two product categories: non-automated and computerized. *Tetrylus* is in the latter category ...

Our market
The market divides into six segments. There are three industry types (construction, mining and petroleum) each divided into large and small companies (the boundary being 2000 manual workers and above). *Tetrylus* is targeting primarily large petroleum companies. The other large companies are secondary targets for us, but are not ruled out. Small companies are currently not viable prospects on cost grounds ...

Tetrylus is operating in Asia-Pacific. Mining and petroleum companies have fairly homogeneous buying characteristics throughout the region, but the construction industry is more fragmented. Hong Kong and China ...

Competitors
Four major international competitors are operating within our territory. Together they dominated 94% of the market last year, as Table 2 indicates:

Table 2. Asia-Pacific HSMCE sales by competitor

Company	Sales, $m	Market share, %
Pacific Link	166	46
Atlantic Watch	87	24
Indian Continental	74	20
Arctic Assets	13	4
Other	21	5
SafeTRAK	1	1
Total	**362**	**100**

However, when taken by market segment the picture is rather different. HSMCE sales by competitor, market segment, and territory are shown in Table 3 ...

Competitive advantages
Our research indicates that there are four areas where *Tetrylus ONE* has distinct competitive advantages. These are ...

By exploiting these advantages we can construct effective barriers to entry which will deter competitors from trying to enter our prime market until ...

8. Strategy and operating plan
See Chapter 6, p.128

Business strategy

Objectives
Our strategic objectives are as follows:

1. Annual sales volumes in the range shown in Table 16, column D.
2. Completion of modifications to hardware as described in Table 17 by the dates indicated.
3. Completion of modifications to software as described in Table 17 by the dates indicated.
4.

Strategy
The market analysis on page 7 indicates that we can take advantage of an unexploited market niche -- automated safety systems for large petroleum companies operating in Asia-Pacific. The main countries ...

We were the first to spot the gap in the market and our exclusive licence for the identification badge locks out the main competitors. We estimate that there will be a 15-month time lag before they are in a position to compete... by which time we have achieved critical mass and the market will be unattractive to them for the reasons explained ... We will also use the revenue from the first sales to develop ...

In essence, our strategy is to:

* Work with ISPs to enable fast deployment of our system using their relationships and resources. We have signed exclusive agreements with ...
* Pursue the strategic sales indicated Table 16, column C that will take us to critical mass most-rapidly and lock out the major competitors.
* Use revenue for the initial sales to erect barriers to entry as shown in ...

Operating plan
There are three main elements to our operating plan, relating to production, marketing and sales, and administrative support. These are considered in the following paragraphs ...

Production ...

Marketing and Sales ...

Administrative Support

9. Sales forecasts *See Chapter 8, p.185*

Sales forecasts
Tetrylus ONE reduces the number of accidents at work and cuts the cost of complying with health and safety legislation. Companies will recover in 10 months their entire initial investment in buying the hardware, licensing the software and implementing the system. Moreover ...

Sales volumes
The limiting factor on sales volumes might be our ability to implement enough systems in a given period of time. We can solve this by selling through ISPs and using *their* technical staff to implement our systems for end-users. This cuts our resource requirements and reduces the sales cycle (since ISP's will leverage existing customer relationships). Moreover, we are increasing the incentive for ISPs to re-sell *Tetrylus ONE* by allowing them to earn a high margin on the product while also earning from sales of their consulting and implementation services.
....
We have already appointed three ISPs, and we expect to recruit one more this year. We will continue to add ISPs -- until we have 20 in year 5. We are working with current ISPs to develop specific prospective sales. We have three pilot sales at contract-negotiation stage, and we will make a total of four sales during this year ...

Our target is to sell an average of 2500 *Tetrylus ONE* identity badges with each sale by year 3. Initial sales will be smaller because ...

Production costs
TechnoWhiz will produce identity badges for us. This will reduce the resources that we require and limit our manufacturing risks -- TechnoWhiz have already produced prototypes that meet or exceed our quality specifications. Initial costs of $50 a badge will fall to $23 in year 2. Our projected volumes allow ...

Pricing
Longer-term, sales will average a little over $100 000 per package. Pilot sales aimed at establishing references sites will be smaller values. The following table shows the composition of a *Tetrylus ONE* package ...

Gross profit from sales
The following table indicates that gross profit from sales will reach ...

10. Financial analysis
See Chapter 11, p.280

Financial analysis

Break even
We pass break even when we sell more than 124 *Tetrylus ONE* packages at a minimum price of $95 000 each ...

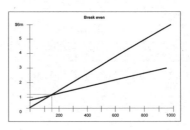

We believe that we can comfortably achieve this break even level even on a worst case scenario with ...

Capital Spending
Production of *Tetrylus ONE* requires the following equipment ... We will minimise capital outlays by leasing ... but we need to own the ... for the strategic opportunities outlined on page 195.

Staff costs
Our major operating costs relate to staffing the ... To minimise our commitments while sales are being established we will sub-contract ...

Other operating costs
Table 20 shows that the largest non-staff operating costs are ...

11. Financial analysis
See Chapter 10, p.238

Income statement/profit & loss account
The revenues and costs described above are brought together in the profit and loss account in Table 12 (full details are in Annex A). The $1.4m net loss in year 1 reduces to $0.2m in year 2 and turns to a net profit of $3.8m by year 3. Sales could …

Balance sheet
A summarized balance sheet is shown in Table 13 (full details are in Annex A). By year 5, retained earnings exceed $12m and net asset value is …

Cash flow and funding requirements
The following chart illustrates our cumulative cash flow projection (Detailed figures are in Annex A). Monthly cash inflows start to exceed outflows by month 14 and we move into a surplus by month 30. Our maximum funding requirement is $1.25 million …

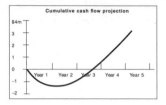

…

Valuation
On a modest price earnings multiple of 10, the implied market value of the equity capital will be nearly $40m by year 3 … This would represent a potential return on investment of … Also …

12. Risk analysis *See Chapter 11, p.280*

RISK assessment

SWOT
We have analysed our strengths and weaknesses, and the opportunities for and threats to the business. The key items are listed below, each with a note explaining how we will cope with, or exploit, the issue …

Critical success factors
We have determined that we must achieve the following targets in order to move our strategy forward. Most critical is the need to source … We are implementing a four-step program to ensure that we meet the requirements … The first step is to …

Limiting factors
There are two things which could limit our sales in year one and … First, there is a constraint on the amount of … that we can source until we have … Of course, these limits are way beyond the sales volumes that we can reasonably hope to achieve. Moreover, …

Specific risks and their solutions
There are eight specific risks to which we should draw attention … We have strategies to deal with each of these risks, as described below.

Production. *Tetrylus ONE* has been successfully prototyped and the feasibility and cost of the manufacturing process is known. The manufacturing is undertaken by a company with quality procedures that meet ISO 9002 standards, and we will conduct our own quality control sampling at their premises … The one remaining uncontrollable factor affecting production is the availability and price of silicon on the world market which …

Alternative scenarios
Our sales forecasts, and projected revenues, costs, and financial statements are based on the lower-end of our most-likely scenario.

As already discussed, there is a range of possible outcomes dependent on a wide range of factors both within and outside of our control. Accordingly, this plan includes two alternative scenarios showing how the business will develop under varying conditions. The low-income scenario assumes that certain unlikely events depress production, sales and prices by … Our calculations show that we will still break even at … and … . We also include a high-income scenario to show how net profit will rise sharply if …

Sensitivity analysis
The following table shows our assessment of the effects of a 1% increase in key variables. A 1% decline will have approximately the opposite effect. You may use this table to assess your own scenarios.

A 1% increase in	Net profit $000	Borrowing $000	ROE %
	Will change these by		
Sales volume	+167	−83	+33
Sales price	+134	−57	+27
Marketing expenditure	+15	−8	+03
Raw material prices	−59	+30	−1.2
Labour costs	−23	+12	−0.5
Other costs	−12	+5	−0.2

13. Conclusion *See Chapter 3, p.50*

Conclusion

We have subjected this business plan to the most rigorous analysis and the business appears to be viable under all realistic scenarios.

We firmly believe that we have identified a solid new business based on a new but tested technology with unique and exciting opportunities. The conclusion from our extensive and detailed market analysis is that competing products are so different that … Based on this analysis, we have developed a solid strategy to rapidly move into the major markets and then consolidate our position.

We have examined the potential risks and have turned many into opportunities, eliminated others, and reduced the remainder to a manageable level …

We have aligned the business organization to our immediate needs and so as to sustain the rapid growth that will follow. We have a well-qualified management team with proven relevant experience … In addition, we have already identified additional personnel of the highest quality to complement our team.

Our financial projections are conservative, yet still indicate a very profitable business. As explained, we believe that we will exceed these projections by a wide margin.

….

14. Annex A1. Production and sales
See Chapter 8, p.186

ANNEX A.1 Production & sales

Note: Depending on the purpose of your plan, you will almost certainly need to include projections for a longer time period than the six months shown here. You may want to show details for the first few months of the future period, and perhaps annual figures for three to five years ahead. You will also include historical figures if the business is already in existence.

Tetrylus Inc Financial plan

Production & sales, first 6 months
Dollars

		Month 1	Month 2	Month 3	Month 4	Month 5	Month 6
G-1	**Costs and prices**						
G-2	Production cost, per unit	0	50	50	50	50	50
G-3	Sales price, per uhi	0	78	78	78	78	78
G-4							
G-5	**Inventory volume**						
G-6	Opening stock (prev 9)	0	0	300	800	350	850
G-7	Addition (production volume)	0	500	500	0	500	0
G-8	Reduction (sales volume)	0	−200	0	−450	0	−600
G-9	**Closing stocks (6 + 7 + 8)**	0	300	800	350	850	250
G-10							
G-11	**Inventory value**						
G-12	Opening stock (prev 15)	0	0	15 000	40 000	17 500	42 500
G-13	Addition (line 2 x line 7)	0	25 000	25 000	0	25 000	0
G-14	Reduction (line 2 x line 8)	0	−10 000	0	−22 500	0	−30 000
G-15	**Closing stock (12 + 13 + 14)**	0	15 000	40 000	17 500	42 500	12 500
G-16							
G-17	**Gross sales**						
G-18	Hardware (line 3 x line 8)	0	15 600	0	35 100	0	46 800
G-19	Software	0	4 400	0	4 900	0	3 200
G-20	**Total sales (lines 18 + 19)**	0	20 000	0	40 000	0	50 000
G-21							
G-22	**Cost of sales**						
G-23	Hardware (line 2 x line 8)	0	10 000	0	22 500	0	30 000
G-24	Software (from software)	0	3 591	0	4 683	0	3 979
G-25	**Total cost (lines 23 + 24)**	0	13 591	0	27 183	0	33 979
G-26							
G-27	**Gross profit, %**						
G-28	Hardware (line 18 − line 23)	0	5 600	0	12 600	0	16 800
G-29	Software (line 19 − line 24)	0	809	0	217	0	−779
G-30	**Total(lines 28 + 29)**	0	6 409	0	12 817	0	16 021
G-31							
G-32	**Gross profit, %**						
G-33	Hardware (line 28 / line 18)	0	36	0	36	0	36
G-34	Software (line 29 / line 19)	0	18	0	4	0	−24
G-35	**Total(line 30 / line 20)**	0	32	0	32	0	32

15. Annex A2. Capital outlays

See Chapter 9, p.203

ANNEX A.2 Capital outlays

Tetrylus Inc Financial plan

Total capital outlays & depreciation, first six months

		Month1	Month 2	Month 3	Month 4	Month 5	Month 6	H1
	CAPITAL OUTLAYS							
C-11	Office fitting	6 500	0	0	0	0	0	6 500
C-12	Office furniture	5 000	0	0	0	0	0	5 000
C-13	Office equipment	0	0	750	0	0	0	750
C-14	Telecoms equipment	0	0	0	0	0	0	0
C-15	Computers, etc	20000	1 500	0	1 000	0	0	22500
C-16	Software	000	0	0	0	0	0	5 000
C-17	Motor vehicles	0	0	0	0	0	0	0
C-00	TOTAL	36,500	1 500	750	1 000	0	0	39750
	DEPRECIATION SCHEDULE							
D-11	Of	0	542	542	542	542	542	2 708
D-12	Of	0	83	83	83	83	83	417
D-13	Of	0	0	0	13	13	13	38
D-14	Telecoms equipment	0	0	0	0	0	0	0
D-15	Computers, etc.	0	556	597	597	625	625	3 000
D-16	Softwae	0	208	208	208	208	208	1 042
D-17	Motor vehicles	0	0	0	0	0	0	0
D-00	TOTAL	0	1 389	1 431	1 443	1 471	1 471	7 204

Notes to the accounts: depreciation policy

Fixed assetsare written-off over their projected working lives using the straight-line method. Office fittings are depreciated over the 12-month term of the office lease;office furniture and equipment is depreciated over 60 months, computers over 36 and software over 24 months

Commentary (extract)

Line S-00 – Total salaries

Total spending on salaries is based on headcount projections and expected salary levels (as described …)

Line S-11 Director stipends

There is a modest $10,000 a month to cover the directors' basic living costs and commitments. This will be increased toward market levels once the business is generating sustained positive cash flow.

Line S-12 Deliberately omitted

Line S-13 Contract staff

To avoid the commitment associated with increasing the permanent staff complement, and to add to the range of resources available, a number of technical staff will be employed on a contract basis. Their costs are shown on page 178 and the total is included in line S-13.

Line E-11 Premises rental and taxes

We have a one-year lease on premises at Millennium Park, The lease is fixed at $12,000 for the period and it is payable monthly in advance commencing in month 1.

Line E-12 Amortisation – leasehold improvements

This is the initial office fitting costs (described on page 178 written-off over the 12-month term of the lease.

Line E-13 Utilities

We estimate spending on electricity and water at a little over $500 a month. There will be an annual price increase in month 11 – we have provided for the maximum likely rise of 10%.

16. Annex A3. Staff costs

See Chapter 9, p.205

ANNEX A.3 Staff costs

Tetrylus Inc Financial plan

Staff costs, first six months

Dollars

		Month 1	Month 2	Month 3	Month 4	Month 5	Month 6	H1
	STAFF NUMBERS							
	Directors/managers	3	3	3	3	3	3	3
	Technical staff	2	4	4	4	4	4	4
	Marketing staff	0	1	1	2	2	2	2
	Administrative staff	2	2	2	2	2	3	3
	Total	7	10	10	11	11	12	12
	STAFF COSTS							
	Staff salaries							
S-1	Technical staff 1	1 200	1 200	1 200	1 200	1 200	1 200	7 200
S-2	Technical staff 2	1 200	1 200	1 200	1 200	1 200	1 200	7 200
S-3	Technical staff 3	.	1 200	1 200	1 200	1 200	1 200	6 000
S-4	Technical staff 4	.	1 200	1 200	1 200	1 200	1 200	6 000
S-5	Sales/distribution manager	.	.	.	1 250	1 259	1 250	3 759
S-6	Marketing assistant	.	750	750	750	750	750	3 750
S-7	Book-keeping, etc.	.	.	.	.	.	750	750
S-8	Receptionist/secretary	600	600	600	600	600	600	3 600
S-9	Messenger/security	300	300	300	300	300	300	1 800
S-00	TOTAL (sum S1 to S9)	3 300	6 450	6 450	7 700	7 709	8 450	40 059
S-11	Directors' stipends	10 000	10 000	10 000	10 000	10 000	10 000	60 000
S-13	Contract staff	10 000	10 000	10 000	10 000	10 000	10 000	60 000
S-14	Staff social security	92	162	162	185	185	208	992
S-15	Staff temporary	0	0	0	0	0	0	0
S-10	TOTAL DIRECT (11 to 19)	23 392	26 612	26 612	27 885	27 894	28 658	161 051
S-21	Staff pension fund	417	417	417	417	417	417	2 500
S-22	Staff termination fund	0	0	0	0	0	0	0
S-23	Staff rent allowances	0	0	0	0	0	0	0
S-24	Staff transport allowances	0	0	0	0	0	0	0
S-25	Staff other allowances	0	0	0	0	0	0	0
S-26	Staff group insurance	0	0	0	0	0	0	0
S-27	Staff medical insurance	500	0	0	0	0	0	500
S-28	Staff other benefits	0	0	0	0	0	0	0
S-20	TOT. BENEFITS (21 to 29)	917	417	417	417	417	417	3 000
S-31	Staff medical expenses	0	0	0	0	0	0	0
S-32	Staff recruitment	0	0	0	0	0	0	0
S-33	Staff relocation	0	0	0	0	0	0	0
S-34	Staff legal expenses	1 500	0	0	0	0	0	1 500
S-36	Staff training	0	0	0	0	0	0	0
S-38	Staff entertainment	70	100	100	110	110	120	610
S-39	Staff sundry	0	0	0	0	0	0	0
S-30	TOTAL OTHER (31 to 39)	1 570	100	100	110	110	120	2 110
S-00	TOTAL STAFF (10+20+30)	25 879	27 128	27 128	28 411	28 420	29 194	166 161

17. Annex A4. Non-staff operating costs

See Chapter 9, p.212

ANNEX A.4 Non-staff operating costs

Tetrylus Inc Financial plan,

Operating costs, first six months

Dollars

		Month 1	Month 2	Month 3	Month 4	Month 5	Month 6	H1
E-11	Premises ental & taxes	1 000	1 000	1 000	1 000	1 000	1 000	6 000
E-12	Amort'n – lease impoevem'ts	0	542	542	542	542	542	2 708
E-13	Utilities – electricity etc.	500	500	500	500	500	500	3 000
E-10	TOTAL OCCUPANCY	1 500	2 042	2 042	2 042	2 042	2 042	11708
E-21	Dep'n – office furniture	0	83	83	83	83	83	417
E-22	Dep'n – office equipment	0	0	0	13	13	13	38
E-23	Small equipment	100	100	0	0	0	0	200
E-24	Stationery & printing	100	25	25	25	25	25	225
E-25	Dues & subscriptions	100	100	100	100	100	100	600
E-26	Books & periodicals	50	50	50	50	50	50	300
E-27	Other of	0	50	50	50	50	50	300
E-20	TOTAL OFFICE	400	408	308	321	321	321	2 079
E-31	Dep'n – coms. equipment	0	0	0	0	0	0	0
E-32	Telephone & fax	2 500	2 500	2 500	2 500	2 500	2 500	15000
E-33	Information services	100	100	100	100	100	100	600
E-34	Postage & courier	250	250	250	250	250	250	1 500
E-30	TOTAL COMMS	2 850	2 850	2 850	2 850	2 850	2 850	17100
E-41	Depreciation – computers	0	556	597	597	625	625	3 000
E-42	Depreciation – software	0	208	208	208	208	208	1 042
E-43	Other software licences	500	0	0	0	0	0	500
E-45	Computer consumables	50	50	50	50	50	50	300
E-40	TOTAL COMPUTERS	550	814	856	856	883	883	4 842
E-51	Product distribution	0	0	500	1 000	300	2 500	4 300
E-52	Brochures and printing	0	5 000	2 500	0	0	0	7 500
E-55	Promotional items	0	2 500	0	0	0	0	2 500
E-59	Other marketing	0	5 000	5 000	0	0	0	10000
E-50	TOTAL MKTG & SALES	0	12 500	8 000	1 000	300	2 500	24300
E-61	Depreciation – vehicles	0	0	0	0	0	0	0
E-62	Rental – vehicles	0	0	0	0	0	0	0
E-63	Motor vehicle expenses	0	0	0	0	0	0	0
E-64	Travel & subsistence	5 100	10 100	10 100	10 100	10 100	10 100	55600
E-65	Entetainment	0	0	0	0	0	0	0
E-60	TOTAL TS&E	5 100	10 100	10 100	10 100	10 100	10 100	55600
E-71	Audit fees	0	0	0	0	0	0	0
E-72	Legal fees	1 000	2 500	1,000	0	0	0	4 500
E-75	Other pofessional fees	0	0	0	0	0	0	0
E-70	TOTAL PROFESSIONAL	1 000	2 500	1 000	0	0	0	4 500
E-83	Insurance	1 000	2 500	0	0	0	0	3 500
E-85	Sundy expenditue	100	100	100	100	100	100	600
E-80	TOTAL OTHER	1 100	2 600	100	100	100	100	4 100
E-00	TOTAL EXPENDITURE	12500	33814	25256	17268	16596	18796	124229

18. Annex A5. Income/P&L and balance sheet

See Chapter 9, p.215

ANNEX A.5 Income/P&L and balance sheet

Tetrylus Inc, Financial plan
Income statement/profit & loss account, first six monthes

Dollars

	Month 1	Month 2	Month 3	Month 4	Month 5	Month 6	H1
Sales	0	20 000	0	40 000	0	50 000	110000
Less: Costs of sales	0	13 591	0	27 183	0	33 979	74753
Gross profit	0	6 409	0	12 817	0	16 021	35247
***Less:* Operating costs**							
Employee cost	25 879	27 128	27 128	28 411	28 420	29 194	166161
Other expenditue	12500	33814	25256	17268	16596	18796	124229
Total operating costs	38379	60942	52384	45679	45016	4 7990	290 390
Net profit (loss) before contingency etc	(38379)	(54533)	(52384)	(32862)	(45016)	(31969)	(255143)
Less: Contingeny	3 838	6 094	5 238	4 568	4 502	4 799	29039
Net profit (loss) before interest and tax	(42217)	(60627)	(57622)	(37430)	(49518)	(36768)	(284182)

Balance sheet
Dollars

		Month 1	Month 2	Month 3	Month 4	Month 5	Month 6
	Assets						
B-1	Cash at bank	1 000	1 000	1 000	1 000	1 000	1 000
B-2	Accounts eceivable	0	20 000	0	40 000	0	50 000
B-3	Deposits pail	2 000	2 000	2 000	2 000	2 000	2 000
B-4	Repayments (ents)	11 000	10 000	9 000	8 000	7 000	6 000
B-5	Inventory	0	15 000	40 000	17 500	42 500	12 500
B-6	Fixed assets at cost	36 500	38 000	38 750	39 750	39 750	39 750
B-7	Less accumulated depciation	0	−1 389	−2 819	−4 263	−5 733	−7 204
B-8	**Memo: net fixed assets**	36 500	36 611	35 931	35 488	34 017	32 546
B-9	**Total assets**	50 500	84 611	87 931	103 988	86 517	104 046
B-10							
B-11	**LIABILITIES**						
B-12	Total loans	91 300	172 031	242 556	268 443	322 573	342 475
B-13	Accounts payable – haware	0	10 000	0	22 500	0	30 000
B-14	Accounts payable – softwar	0	3 591	3 591	8 274	8 274	12 253
B-15	Accuals (staf pensions)	417	833	1 250	1 667	2 083	2 500
B-16	**Total liabilities**	91 717	186 455	247 397	300 884	332 931	387 228
B-17							
B-18	**CAPITAL & RESERVES**						
B-19	Shae capital	1 000	1 000	1 000	1 000	1 000	1 000
B-20	Unremitted P&L	−42 217	−102 844	−160 467	−197 896	−247 414	−284 182
B-21	**Total capital and reserves**	−41 217	−101 844	−159 467	−196 896	−246 414	−283 182
B-22							
B-23	**Total liabilities and equity**	50 500	84 611	87 931	103 988	86 517	104 046

19. Annex A6. Cash flow
See Chapter 10, p.236

ANNEX A.6 Cash flow

Tetrylus Inc Financial plan

Cash flow, first six months
Eurodollars

		Month 1	Month 2	Month 3	Month 4	Month 5	Month6
F-1	Net profit	–42 217	–60 627	–57 622	–37 430	–49 518	–36 768
F-2	Adjustments for changes in:						
F-3	Cash at bank	–1 000	0	0	0	0	0
F-4	Accounts receivable	0	–20 000	20 000	–40 000	40 000	–50 000
F-5	Deposits paid	–2 000	0	0	0	0	0
F-6	Prepayments (rents)	–11 000	1 000	1 000	1 000	1 000	1 000
F-7	Inventory	0	–15 000	–25 000	22 500	–25 000	30 000
F-8	Fixed assets	–36 500	–1 500	–750	–1 000	0	0
F-9	Depreciation	0	1 389	1 431	1 443	1 471	1 471
F-10	Accounts payable - hardware	0	10 000	–10 000	22 500	–22 500	30 000
F-11	Accounts payable - software	0	3 591	0	4 683	0	3 979
F-12	Accrued pensions	417	417	417	417	417	417
F-13	Equity	1 000	0	0	0	0	0
F-14	**Cash flow**	–91 300	–80 731	–70 525	–25 887	–54 130	–19 902
F-15	Cumulative cash flow	–91 300	–172 031	–242 556	–268 443	–322 573	–342 475

Notes:
F-3 – thee is povision for a working bank balance of $1000.
F-4 & F-10 – 30 days credit is allowed to customers and provided by the hardware supplier.
F-5 – a returnable deposit equivalent to two months' rent was required by the lessor of the office premises.
F-6 – office rent is payable 12 months in advance.
F-11 – software licence fees are paid to the supplier annually

20. Annex B. Management biographies
See Chapter 4, p.75

ANNEX B Management biographies

Niccolò Machiavelli, Chief Executive Officer
Born 3 May, 1469 in Florence, Italy. Niccolò gained fame for his controversial pamphlet *The Prince*, which he wrote to gain influence with the ruling Medici family. Initially a secretary in the Florentine government, he engaged in diplomatic missions and rubbed shoulders with the great and famous. He brings strategic insight which will help the company to gain market share … His other publications include *The Art of War* and *Discourses on Livy* …

Karl Marx, Director of Sales
Born 1818 in Trier, Prussia. Karl studied law and philosophy at Bonn University and Jena. He bagan his career as a lecturer before becoming a political journalist and subsequently editor of *The Rhenish Gazette*. He was exiled for his views and he moved to London in 1850 … His works include *Das Kapital* which became the justification of modern socialism …

Adam Smith, Director of Production
Born 1768 in Kirkcaldy, Scotland. After a scholarship at Oxford, Adam was appointed Professor of Logic at Glasgow University – and later Professor of Moral Philosophy. He is the founder of classical and political economics. His works include *Inquiry into the Nature and Causes of the Wealth of Nations* which introduced the concept of the invisible hand of capitalism …

René Descartes, Director of Research & Development
Born March 31, 1596 in Touraine, France. Famous for coining the phrase 'cogito, ergo sum' ('I think, therfore I am'), Descartes is widely held as the founder of modern philosophy; however, he was also a brilliant mathematician. Aside from his philosophical works, including *Meditations on First Philosophy*, he wrote *La Géométrie* applying algebra to geometry – the foundation of cartesian geometry …

If you would be a real seeker after truth,
it is necessay that at least once in your life
you doubt, as far as possible, all things
René Descartes

Index